A SOCIOLOGY OF PRAYER

Ashgate AHRC/ESRC Religion and Society Series

Series Editors:

Linda Woodhead, University of Lancaster, UK
Rebecca Catto, University of Coventry, UK

This book series emanates from the largest research programme on religion in Europe today – the AHRC/ESRC Religion and Society Programme which has invested in over seventy-five research projects. Thirty-two separate disciplines are represented looking at religion across the world, many with a contemporary and some with an historical focus. This international, multi-disciplinary and interdisciplinary book series will include monographs, paperback textbooks and edited research collections drawn from this leading research programme.

Other titles in the series:

Religion Italian Style
Continuities and Changes in a Catholic Country
Franco Garelli

The Changing Soul of Europe
Religions and Migrations in Northern and Southern Europe
Edited by Helena Vilaça, Enzo Pace, Inger Furseth and Per Pettersson

Religions as Brands
New Perspectives on the Marketization of Religion and Spirituality
Edited by Jean-Claude Usunier and Jörg Stolz

Everyday Lived Islam in Europe
Edited by Nathal M. Dessing, Nadia Jeldtoft, Jørgen S. Nielsen
and Linda Woodhead

Media Portrayals of Religion and the Secular Sacred
Representation and Change
Kim Knott, Elizabeth Poole and Teemu Taira

A Sociology of Prayer

Edited by

GIUSEPPE GIORDAN
University of Padua, Italy

and

LINDA WOODHEAD
University of Lancaster, UK

ASHGATE

A SOCIOLOGY OF PRAYER

An astonishing array of insights about something generally neglected and taken for granted: what are people up to when they pray? The fresh, empirically-based contributions will engage and inform readers. Most importantly, the collection helps move forward the only recently-opened discussion about the sociality and relationality of prayer, a practice that persists within and on the borders of the sacred and the secular.

Abby Day, Goldsmiths, University of London, UK

Insightfully, in her conclusion, Linda Woodhead considers prayer as "changing the subject". The chapters brought together in this book help us to understand why. Each of them makes a distinctive contribution to a topic that is insufficiently understood by sociologists.

Grace Davie, University of Exeter, UK

For those living within western cultures, prayer remains one of the most perplexing of religious phenomena. This collection of essays approaches prayer as a social fact, as patterns of behaviour that confer meaning within the lives of individuals and communities across the globe. It takes seriously the ways in which acts of prayer are shaped by their social context, and as such, challenges the assumption that prayer is always individual and self-serving, instead highlighting its social consequences, such as the cultivation of relationships and civic responsibility, and the reinforcement of community boundaries. These essays are international in scope, and offer an important contribution to the international sociology of religion. Those who want to understand better why prayer endures as a social phenomenon would do well to engage seriously with this book.

Mathew Guest, University of Durham, UK

Prayer is a central aspect of religion. Even amongst those who have abandoned organized religion levels of prayer remain high. Yet the most basic questions remain unaddressed: What exactly is prayer? How does it vary? Why do people pray and in what situations and settings? Does prayer imply a god, and if so, what sort? A Sociology of Prayer addresses these fundamental questions and opens up important new debates.

Drawing from religion, sociology of religion, anthropology, and historical perspectives, the contributors focus on prayer as a social as well as a personal matter and situate prayer in the conditions of complex late modern societies worldwide. Presenting fresh empirical data in relation to original theorising, the volume also examines the material aspects of prayer, including the objects, bodies, symbols, and spaces with which it may be integrally connected.

Published by
Ashgate Publishing Limited
Wey Court East
Union Road
Farnham
Surrey, GU9 7PT
England

Ashgate Publishing Company
110 Cherry Street
Suite 3-1
Burlington, VT 05401-3818
USA

www.ashgate.com

British Library Cataloguing in Publication Data
A catalogue record for this book is available from the British Library

The Library of Congress has cataloged the printed edition as follows:
A Sociology of Prayer / edited by Giuseppe Giordan and Linda Woodhead.
        pages   cm. – (Ashgate AHRC/ESRC Religion and Society Series)
    Includes index.
    1. Prayer. I. Giordan, Giuseppe. II. Woodhead, Linda.
    BL560.S58 2015
    306.6–dc23   2014046387

ISBN: 9781472427670 (hbk)
ISBN: 9781409455851 (pbk)
ISBN: 9781472427687 (ebk – PDF)
ISBN: 9781472427694 (ebk – ePUB)

Printed in the United Kingdom by Henry Ling Limited,
at the Dorset Press, Dorchester, DT1 1HD

Contents

List of Tables and Figure

Tables

Figure

List of Contributors

Peter Althouse, PhD (University of St Michael's College at the University of Toronto), is Professor of Religion and Theology at Southeastern University, Florida, as well as co-editor for *Pneuma: The Journal of the Society for Pentecostal Studies*. Publications include *Catch the Fire: Soaking Prayer and Charismatic Renewal* (with Michael Wilkinson), *Spirit of the Last Days: Pentecostal Eschatology in Conversation with Jürgen Moltmann*, and *The Ideological Development of Power in Early American Pentecostalism*, as well as numerous journal articles and chapters.

Tania ap Siôn is Senior Lecturer in Pastoral Sciences at Glyndŵr University, Wales, Director of the St Mary's and St Giles' Centre, Wales, and Senior Research Fellow at the Warwick Religions and Education Research Unit at the University of Warwick, England. Her research includes publications on intercessory prayer, religious experience, and religion and education.

Andrea Borella received his PhD degree in Anthropology from the University of Turin–Italy. He was Doctoral Fellow at the Young Center for the Anabaptist and Pietist Studies of the Elizabethtown College, Elizabethtown, PA. His PhD dissertation focuses on the relationship between the Amish soteriology and the *Ordnung*. He is the author of two books: 'Gli Amish' (*The Amish* – 2009), and '101 modi per allenare la fede e lo spirito' (*101 ways for training faith and spirit* – 2011). He has also published a number of articles on the Amish culture, the religion in the United States of America, and the anthropological theories of communitarism, de-growth and anti-modernity.

Peter Collins is Senior Lecturer in Anthropology at Durham University. His research interests include religion, ritual and symbolism, space and place and narrative theory. He recently published *Quakers and Quakerism in Bolton, Lancashire 1650–1995: The History of a Religious Community*, and co-edited *The Quaker Condition: the sociology of a liberal tradition* (with Pink Dandelion), *Locating the Field: Space, Place and Context in Anthropology* (with Simon Coleman), *Texts and Religious Contexts* (with Elisabeth Arweck) and *The Ethnographic Self as Resource* (with Anselma Gallinat). He has conducted fieldwork among Quakers, local government employees and hospital chaplaincies in the North of England.

Yannick Fer is a French sociologist, CNRS researcher (GSRL, Paris), specialist in Polynesian Pentecostal/Charismatic movements and Evangelical missionary networks. He notably published in 2010 *L'offensive* évangélique, *voyage au coeur des réseaux militants de Jeunesse en Mission* (Geneva) and edited in 2012 a special issue of the *Archives des sciences sociales des religions* (62), "*Christianismes en Océanie / Changing Christianity in Oceania*".

Carlo Genova, PhD in comparative social research, is assistant professor at the University of Turin, where he teaches Sociology of culture and Lifestyles and social spaces. His main study interests relate to youth cultures, lifestyles and subcultures theories, and social space dynamics. Focusing on youth, his main empirical research fields have been social and political activism, forms of religious participation, artistic scenes, forms of distinctive consumption. He is a member of the European Sociological Association, RN: Sociology of Culture, Youth and Generation; of the European Consortium for Political Research, SG: Forms of participation; and of the Interdisciplinary Network for the Study of Subcultures, Popular Music and Social Change.

Giuseppe Giordan is Associate Professor of Sociology of Religion at the University of Padua (Italy). He is Co-Editor of the *Annual Review of the Sociology of Religion* (Brill), elected member of the *Executive Council* of the *Association for the Sociology of Religion*, and served as General Secretary of the *International Society for the Sociology of Religion* from 2009 to 2013. His books include *Identity and Pluralism. The Values of the Post-Modern Time*. New York, 2004; *Vocation and Social Context* (ed.), Leiden, 2007; *Conversion in the Age of Pluralism* (ed.), Leiden, 2009; *Youth and Religion, Annual Review of the Sociology of Religion* (ed.), 1, Leiden, 2010; *Religion, Spirituality and Everyday Practices* (ed. with William H. Swatos, Jr.) New York, 2011.

Julia Day Howell is Professor of the Sociology attached to the Religion and Society Research Centre of the University of Western Sydney. She has researched religious reform movements and marginal religions in Indonesia and Western societies since the 1970s. Recently she has focused on the revalorisation of Sufism amidst the wider Islamic revival and examined new forms of Islamic piety in modern, media saturated social settings. Her work contributes to the comparative sociology of Islam and addresses issues of Islam and pluralism in democratic states.

Emir Mahieddin is a doctoral student in social anthropology at Aix-Marseilles University and a member of the Institut d'Ethnologie Méditerranéenne Européenne et Comparative (IDEMEC-CNRS-UMR 7307). His research deals with the construction of moral subjects in the Pentecostal and charismatic movements in contemporary Sweden. He taught anthropology at Aix-Marseilles University between 2009 and 2014.

Michael Mason is an Adjunct Professor at Australian Catholic University in Melbourne, Australia. He works across the fields of sociology, religion studies and theology, using multidisciplinary and mixed-method approaches in research. He has been a principal investigator in several national sociological surveys on religion and spirituality. The data analysed in this chapter were collected in a research project undertaken by the author with colleagues Ruth Webber of ACU and Andrew Singleton, now of Deakin University, on the spirituality of the Australian and international youth who attended World Youth Day in Sydney in 2008.

Jayeel Serrano Cornelio has been recently appointed Director of the Development Studies Program at the Ateneo de Manila University, Philippines. In 2012–14, he was a postdoctoral research fellow at the Max Planck Institute for the Study of Religious and Ethnic Diversity in Göttingen, Germany. He has written on youth, religion, education, and urban studies and edited the special issue of *Philippine Studies: Historical and Ethnographic Viewpoints* (2014) on Filipino Catholicism. Under contract with Routledge, his current project is a monograph on being young and Catholic in the Philippines.

Martin Stringer is Pro-Vice Chancellor and Professor in the Sociology of Religion at the University of Swansea. He has worked in both the study of Christian Worship and the Sociology of Religion and has published widely in both disciplines. His most recent books include *Discourses on Religious Diversity* (Ashgate, 2013) and *Rethinking the Origins of the Eucharist* (2011).

Michael Wilkinson, PhD (University of Ottawa), is Professor of Sociology and Director of the Religion in Canada Institute at Trinity Western University. He has published extensively on Pentecostal-Charismatic Christianity, including *The Spirit said Go: Pentecostal Immigrants in Canada* (2006),

Canadian Pentecostalism: Transition and Transformation (2009), *A Liberating Spirit: Pentecostals and Social Action* (2010), *Winds from the North: Canadian Contributions to the Pentecostal Movement* (2010), *Global Pentecostal Movements: Migration, Mission, and Public Religion* (2012) and *Catch the Fire: Soaking Prayer and Charismatic Renewal* (2014).

Linda Woodhead is Professor of Sociology of Religion at Lancaster University. Her books include *A Sociology of Religious Emotion*, with Ole Riis, Oxford, 2010; *The Spiritual Revolution: Why Religion is Giving Way to Spirituality*, with Paul Heelas, 2005; *An Introduction to Christianity*, 2004. Edited and co-edited books include *Religion and Change in Modern Britain*, London, 2012; *Religions in the Modern World* 2nd edition, London, 2009; *Congregational Studies in the UK*, Aldershot: Ashgate, 2004; *Predicting Religion: Christian, Secular and Alternative Futures*, Aldershot: Ashgate, 2003; *Peter Berger and the Study of Religion*, London, 2002; *Reinventing Christianity: Nineteenth Century Contexts*, Aldershot: Ashgate, 2001; *Religion in Modern Times*, Oxford, 2000.

Introduction

You Never Know. Prayer as Enchantment

Giuseppe Giordan

Prayer, or something like it, seems to be at the core of every religion. Even more, it is the core of any relationship with the transcendent, however we wish to define it, within and outside the organized religious traditions. And, since even many who don't believe in a transcendent being pray, prayer seems to be deeply rooted in the human condition. Like the heart, it works even when the electroencephalogram is flat: even when dogmas are believed with much reservation, moral norms are ignored or considered obsolete, and rites are attended sporadically, it seems that prayer remains part of the lives of many people today.

I often hear students in my sociology course saying that, just before their exams, they go to Saint Anthony's basilica, just beside the department, to pray to the Saint to help them obtain positive results. When I ask them whether they really believe that saying a prayer, giving an offering or lighting a candle, is effective in passing the exam, their answer is almost always 'you never know'. Many of them, although they call themselves Catholic, have not attended Mass for years; some of them cannot even say whether they believe in God. But when it comes to prayer they remain open to the possibility that it may work.

In all probability the attitude of Pope Francis was quite different when, at the beginning of June 2014, he invited the Palestinian president Abu Mazen and the Israeli president Shimon Peres to the Vatican to pray for peace. But even in this case, were the participants in this meeting really persuaded that prayer was capable of solving the problems between the Israeli and Palestinian people, a conflict that has been dragging on for decades and that all the peace negotiations and the most diverse diplomatic initiatives have not been able to settle? Even in this case one might say pragmatically: you never know!

Even more complex is what happened in Ukraine in the middle of the crisis that has deepened in 2014: on the occasion of the Orthodox Easter the Kiev government allowed a truce in the military operations against the pro-Russian secessionists in the south-eastern area of the country. Kirill, Orthodox Patriarch of Moscow and Filarete and head of the autocephalous Orthodox Church of Kiev, prayed that God 'stop the plans of those who want to lacerate Holy Russia, either with political means or with armed forces, attempting to acquire military and political superiority'. The reply from the Kiev Patriarch, who also invited the people to pray for peace, does not leave space for doubts about the role that God should take: 'The Country that had granted territorial integrity to us has made an aggression against us. God cannot take the side of evil, for this reason the enemy of the Ukrainian people is condemned to failure'.

Will the prayers of my students in Padova help them to pass their exams? Will the prayers of the Israeli and Palestinian presidents with the Pope succeed where all the attempts at a diplomatic solution failed? Which prayers will God listen to in the Ukraine crisis: those of the pro-Russian separatists or those of the pro-Western nationalists? Why is prayer common to those who belong to different religious traditions and those who do not identify with them, and to those who believe in God and some of those who do not (or not completely)? The book you have in your hands will not settle these questions, but will illustrate how intriguing the subject of prayer is in a world in which a rationalistic mentality was meant to have removed the possibility of explaining reality in ways that do not refer to worldly cause–effect relationships, and in which people are meant to be either secular *or* religious.

Some of the questions asked about prayer are enduring ones: why do people pray? Why do they continue praying even if their requests are not fulfilled? Is prayer capable of changing reality? And, if we answer this last question affirmatively, how does it change reality? Is it capable of changing the world 'out there', or does it just change the way we see it, interpret it, experience it? Other questions relate to historical and social change, and ask whether prayer has changed over time, and if so what distinguishes contemporary forms of prayer?

The growing number of studies carried out in the last decades tell us that prayer is indeed capable of changing reality, but this often happens as a consequence of the change in the 'inner' world of the person who prays: a change that challenges the rules of logic, and that is capable of working even if 'seemingly' the requested results do not take place. Prayer may well have to do with the reality of life, but it surely has much more to do with the meaning that social actors ascribe to the large and small events of their lives.

It was Marcel Mauss, in his pioneering work of 1909 (1968[1909]) – referred to by many of the contributions which follow – who highlighted that prayer is an eminently social fact within which individuals as well as groups ritualize their beliefs. Prayer is linked to the social and cultural contexts in which it is expressed: what can we ask, how we have to ask for it, which posture of the body is correct, who we have to address to have our invocations to, how we interpret the outcomes of the prayer itself. According to Mauss, even if prayer is a purely individual act, it is never the exclusive production of an individual because the meaning of the words that are uttered is socially determined, and each prayer is part of a ritual that, although it may appear to be private, is nevertheless codified according to socially established norms.

As demonstrated by David Nicholls (1993), the language used in traditional petitionary prayer within the Christian tradition derives from the political rhetoric: the believer addresses God as a subject addresses the king, asking God what is appropriate to ask a monarch. In monarchial societies God was addressed according to a court protocol – with reverence and sometimes with dread and fear. As the political context changed, the way in which we represent God changed, with the deity becoming less a king and judge and more and more a father, benefactor and, sometimes, therapist or lover. As a consequence, even the language used to address him and its modalities change: the language becomes less formal and more and more spontaneous, more linked to immediate feelings than precise formulae.

After Mauss's work, and until the 1980s, most studies of prayer took a psychological approach. Numerous empirical studies have investigated the relationship between prayer and health, and in particular the link between praying and 'coping'. The outcomes of this mass of scientific investigation have been summarized by James Nelson (2009): the practice of praying can support and promote a healthy lifestyle, discouraging destructive behaviours such as smoking or overindulging in alcoholic drinks; it can reinforce positive beliefs such as an optimistic approach to reality reducing the anxiety caused by the uncertainties of life; it can support positive emotions balancing and stabilizing the emotional life of people who are passing through particularly difficult experiences.

To Kenneth Pargament (1997), prayer is a continuous process capable of transforming the activities of everyday life and endowing them with meaning: it is not an accessory or a luxury, but a fundamental practice that requires hard preparatory work. While offering meaning to everyday activities, prayer is a powerful instrument to improve and increase well-being, not least in situations of suffering and grief – in other words, in precisely those situations in which it is hardest to find meaning in life.

Increasingly since the 1980s sociologists have also started to pay attention to prayer as a scientifically relevant theme. William Swatos Jr (1982) highlights well how the sociological approach to prayer should be capable of adding evidence about power and institutions which can extend our understanding of the meaning of the prayer. When subjects pray, they address transcendent power(s), and this power is capable of 'empowering' the person who prays. Much research on prayer highlights the high percentage of those who believe that their prayers have a positive outcome, and one way to explain this is in that people feel that they have connected with some source of power beyond what is normal.

The many studies that appeared in recent decades have also developed new instruments to classify different forms of prayers and analyse their contents (e.g. Poloma and Gallup 1991 and several chapters in this volume), and have discovered how different socio-cultural variables help explain how prayer works for diverse categories of people (Baker 2008). Such work shows that as representations of worldly and religious power have changed, so modalities of praying have changed too. The shift from hierarchical authority to flatter structures has turned the all-powerful monarch or inaccessible and ineffable mystery into a friend at hand, with whom one can converse without fear, and the fellow-traveller to whom one can open one's heart without fear of being judged. The shift 'from the age of revelation to the age of information' (Turner 2008), where all can be said and debated within the democratic context, does not leave prayer untouched.

In order to build upon this work, Linda Woodhead and I proposed a panel session at the conference of the International Society for the Sociology of Religion that was held at Aix-en-Provence in 2011. More than forty scholars from all over the world participated in that panel, presenting the outcomes of their research on a theme that was ripe for discussion from a wide range of social science perspectives. The amount of interest in the topic persuaded us to issue a further call for those who could not attend the conference, and this has allowed us to widen still further the themes and perspectives of study. We have collected the contributions which exemplify the most interesting findings and directions of enquiry in two volumes: the first was published in 2013 (Giordan and Woodhead), and this one is its companion. Both illustrate, from an international perspective, the maturing of this field of study and the development of an increasingly developed body of work with clear advances in terms of methods, concepts and schemes of classification, research agendas – and emerging theoretical frameworks.

In the first chapter Carlo Genova proposes the possibility of interpreting some acts of prayer as practices, defining 'practice' as a social activity habitually carried out by an individual or a group. The fundamental element which characterizes a practice as distinct from a more general 'social action' is therefore reference to 'habit', to learned, recurrent patterns of behaviour enacted with minimal reliance on conscious resources. But as with every social action, prayer practices are also connected with a sense, a meaning: the 'full meaning' of prayer can consequently emerge only from its semantic relations with other everyday life activities. The article develops this hypothesis, referring to concrete case studies and offering an analytical approach for this interpretative perspective.

In the following chapter Michael Mason developed Mauss's work by showing how all forms of prayer, even those which are apparently 'private', are profoundly social. Drawing on a recent survey of a large sample of English-speaking youth from many different countries, he finds that the purpose of prayer is rarely the securing of worldly benefits. Predominantly, prayer is understood as the cultivation of a loving personal relationship with God. Factors influential in shaping a person as one who prays frequently are found to be age (beyond school age), gender (female), socialization in a country with a strong traditional Catholic culture, mother's high enthusiasm for her religion, having friends who attend services regularly, and especially one's own previous religious experiences. An interesting finding is that those who pray more frequently are not 'other-worldly', but show higher civic engagement in volunteering and charitable giving.

Drawing from observations and interviews collected within the Assemblies of God of French Polynesia since 2000, Yannick Fer examines three distinct registers of Pentecostal prayer in order to specify the mechanisms of this articulation between individual, community and institution. Pentecostal believers get to 'communicate' with God in their personal prayer through a set of institutional and collective mediation apparatuses that enable them to 'stay online' and to be guided by the 'voice of the Holy Spirit' in their everyday life. In this religious paradigm of constant and transparent communication, prayer in tongues provides a second register of prayer, which facilitates the establishment of what the Palo Alto school has described as a 'metacommunication'. Finally, prayer as a 'spiritual warfare' contributes to the conversion of this enchanted individual relationship with God into collective forms of engagement, notably through rituals of intercession performed in the frame of evangelistic campaigns.

Martin Stringer begins his chapter with evidence about the way in which individuals engage with the non-empirical 'other' through intimate conversations. Whether this 'other' is God, a dead relative, or some other being, it is constructed as being immediate, concerned and engaged in the lives of the individual involved in the conversation. Given that such conversations constitute a substantial element of what might be called 'prayer' in contemporary British society, Martin looks at the way this conversational prayer engages with the public prayer of Christian and other forms of worship. It is still the case that much public prayer – and study of prayer – assumes a transcendent being, very different from the intimate immanent other of the conversational prayer. Drawing on a number of years of ethnographic engagement with both contexts, and specifically with those who engage in both forms of prayer, this chapter addresses the relationship and conflicts that are inherent in the negotiation between the two kinds of others in individual's religious lives.

In the fifth chapter Emir Mahieddin observes that praying has changed in the Swedish Pentecostal churches since the 1980s: a contrast has developed between the Sunday service, which progressively 'de-charasmatized', and the cell groups, which now appear as the more emotive and expressive sphere of Pentecostal religious life. One does not pray the same way in public and in private – the former being more formal, the latter more intimate. This contrast did not exist in such a sharp way in the earlier years of the movement. Mahieddin proposes an interpretation which relates these changes to the religious and political history and culture of Sweden, and reflects on more general implications for understanding prayer.

The following chapter, by Julia Day Howell, concerns the emotional regimes cultivated through certain Islamic prayer practices – the repetitive litanies (*dzikr*) associated with Sufism, within the context of the contemporary global Islamic revival. Traditionally, *dzikr* litanies, potentially conducive to meditative and ecstatic states, have been added to the obligatory five daily prayers (*sholat wajib*) as acts of intensified devotion with the hope of gaining boons from the Almighty or to foster a sense of closeness to Him. Although these litanies are disapproved of by puritanical Islamic revival movements around the world, they have been reframed for modern sensibilities and have found new popularity with Muslim urbanites separated from a taken-for-granted communal religiosity. Julia shows how *dzikr* litanies are promoted by popular leaders and given very new uses and emotional registers on various kinds in the process.

The chapter by Andrea Borella is based on anthropological research in a community of the Old Order Amish in Lancaster County, Pennsylvania. His access to this community is exceptional. He argues that the different forms of prayer evident among the Old Order Amish – spoken, silent, sung, communitarian or personal – relate to a deep emotional trope of Amish religiosity which can be summed up by the concept of *Gelassenheit*. This is a Pennsylvania Dutch term which can be translated as humility, submission and abandonment to the will of God. The chapter suggests that, as well as shaping individual sensibilities and internal social hierarchies, this ethos – fostered centrally through public prayer – helps maintain Amish distinctiveness and underline the boundary with non-Amish society.

The research presented in chapter eight by Jayeel Serrano Cornelio was carried out with undergraduates involved in Catholic organizations in various universities in Metro Manila. It demonstrates how prayer is treated as a conversation with God, and presents an additional angle by giving attention to the different ways prayers are perceived to be answered. For many informants, God answers through people, circumstances, and even mediating technologies such as the radio and the internet. Personal 'revelations' drawn from these are not just food for thought: they are taken as divine answers and help. By looking at the nuances of answered prayers and how God is perceived by informants to respond to their prayers, Cornelio argues that God 'does not speak in mysterious ways'. He is immanent though intervening in daily affairs as a personal friend, and through various everyday media including new technology.

Research investigating prayer in Charismatic Christianity has received minimal social scientific attention. In the next chapter Michael Wilkinson and Peter Althouse explore one type known as 'soaking prayer', which is a development from the Toronto Blessing – which has now become 'Catch the Fire Ministries'. Using the theme of embodiment, the authors focus on how Charismatic Christianity is experienced and expressed through bodies which become a vehicle for signifying the presence of the Spirit. In turn, embodiment allows the researcher a view of prayer that can be researched through observation as well as conversational investigation. Comparisons are made with other types of Pentecostal prayer such as Spirit Baptism, speaking in tongues, deliverance, healing, intercession and prophecy.

The last two chapters are based on the analysis of prayer requests posted on the prayer boards in churches and hospital chapels. As Tania ap Siôn underlines, there is an absence of a recognized analytic framework through which these data have been analysed: in her chapter, Tania presents first of all the ap Siôn Analytic Framework for Intercessory Prayer (apSAFIP), and then applies it to a sample of 1,627 prayer requests taken from over 10,000 prayer requests systematically harvested from Lichfield Cathedral in Great Britain.

The following chapter, by Peter Collins, is based on research carried out in two National Health Service acute hospitals situated in the north-east of England: he illustrates a classification and a preliminary analysis of over 3,000 prayer requests left by patients, visitors and staff in the chapels. This collection is significant because it indicates the importance of religion/spirituality even in the most rational and secular of environments – the acute hospital: it suggests that talk of secularization, even in the most hostile environments, needs to be tempered according to context.

In the conclusion Linda Woodhead draws out the framework for a sociology of prayer in the contemporary world, and discusses what this means for future studies of prayer, and where there is still need for more research. Linda highlights some dimension of variations: prayer may be classified along a spectrum from the more private to the more social, always acknowledging that some element of each will be present; it varies by its relation to the body, bodily posture and ritual practice and, finally, it varies in relation to different material and spatial settings and symbolic objects.

This book is not the definitive sociology of prayer. It does not even claim to be the last word on prayer in contemporary societies. Its purpose is to take stock of the recent international flowering of work on prayer in many societies across the world, to identify main themes and new agendas. As such, its acts as a resource for those who want to see what the 'state of the art' is in order to continue the exciting and fast-developing work of constructing a richer sociological understanding of prayer.

References

Baker, Joseph (2008). 'An investigation of the sociological patterns of prayer frequency and content'. *Sociology of Religion* 69/2: 169–85.

Giordan, Giuseppe and Linda Woodhead (eds) (2013). 'Prayer in Religion and Spirituality'. *Annual Review of the Sociology of Religion* 4.

Mauss, Marcel (1968[1909]). 'La prière et les rites oraux'. In Karady, V. (ed.), *Oeuvres I : Les fonctions sociales du sacré*. Paris: De Minuit, 355–548.

Nelson, J.M. (2009). *Psychology, religion and spirituality*. New York: Springer.

Nicholls, David (1993). 'Addressing God as ruler: prayer and petition'. *The British Journal of Sociology* 44/1: 125–41.

Pargament, K.I. (1997). *The psychology of religion and coping: Theory, research and practice*. New York: Guilford.

Poloma, Margaret M. and George Gallup (1991). *Varieties of Prayer: A Survey Report*. Philadelphia: Trinity Press International.

Swatos Jr, William H. (1982). 'The power of prayer: A prolegomenon to an ascetical sociology'. *Review of Religious Research* 24: 153–63.

Turner, Bryan S. (2008). 'Religious Speech. The Ineffable Nature of Religious Communication in the Information Age'. *Theory, Culture & Society* 25(7–8): 219–35.

Chapter 1

Prayer as Practice:
An Interpretative Proposal

Carlo Genova

Against the common view that prayer is first and foremost a matter of religious belief and interiority, this chapter argues that it is possible to interpret some forms of prayer as 'social practices' i.e. repeated activities that do not require explicit processes of reflection, and which, for the actor, can have a meaning that transgresses the boundaries of religion, sometimes completely.

After having made a brief overview of relevant ideas put forward by classical sociologists who have dealt with religious phenomena I shall, first of all, comment on the reflections of Mauss, who was the first to face the question whether the activity of prayer 'makes sense'. Reference will then be made to some authors who have been involved in the social analysis of prayer more recently, in order to show how thinking has developed over time. I pay particular attention to authors who have considered prayer as social practice. The final section of the chapter considers the feasibility of applying the concept of practice to the analysis of actual forms of prayer, to facilitate a more adequate interpretation.

1. First Reflection on Prayer as Social Phenomenon

The phenomenon of prayer might seem to be one of the most fundamental subjects for the sociology of religion to deal with. If we go beyond definitional questions which are not included in the scope of this contribution, it seems possible to affirm that every religious tradition expresses itself through activities which can be interpreted as prayers. It would then be logical to suppose that a discipline that deals with religious phenomena would give first priority to the analysis of the geographic, social, historical and cultural variability of prayer. However, if this rather naive hypothesis were tested by a general overview of the classical texts of the sociology of religion, and the most well-recognized textbooks dedicated to this field, it would become evident that the reality is completely different. Not only is it extremely difficult to find introductory texts which deal with the question of prayer, it is also rare to find a serious analysis of this phenomenon in works by authors considered to be 'classical'.[1]

From a sociological perspective, even though Comte refers to this issue in *Catechisme positiviste*,[2] he does so mainly from a prescriptive angle – and he hardly mentions it at all in *Cours de philosophie positive*;[3] Durkheim speaks of it in *Formes elementaires de la vie religieuse*, but it is neither structured nor organic;[4] Simmel makes only brief mentions of prayer in some passages in *Beiträge zur Erkenntnistheorie der Religion*, in *Die Gegensätze des Lebens und die Religion* and in *Die Religion*;[5] Weber mentions the issue briefly in only a few passages of *Wirthschaft und Gesellschaft*[6] and *Die Protestantische Ethik und der Geist des Kapitalismus*,[7] and in *Der Wirthschaft der Weltreligionen*. From a more anthropological perspective, some consideration of the topic is found in *Lectures on the Religion of the Semites* by Robertson Smith,[8] in *Structure and Function in Primitive Society*[9] and *African Systems of Kinship*[10] by Radcliffe Brown, in the various volumes of *The Golden Bough* by Frazer, and above all in the pages of *Primitive Mentality* by Lévy-Bruhl.[11] Nevertheless, the question is not dealt with in a direct or explicit manner in any of these texts.

In many of these texts we find interesting descriptive elements of specific forms of prayer along with some more general reflections on prayer as a characteristic activity of the religious field – but structured, systematic reflections are lacking. The great exception to this rule is the contribution made by Mauss,

---

[1]   By this we do not imply that there are no sociological reflections or researches on the question of prayer but rather that, to date, this particular field of study is still poorly organic and structured.

[2]   Comte (1858): 25, 38, 93, 105–11, 115, 117, 119, 124–7, 140, 149, 314, 333.

[3]   The only notions are to be found in Comte (1892): vol. IV, 538, 555; vol. VI, 210.

[4]   Durkheim (1912): 41, 42, 46, 47, 58, 73, 75, 112, 260, 264, 285, 313, 396, 412, 440, 445, 481, 621.

[5]   Simmel (1997): chapters 5, 10, 11.

[6]   Weber (1978): vol. I, 23, 339, 434.

[7]   Weber (2001): 44 f. 29, 61 f. 32, 98 f. 219, 105 f. 20, 106, 112 f. 69.

[8]   Robertson Smith (1894): 82, 108, 111, 117, 164, 165, 168, 178, 195, 200, 213, 258, 277, 321, 359, 364, 457, 481.

[9]   Radcliffe Brown (1952): 28, 157, 161, 173.

[10]   Radcliffe Brown, Forde (1950): 37, 114, 120, 127, 130, 136, 228, 237, 249, 316.

[11]   Lévy-Bruhl (1922): 33, 71, 81–4, 116, 134, 136–7, 141, 143, 175, 176, 180, 199, 201–2, 204–8, 220, 223, 225, 243, 336, 338, 348, 349, 354, 359, 360, 366, 368, 377, 397, 419, 433, 439, 470.

who dedicated a book, although uncompleted, to the subject – *On Prayer*. It is this text which offers us a useful starting point for reflection.

From Mauss's point of view, prayer is an activity which involves both belief and ritual at the same time. The religious person both thinks and acts in the prayer; the ritual and mystic components are inseparable one from the other and bear the same weight (Mauss 1969–74 vol. I: 359–60). Mauss suggests that if all religious rites were divided into manual activities such as body movements and the moving of objects, and oral activities such as repeated phrases, then prayer would tend to be located within the latter category, whilst also sharing some aspects retaining of the former. Prayers are oral religious rites that aim at modifying something profane by conferring a sacred characteristic upon it (Mauss 1969–74 vol. I: 413–14).

In this sense, each and every prayer expresses religious sentiments and ideas: a prayer is an attitude and an act adopted toward sacred things. That is, a prayer is an attempt to communicate with the divine in an attempt to influence: some form of outcome is expected from a prayer. Prayer involves the use of words which have an objective and an expected effect. It is an 'action instrument' that works through the expression of ideas and sentiments. Therefore, prayer incorporates both acting and thinking. It unites ritual, cult and belief, and embraces both meaning and efficacy.

In this perspective, a rite acquires a *raison d'être* only once its meaning (i.e. the notions and ideas it has been based on and the belief it corresponds to) has been discovered (Mauss 1969–74 vol. I: 358). Likewise, prayer finds its reason to exist in the notions and beliefs from which it derives. In most cases prayer has clearly expressed reasons, circumstances and motives for being uttered. However, both the form and meaning of prayer should always be taken as a phenomenon which is not simply traceable to a single individual, but something of a fundamental social nature. Indeed, according to Mauss, even if the prayer is individualistic and free, and even if the individual chooses how and when to pray, the words and their meaning are consecrated and, therefore, social. The more a prayer is social in its content and form, the less it exists outside a ritual. It is related to collections of phrases handed down from one generation to another and often inscribed in written texts. The same applies to the circumstance, the moment, the place and the attitude taken towards the prayer, all of which are often strictly defined. Each prayer is a ritual speech adopted by a religious society, a series of words with a determined order and sense. Even the most personal and free form of prayer follows prescriptions (Mauss 1969–74 vol. I: 375–80).

It goes without saying that, even if prayer is a social phenomenon, this does not mean it is not also an individualistic, personal one. However, personal prayer is not primary over collective prayer, but rather the opposite. Historically, prayer was first of a collective nature, even if personal prayer was not forbidden. Moreover, it is collective not only in form, but also inasmuch as it has both juridical and moral aspects. Although recitation and prayer did become more and more individualistic with the passing of time, this never eliminated their social content. The original contribution of each individual in prayer does not annihilate its essentially collective character, as even personal prayer is strongly influenced by the cultural forms the individual who uttered it is part of. Moreover, the community that practices the prayer not only determines its characteristics, but also its efficacy (Mauss 1969–74 vol. I: 380–84).

It is the social dimension of prayer that brings about a weakening of its sense when it is reproduced individually. If, indeed, the sense of prayer is first and foremost one of a social nature and only afterwards does it take an individual form, then at the moment it is adopted by an individual there is the risk of it becoming detached from its original sense. And a practice which is not linked to its origin can be only a mechanical sequence of traditional movements.

If then, from a historical perspective, prayer was at first chiefly social and bodily with little to do with any thought process, it later became a more completely mental and interior process. However, this process is not an irreversible one. Indeed, at times prayer starts off as being wholly spiritual only to become a form of recitation void of any personal content. Therefore, there are certain oral rites that have become manual rites after a degradation process (Mauss 1969–74 vol. I: 413). Prayers repeated constantly, time after time, recited in a language that can't be understood, formulas that have lost every meaning, with words so outdated as to be incomprehensible, unrecognizable, are clear examples of such a regression. Moreover, we also see some cases where prayer has been reduced to a mere material object e.g. the rosary, the prayer-tree, the prayer wheel, the amulet and ex-votos, are all materialized prayers. This kind of materialization can then easily translate into a weakening of the known sense of the prayer. In neither case is the distinction between a prayer pregnant with meaning or devoid of it absolute, but rather refers to states of the same prayer in different moments (Mauss 1969–74 vol. I: 357). According to Mauss, once prayer, inasmuch as it is a rite, loses its tie to the notions and beliefs that generated it, it also loses its meaning.

2. Prayer in Recent Scholarship

Mauss's work on prayer, despite constituting a fundamental starting point for this field of study, can, of course, only be correctly interpreted in terms of its peculiar historical and cultural background. When more recent contributions to a social analysis of prayer are taken into account it is clear that the question of meaning becomes more complex. However, even within this literature we can still find reference to the idea that only when a prayer is accompanied by explicit reflection on the meaning of the gestures and words it contains are we dealing with meaningful prayer. Conversely, we find the idea that when a recitation – whether physical, vocal or mental – is less tied to a reflection on meaning, then prayer lacks meaning.

It is helpful to begin by looking at classifications used in this more recent literature to distinguish the various types of prayer (Khoury 2004: 564; Cipriani 2011; Janssen, De Hart, Den Draak 1990: 104; Poloma, Pendleton, 1989: 48–51; Ladd, Spilka 2006: 233). Taking these together, prayer is described as:

- request: asking for something that you don't have at that moment, whether it be spiritual or material;
- intercession: when you advocate and ask for something for someone else;
- confession: asking for forgiveness for one's own sins;
- praise, worship and adoration: where God is praised;
- relationship: where contact with the Creator is sought;
- thanksgiving;
- meditation: where order can be established in one's thoughts;
- rite or ceremony;
- communication: where a dialogue is established with the Divine, with 'the other' or with oneself.

Of course these characteristics can be present simultaneously and are not mutually exclusive.

Even if this typology is necessarily partial and incomplete, it does allow the diversity of the phenomenon to be grasped. It also shows that different types of prayer are defined on the basis of the function they are believed to fulfil. A significant number of definitions of what a prayer 'is' make specific reference to these functions. Thus prayer is defined as: a communication technique (Headley 1994: 11; Swatos Jr 1982: 157; Khoury 2004: 561; Chauvin 1970: 111); an instrument to help cope with difficulties, both in the sense of making reality more acceptable and that of intervening in it (i.e. a coping mechanism, in the sense of the management process of internal and external problems) (Janssen, De Hart, Den Draak 1990: 105; Baker 2008: 170–71); a means to divine aid and guidance (Baker 2008: 171; Chauvin 1970: 113); a means to define, redefine or reactivate the mutual position of the divine and earthly (Headley 1994: 11); a means of construction and interpretation of reality and individual experience (Janssen, De Hart, Den Draak 1990: 105–6).

It is clear that the frameworks for understanding prayer as a social phenomenon have become more complex and developed since the pioneering reflections made by Mauss. There is however one element that seems to remain unaltered, i.e. the hypothesis that only the 'reflexive' type of prayer which connects the act of recitation (be it vocal or mental) to meditation on the meaning of the words uttered may be considered meaningful. This is particularly true for research carried out in the last few years (rather than that done in the past which tended to deal more with the question of the frequency of prayer) where the importance of an analysis of this type has often been emphasized (Poloma, Pendleton 1989: 51; Baker 2008: 171). Similarly, analysis of the contents of a prayer is taken to be a fundamental element in the reconstruction of the motivation and therefore the sense of prayer. It is commonly held that the connection between the act and thought, between the body, the voice and the mind of the individual praying, is crucial. If a prayer were to be recited without understanding the meaning of the words used, then it would lose most of its substance (Khoury 2004: 565).[12] Consequently, when it is said that praying requires silence, isolation and concentration, it is because it is said to be because a genuine mental connection is thereby established with the divine and/or that this offers the possibility to understand oneself and others more fully (Benson, Wirzba 2005: 89–91).

Of course, the difficulty and complexity of prayer, which is often contradictory in its constitutive elements, cannot be eliminated even under the best of conditions. Often, even for the truest of believers, the invocation of the divine is familiar and incomprehensible at the same time, both with regard to form and content (Headley 1994: 7). Indeed, as prayer should plumb deeper significance, its meaning may be unclear even to those who pray with deep reflection (Benson, Wirzba 2005: 3). Also, it is not always clear who the dialogue developed in prayer is intended to engage, nor what the level of awareness of the meaning attached to the act of prayer really is (Headley 1994: 8).

---

[12]   In this sense it is emphasised how several chapters in the Koran for example express a truly condemning attitude towards a prayer which is not able to establish an intimate relationship with the divine (Khoury 2004: 566).

As can be seen, all these interpretations tend to identify the sense of the prayer in the connection between words, or even bodily gestures and thoughts, in particular with reference to the meaning that particular gesture or word is given by the doctrinal system of which prayer is a part. Therefore, in some cases, the fact that a prayer does not meet the requirements of such a connection and reflection is taken to mean that it cannot make sense.

However, it is useful to think critically about this line of analysis. In principle, the act of prayer may be wholly individual and spontaneous: the individual may pray through words and gestures chosen completely freely. However, a social and historical analysis of prayer has clearly shown that it is done with more or less homogeneous characteristics within specific communities that share the same religious beliefs. The act of praying is mainly carried out through traditional formulas acquired through the process of religious socialization; prayer models are reproduced over time starting from the mnemonic use of gestures and texts picked up from others (Cipriani 2011). In the Islamic context, for example, prayer is recited at five determined moments of the day: Salat al-fajr: dawn, before sunrise; Salat al-zuhr: midday, after the sun passes its highest; Salat al-'asr: the late part of the afternoon; Salat al-maghrib: just after sunset; Salat al-'isha: between sunset and midnight. Most of the texts used in such prayer come from the Koran. They are uttered in Arabic all over the world, according to an identical scheme and, even if the contents are not particularly complex, many of those who recite the words do not understand them. The complete act of prayer is to be said with 17 bowing movements, 17 genuflections and 5 prostrations, each of which is to be repeated twice and accompanied by physical cleansing and physical education.[13]

In a Christian context also, the principles of prayer are defined in written texts officially recognized by churches, and their recital is often connected to precise rules as to times and modalities. Moreover, there was a long-lasting Catholic tradition which advocated the transmission of prayers with rigidly defined words that could not be altered as they were identified as sacred (Châtellier 2000: 639).[14]

Moreover, many religious traditions share the assumption that addressing a divinity, conversing with a divinity apart from the sense the words usually mean, must, without doubt, require the adoption of special techniques. Therefore,

---

[13]   Along with the compulsory prayers there are also spontaneous prayers, for thanksgiving, worship and aspirations.

[14]   Despite this, although the Christian prayer is based on writings, it is also in continuous expansion and blends predefined formulas with impromptu speeches without opposition.

texts and prayer modalities must be significantly formalized (Headley 1994: 7). The spread of prayer is mainly tied to the action of the educative structure of religious confession that transmits form and content. Consequently, the various forms of dialogue with the divine do not constitute spontaneous acts, but are rather the result of historical processes of sedimentation, and religious organizations favour the persistence of some specific models (Cipriani 2011). It is not uncommon for the faithful to find themselves adopting codified gestures and formulas which have often been coined in historical eras prior to their own, and perhaps in a language which they know little if at all.

This does not mean that forms of prayer are not subject to individual personalization, just as the historical transformations a prayer undergoes over time are not eliminated. Prayer, in its concrete manifestation, takes place mainly as a variation on a theme, as an intermediate point between rules and improvisation (Fabre 2010: 956); it should always be remembered that there is a difference between the text of a prayer and the complexity of its concrete performance. However, because prayers in different religious traditions often follow rather rigidly-set texts and modalities of recitation, which are often handed down in written form, and may involve strongly codified formula and gestures, the religious believer may have difficulty in getting back in touch with their original doctrinal significance.

3. The Concept of Practice

As mentioned before, much research and reflection on the phenomenon of prayer within and outside the social sciences has concentrated mainly on its diffusion and frequency in a determined population and on the socio-cultural factors that influence these variables. Indeed, it is only recently and to a lesser extent, that there seems to have been an interest in dealing with the sense the religious believer attributes to the act of prayer. However, more often than not, these interpretative proposals have supported the idea of a close connection between the sense of the prayer, the reflexive state of mind of the person praying, and the tie between the wording of the prayer and the doctrine it refers to.

The contribution being made here proposes a partly different approach by expanding the understanding of prayer to include instances when there is no direct connection between the words recited or the gestures made and the doctrinal meaning, or when there is no explicit reflection on those words or gestures. Even in such cases, the act of praying may still make sense for the actor and, moreover, may make sense as a social practice.

But what is a social practice? It is a concept which is both widespread and poorly defined within the social sciences (Chaiklin, Hedegaard, Jensen 1999: 19). In Ansart's definition (1999: 416), 'practice' refers to conduct classified as 'trivial' day-to-day activities (De Certeau 1984: XI), whether carried out by an individual or a group (Giddens 1977: 75). A distinguishing feature of such conduct is the fact that it does not require the actor to make any explicit reflection when it is being done, yet, despite this, it has elements of intentionality and meaning. Even the habitual, routine, day-to-day activities that do not prompt the individual to pose problems of explicit reflection on the whys and wherefores still have an element of intentionality. Yet, such intentionality of action is not connected to the actor's ability to formulate the knowledge applied to it in the form of abstract proposition, nor is it necessary that such a knowledge be valid (Giddens 1977: 76). That is to say, the repetition that frequently characterizes conduct in social practice does not eliminate the intentional nature of such conduct (Tuomela 2002: 63). That is what Bourdieu means when he writes that the key element is that practices cannot always be traced back to purely mechanical reactions, or to purely intentional actions, as there are a multiplicity of 'reasonable' practices that are not fruit of a reasoned plan, or a conscious calculation, but are related to a practical sense, a kind of socially-constituted 'sense of the game' (Bourdieu 1992).

Although practices which are essentially individual do come to mind (despite the fact that their form and meaning are always influenced by the social context), it does seem that most 'practices' are of a social nature, collectively shared. Moreover, according to some authors, social life contains above all social practices. It is in this perspective that social practices are intended as collective social actions that are repeated according to shared attitudes (Tuomela 2002: 1, 63).

But what do we mean when we say these practices are social and shared by more than one individual? In principle it could simply be considered as different individuals acting out the same action repeatedly. However, some authors are of the opinion that if we are to speak of practice, then it must essentially be something that goes beyond the simple individual habit which stems from the individual repetition of the same act (Turner 1994: 100, 105). The actors may undertake even complex practices without having a completely explicit knowledge of what they are doing, however they must, in any case, share knowledge, which, although pragmatic and non-propositional, constitutes shared assumptions in their performance (Bohman 1997).[15] If individuals share a practice, then they also share an unspoken knowledge, even if the sharing of knowledge in a 'community of practice' derives from the sharing of these practices (Seely Brown, Duguid 2001: 204–5).[16]

As Reckwitz argues in more detail, the concept of social practice refers to a model that may be interpreted by a multitude of single individual actions that reproduce the practice. The practice in this sense is then 'social', inasmuch as it is a 'type' of conduct and understanding that emerges in different places and at different times, developed by different individuals (although this does not necessarily presuppose forms of interaction) (Reckwitz 2002: 249–50). Thus a social practice is both a physical and mental activity that has been routinized and is produced by a particular 'training' of the body according to a specific way of understanding, preference, emotion, mutually-connected desires, particular ways of understanding the world (i.e. the objects, human beings and oneself). It is historically and culturally influenced, collective and shared (Reckwitz 2002: 252–3).[17]

However, it is obvious that the sharing of thought and action models amongst many individuals cannot be considered a spontaneously emerging element within a social context. Day-to-day conduct, be it mental or physical, is a fundamental component of social practices, indeed, it stems from both individual repetitive processes and, above all, from learning processes (Tuomela 2002: 58).[18] Therefore, so that a practice may be shared, it must basically be transmitted, taught and learnt, even if the same practice may be acquired in different manners (Turner 1994: 39, 43, 65–6) and the transmission mainly takes place through day-to-day actions that are carried out as routine. The question of the similarity of practices adopted by different persons must be kept distinct from that of their transmission: the history of the practices' acquisition is separate from the coincidence of the shared practices. The term 'practice'

---

[15]   On this subject, Bohmann emphasises how, despite the fact that the actors do not explicitly have this knowledge, it can be reconstructed by examining the regularity of the conduct, even if, in this way, the results obtained are more vulnerable.

[16]   And in this sense one may speak of 'community of practice' inasmuch as it is an entity that is defined by shared practices and common knowledge on how such practices are carried out and developed. However, it is a very broad question and most certainly goes beyond the intent of this contribution.

[17]   Objects may also be considered fundamental components of many practices: the routine acting out of a practice often implies the use of specific objects in a specific way.

[18]   As Friedmann emphasises (1978: 86), in social practice, action and knowledge are united in a single learning process.

refers to the idea of behavioural models that an observer sees as similar and that seem to have been handed down amongst persons who live together (Turner 1994: 117).

It is this very aspect of the reproduction of the practice that is fundamental for their connection with the social structure. In fact, the structure emerges and develops with the reproduction of the practices: the structure may be considered as a series of reproduced practices (Giddens 1977: 121, 161). Therefore, social practices are pivotal for the creation, the maintenance and the renewal of the social system and its structure (Tuomela 2002: 2). More precisely, according to the theory of practice, social structures are routinizations and social practices are those routines (Reckwitz 2002: 255). It has been emphasized that, although practices can be multiform and fragmentary, they follow implicit rules and models, and depend on a union of procedures intended as operational schemes and technical manipulations (De Certeau 1984: XV, 43).

Such a theory of practice may be seen as a way to account for social life through the synthesis of social structure and personal individual inclinations (Mahar 2008: 418). As suggested by Thévenot, practices cannot be only regularities of conduct stemming from habits or individual inclinations, inasmuch as they both influence and are influenced by the framework of social rules they are inserted into (Schatzi, Cetina, Savigny 2001: 16).

4. Conclusion: Prayer as Social Practice

The brief references made to some authors who have discussed the nature of social practices are not intended to provide an overview of the subject, but are an attempt to lay useful foundations for interpreting some forms of prayer as social practices.

In one perspective on prayer as a social phenomenon it seems as if the connection between action, both physical and linguistic, and the believer's thoughts is fundamental. This is the tendency to refer to prayer as an act that expresses religious ideas and sentiments, where the meaning stems from the believer having inserted the act into a specific framework of notions and beliefs. From this point of view, both the modality and the meaning of the prayer are strictly connected to the processes of religious socialization, to the traditional models individuals are exposed to. Therefore, if, on the one hand, the prayer and its meaning are often defined as starting from the function they perform, assigning a particular relevance to the reflexive dimension, on the other hand, it is explicitly emphasized how repeated use trivializes prayer, as does its progressive historical and cultural decontextualization, which may lead to a loss of sense, taken as a clear dividing line between action and thought, and, moreover, a split between action and doctrine.

It is useful to linger a while over some distinctions in this type of interpretation. Firstly, a distinction is to be made between the connection of words and gestures that characterize the prayer with the religious doctrine it belongs to, and the connection of words and gestures with individual cognitive schemes. Indeed, although a believer may not be able to identify the sense the bodily and linguistic expressions of a prayer have in connection to the doctrine it can be traced back to, he/she can realize that these elements do have an explicit sense for his/her own personal religious references. Secondly, a distinction is to be made between the religious and the non-religious sense a prayer may have for the individual in question: as can be seen from the previous notes in this chapter, individual personal prayer may have multiple functions, some of which are completely outside the boundaries of the religious field. Lastly, the individual capacity to explicitly express the meaning attributed to the act of prayer is not to be confused with an absence/presence of that meaning: even where the individual is not able to verbalize the meaning he/she imparts to the wording and gestures used in the prayer, this does not necessarily mean that there is no meaning.

Therefore, on the basis of such elements, certain acts of prayer that may be brimming over with meaning for the actor, may partly, or entirely, be of a non-religious nature, disconnected from a more ample doctrine and not explicitly expressed. The recitation of a prayer that contains words that make no sense to the actor (as was the case for the Catholic mass held in Latin, or for some formulas used in Buddhist groups in the west) may however still be an act pregnant with religious meaning for the believer, whether it takes on an individual form or a collective one. Consequently it would seem useful to interpret these acts of prayer as social practices, because, as can be seen from the previous notes herein reported, they possess elements that characterize this particular form of action.

Whether or not, during the recitation of a prayer, the believer reflects on the literal or doctrinal significance of the terms and gestures involved in it, it may hold a strong sense for him/her: it may be an instrument of psychological support, it may help to organize the 'everyday time' (as was the case for Christian monks, even if in a less rigid form), it may mark the relevance, or exceptional quality, of specific events and moments. It is the religious organization itself that, in some cases, recognizes this type of prayer. When faced with the difficulties the believer has to deal with, the priest advocates prayer being fully aware that this will activate psychological processes of coping; in numerous new religious movements the new participants are spurred to pray before and without even considering whether or not the significance of the wording involved in the formula and the doctrine it belongs to have been fully understood; likewise in the Catholic use of the rosary the priest invites thought which is not projected towards the meaning of the words pronounced, but rather towards the 'mysteries' it refers to. In all these and yet more examples, the fact that the believer finds a reason, a sense for the prayer, does not necessarily mean that, at the same time, the believer is able to voice this sense. The believer prays sure that praying has a sense, but this does not mean that he or she has developed a reflection process on it.

Therefore the interpretation of an act of prayer as a social practice allows for the identification of a meaning for that act, a meaning that might otherwise have remained undiscovered. The perspective is that of looking for a meaning for the acts of prayer beyond the boundaries of the doctrine it refers to and, in a more general sense, of the religious field. Such a sense may, in fact, come to light by inserting such an act within the individual's personal cognitive framework, i.e. in the individual's semantic relationship with other activities that characterize his/her everyday life. And, in this sense, it cannot be taken for granted that there is some predominant principle in the religiously-oriented interpretation of acts of prayer.

Taking some points from the previous pages, an act of prayer may, therefore, constitute a social practice as a social activity practised habitually by an individual, or a group, which, even if it does not necessitate any explicit reflection by the actor/s for it to be acted out, nor any skill to explicitly formulate its underlying knowledge, still has intentional elements and meaning *in situ*. Moreover, prayer as a social practice may be configured as an interpretative model that stems from a multitude of individual actions that reproduce it, with learning and imitation processes at its base in equal measure. And, if on the one hand the model of the single prayer develops from its expression by each individual, on the other it is this individual reproduction per se that follows such a model, along a circular pathway twining between actor and structure, where there is no clear dividing line, no priority component.

Acknowledgment

The author would like to thank Barbara Wade for her linguistic advice.

References

Ansart, Pierre (1999). 'Pratique', in André Akoun and Pierre Ansart (eds), *Dictionnaire de Sociologie*, Paris: Le Robert-Seuil, 416–17.

Baker, Joseph O. (2008). 'An Investigation of the Sociological Patterns of Prayer Frequency and Content', *Sociology of Religion*, 2: 169–85.

Benson, Bruce Ellis and Norman Wirzba (2005). *The Phenomenology of Prayer*, New York: Fordham University Press.

Bohman, James (1997). 'Do Practices Explain Anything? Turner's Critique of the Theory of Social Practices', *History and Theory*, 1: 93–107.

Bourdieu, Pierre (1992). *Réponses. Pour une anthropologie réflexive*, Paris: Seuil.

Chaiklin, Seth, Hedegaard, Mariane and Uffe Juhul Jensen (1999). *Activity Theory and Social Practice: Cultural-Historical Approaches*, Aarhus: Aarhus University Press.

Châtellier, Louis (2000). 'De la prière interdite à la prière impossible', *Revue de l'histoire des religions*, 3: 639–48.

Chauvin, Rémy (1970). 'Un antique mode de communication: la prière', in *Communication et langages*, 6: 111–18.

Cipriani, Roberto (2011). 'Diffused Religion and Prayer', *Religions*, 2: 198–215.

Comte, Auguste (1858). *The Cathechism of Positivism*, London: Chapman.

Comte, Auguste (1892). *Course de philosophie positive*, Paris: Société Positiviste.

De Certeau, Michel (1984). *The Practice of Everyday Life*, Berkeley: University of California Press.

Durkheim, Émile (1912). *Les formes élémentaires de la vie religieuse*, Paris: Alcan.

Fabre, Pierre Antoine (2010). 'Prière', in Azria, Regine and Daniele Hervieu-Léger (eds), *Dictionnaire des faits religieux*, Paris: Puf, 955–8.

Friedmann, John (1978). 'The Epistemology of Social Practice: A Critique of Objective Knowledge', *Theory and Society*, 1: 75–92.

Giddens, Anthony (1977). *New rules of sociological method*, London: Hutchinson University Library.

Headley, Stephen C. (1994). 'Pour une anthropologie de la prière', *L'Homme*, 132: 7–14.

Janssen, Jacques, De Hart, Joep and Christine Den Draak (1990). 'A Content Analysis of the Praying Practices of Dutch Youth', *Journal for the Scientific Study of Religion*, 1: 99–107.

Khoury, Adel Theodor (2004). 'Preghiera', in Khoury, Adel Theodor (ed.), *Dizionario delle religioni monoteistiche*, Casale Monferrato: Piemme.

Ladd, Kevin L. and Bernard Spilka (2006). 'Inward, Outward, Upward Prayer: Scale Reliability and Validation', *Journal for the Scientific Study of Religion*, 2: 233–51.

Lévy-Bruhl, Lucien (1922). *La mentalité primitive*, Paris: Alcan.

Maha, Cheleen Ann-Catherine (2008). 'Practice theory', in William A. Darity (ed.), *International Encyclopedia of the Social Sciences*, New York: Macmillan-Gale, 418–19.

Mauss, Marcel (1969–74). *Oeuvres*, Paris: Minuit.

Poloma, Margaret M. and Brian F. Pendleton (1989). 'Exploring Types of Prayer and Quality of Life: A Research Note', *Review of Religious Research*, 1: 46–53.

Radcliffe Brown, Alfred Reginald and Cyril Daryll Forde (1950). *African Systems of Kinship and Marriage*, London: Oxford University Press.

Radcliffe Brown, Alfred Reginald (1952). *Structure and Function in Primitive Society*, Glencoe: Free Press.

Reckwitz, Andreas (2002). 'Toward a Theory of Social Practices. A Development in Culturalist Theorizing', *European Journal of Social Theory*, 2: 243–63.

Robertson Smith, William (1894). *Lectures on the Religion of the Semites*, London: Black.

Schatzi, Theodore R., Cetina, Karin Knorr and Eike von Savigny (2001). *The Practice Turn in Contemporary Theory*, London: Routledge.

Seely Brown, John and Paul Duguid (2001). 'Knowledge and Organization: A Social-Practice Perspective', in *Organization Science*, 2: 198–213.

Simmel, Georg (1997). *Essays on Religion*, Yale: Yale University Press.

Swatos Jr, William H. (1982). 'The Power of Prayer: A Prolegomenon to an Ascetical Sociology', *Review of Religious Research*, 2: 153–63.

Tuomela, Raimo (2002). *The Philosophy of Social Practices*, Cambridge: Cambridge University Press.

Turner, Stephen P. (1994). *The Social Theory of Practices*, Cambridge: Polity Press.

Weber, Max (1978). *Economy and Society*, Berkeley: University of California Press.

Weber, Max (2001). *The Protestant Ethic and the Spirit of Capitalism*, Chicago: Dearborn.

Chapter 2

For Youth, Prayer is Relationship

Michael C. Mason

Introduction[1]

Prayer should be understood as the most fundamental of all religious activities, because it is through prayer that the sacred world becomes real for believers – prayer actualises their relationship with their God. Religious faith, at its most basic level, is the acknowledgment of the *reality* of a transcendent Being or Power. This is prayer in its simplest form.[2]

This chapter reports on a recent empirical investigation of prayer among a large group of young people from both Western and Asian societies, which explored the forms of prayer they used, the content or themes of their prayers, the relationship between prayer and civic engagement, and the influences which contributed to shaping most of them as people who prayed frequently.

Sociological Research on Prayer

After reviewing sociological theories of prayer, Mason (2013) concludes, following Mauss (2003) that all prayer – even 'private' prayer – is a profoundly social activity. Prayer in solitude has a special significance in being more

---

[1]   The project which gathered the data on which this paper is based was the work of a research team comprising Michael Mason (Australian Catholic University), Andrew Singleton (Monash University) and Ruth Webber (Australian Catholic University). The project was assisted by a grant from the Sydney 2008 World Youth Day Administration, and by personnel and infrastructure support from the Australian Catholic Bishops Conference, Australian Catholic University and Monash University. Support from all these sources is gratefully acknowledged. For more detail on the project and its findings, see the reports, questionnaires and background materials on the website: http://dlibrary.acu.edu.au/research/wyd/.

[2]   A fuller discussion and review of theories of prayer – its place in religion, and how it achieves its effects – especially how it 'makes the sacred world real to believers' can be found in Mason (2013).

voluntary and spontaneous than prayer in others' company; it is relatively less constrained in its exercise and its content, so may be taken more confidently as an indicator of a person's religious sentiments; whereas prayer in the presence of others is more likely to involve multiple motives, so is more open to being performed for non-religious reasons.

In his comparative sociological study of religion, Max Weber examined prayer in a variety of cultures, Eastern and Western, tracing its origins to magic: the attempt to coerce spiritual beings or powers to serve human ends. As people's ideas of gods became more elevated, the latter were seen as overlords who could not be constrained by magical means, but had to be entreated and given gifts. Weber maintained that, in prayer:

> The pervasive and central theme is: *do ut des* [*I give (to you) so that you will give (to me)*]. This aspect clings to the routine and mass religious behavior of all people at all times and in all religions. The normal situation is that the burden of all prayers, even in the most other-worldly religions, is the aversion of the external evils of this world and the inducement of the external advantages of this world (Weber [1922] 1964: 27).

Many sociological researchers[3] follow Weber in this, defining prayer as intended to persuade a spiritual power to grant worldly favours. Many studies have sought to show that the frequency and content of prayer are strongly influenced by disadvantage: that economically or socially disadvantaged people are more likely to pray, either in the hope of advancing in wealth or social status, or seeking otherworldly compensation for earthly deprivations.[4]

Baker (2008) analysed data from the Baylor Religion Survey (2005) to show that in the USA, women, African–Americans and those with lower incomes pray more often. Four variables were employed to indicate the content of people's most recent prayer; the model also included a frequency of prayer variable (which combined prayer and meditation), demographics and religious control variables (religious tradition and Biblical literalism). In Baker's analysis, Pargament's (1997) 'coping mechanism' theory of religion is applied to prayer: those who

---

[3]   Psychological research has tended to focus on prayer as a coping mechanism (Pargament 1997) especially for those in deprived, oppressed or less privileged social strata, and on the relationship between prayer and physical or psychological benefits such as health (McCullough 1995), well-being, reduction of anxiety, sense of purpose in life, improved self-esteem.

[4]   For example Stark and Bainbridge (1996), Norris and Inglehart (2004) and Baker (2008).

pray seek primarily an improvement in their material circumstances. Prayers for forgiveness or 'about your spiritual life / relationship with God' are interpreted by Baker as attempts at 'securing favour with the supernatural' (2008: 171) – a means of obtaining otherworldly benefits as compensation for this-worldly deprivation. The results were claimed to replicate Norris and Inglehart's (2004) findings (Baker 2008: 175). However it is notable that in Baker's data, as in ours, prayers for financial security were by far the least frequent content theme. Prayers for family and friends, and prayer that was about one's relationship with God were more than twice as frequent, among those who prayed at all. The (negative) relationship of prayer frequency with income retained its significance in logistic regression when controls were introduced, but the relationship was weak.

If there is indeed a statistical association between prayer and economic disadvantage which remains when differences in culture and spiritual style between rich and poor have been taken into account, there are still alternative explanations to that *assumed* by the authors just cited: that the poor pray more frequently because they seek material relief (or compensatory otherworldly benefits).[5] Several religious traditions propose a contrasting interpretation: that wealth tends to blind the rich to spiritual values, so that they are disinclined to pray; whereas the 'poor in spirit' are better placed to appreciate the Gospel message of the transitory quality of earthly possessions, and more likely to value their relationship with God.

Several studies have advanced the investigation of prayer by moving away from an exclusive focus on prayer of petition, and exploring multiple dimensions of prayer: its detailed content, its social setting, its length and purpose, and beliefs about its efficacy. One of the most comprehensive sets of measures was that utilised by Poloma and Pendleton (1989) for a study of prayer and well-being. Fifteen questions on the content of prayer were developed, (subsequently reduced by factor analysis to four factors), and accompanied by a battery of measures of happiness and well-being, an indicator of religious satisfaction, the standard question about frequency of prayer, and most usefully, by five questions about religious experiences occurring during prayer. It was the latter that turned out to be the most powerful predictors of well-being; the content factors were not as strong in their effects.

Poloma and Gallup (1991) presented a book-length report of a US national survey on prayer (N=1030) utilising similar, admirably varied, measures as in the project just reviewed. However both studies have some limitations in the

---

[5]   The studies reviewed have not shown precisely that disadvantage is related to prayer of petition for material advantage.

way forms of prayer are classified. To label as 'ritual' prayers which follow a written or memorised formula, but are neither collective nor accompanied by any visible expression, conflicts with the common understanding of ritual in anthropology and religion studies as involving performative action, or at least perceptible symbols (Grimes 1990). The classification of 'forms of prayer' as ritual, petitionary, conversational and meditative is logically inconsistent. These 'forms' mix *methods* of prayer with *contents* of prayer, so the categories are not mutually exclusive: a so-called 'ritual' (memorised) prayer may also be 'petitionary' (1991: 26).

Krause and Chatters (2005) noted that the effects of race had been neglected in sociological research on prayer in the USA, and contrasted older African–Americans and older whites on a battery of 17 measures of prayer, 8 of which focused on content. The African–American group were significantly more involved in prayer on 16 of the 17 measures. The study is particularly valuable for the large set of measures of prayer employed, and for its attempt to take account of cultural as well as social structural factors.

Mason, Singleton and Webber (2007) studied Australian youth of any or no religion, conducting a telephone survey in 2005 of a probability sample of Australians aged 15–24. The survey canvassed the young people's worldviews, values, religious and 'spiritual' beliefs and practices as well as their forms of civic engagement. Prayer was not the main focus of the study, but it provided a measure of frequency of 'private' prayer among youth in the general Australian population which proved useful as a baseline against which to profile respondents of the present study, which took place three years later.

Research Design

The investigation of prayer described in this chapter is based on the understanding of prayer we had tentatively arrived at on the basis of previous theory and research, and analysis of the lengthy interviews which constituted the first stage of the earlier project. In the present investigation, first, a research problem was specified and then several hypotheses were developed to express specific aspects of the research question, so that operational measures of relevant variables could be implemented.

1. Research Problem

What influences can be discerned that shape the observed variations in form, content and frequency of prayer?

The following hypotheses or expectations were formulated to serve both as statements of the principal elements of our understanding of prayer, and to provide measurable criteria for testing each element.

2. Hypotheses

1) The *content* of prayer

> a) is that of a personal relationship with God; seeking worldly advantages will play a minor role;
> b) will be found to be influenced by age, frequency of prayer and country of residence.

2) The frequency of prayer will be positively associated with other religious practices such as church attendance and attendance at Reconciliation (Confession), with strong Catholic identity, orthodox Catholic beliefs and moral values, and a strong sense of personal security and well-being.
3) Those who pray more frequently will show higher civic engagement in volunteering and charitable giving.
4) Higher frequency of prayer will be influenced by:

- Age of the respondent
- Traditionalism of the Catholic culture in home country
- Parents' frequency of church attendance and 'enthusiasm for their religion'
- Having friends who attend services regularly
- Membership in a church group such as a youth group or prayer group
- Previous religious experiences.

Method

In this section the method of the study and the characteristics of the sample obtained will be briefly described, then the methods used in this analysis.

The data are drawn from a study of young people who registered to attend the Catholic youth festival known as 'World Youth Day' (WYD) which in 2008 took place in Sydney, Australia, during the week of July 15–20. Stage I of the research, prior to the event, consisted of 49 semi-structured interviews with Australian youth intending to attend WYD. Next, all English-speakers who had registered to attend as of early May, 2008, were invited to complete a survey on a research website canvassing their worldviews, values, spiritual background, past civic engagement and hopes for WYD. Responses were received from 12,275 registrants. The responses obtained were representative of those registered at the time, and the sample characteristics closely match those of the target population.[6]

Confining our attention to those who were Catholic (nearly all of those registered) and were under 35 years of age leaves 9,536 cases. Sixty-five per cent of these respondents were female, 35 per cent male. WYD attracted many more young women than young men. The greatest imbalance was in the school-age group, who were mostly from Australia, in which there were more than twice as many girls as boys.

Table 2.1   WYD attenders aged 15–34 – Age by gender (% of age-group within gender)

		Age-group			Total
		15–18	19–24	25–34	
SEX	Male	1091	1151	1091	3333
		30.3%	34.0%	42.8%	35.0%
	Female	2509	2234	1460	6203
		69.7%	66.0%	57.2%	65.0%
Total		3600	3385	2551	9536
		100.0%	100.0%	100.0%	100.0%

Attenders came from a wide variety of nations. The following table summarises countries of residence into seven regional groups:

---

6   Fuller details of sampling and response rates are contained in the report on Method on the project website (see note 1 above).

Table 2.2   Main countries of residence[7]

	Frequency	Per cent
1 Aus	4447	46.6
2 NZ	518	5.4
3 USA	1398	14.7
4 Can	496	5.2
5 UK/etc.[1]	483	5.1
6 Asia[2]	1044	10.9
7 Other[3]	1150	12.1
Total	9536	100.0

Notes:

[1] Grouped with the UK respondents here are those from the Republic of Ireland and a small number of English-speaking respondents from other countries of Europe, especially Germany.

[2] The principal countries in the 'Asia' category were the Philippines, Singapore, India, Indonesia, Vietnam, Hong Kong, China. Only English-speaking attenders from these countries were surveyed.

[3] 'Other' country of residence was a residual category comprising a large number of (mostly less-developed) countries, each contributing a small number of WYD attenders. Their communities of origin tended to be strongly 'traditional' in their Catholicism.

Obviously, the highest number of attenders by far was from Australia. These differed from overseas visitors in some important respects: Australian attenders had the least distance to travel; their attendance was strongly urged and often subsidised; a higher proportion of them were secondary school students. Groups from other countries had to raise funds for costly travel,[8] and arrange for a longer absence from work or study. The filtering effect of these costs resulted in the selection of older and more highly committed attenders from overseas than from the host country.[9]

---

[7]   The population of every table is Catholic WYD attenders aged 15–34 unless otherwise noted.

[8]   Registration costs and some travel costs were subsidised for attenders from developing countries.

[9]   These considerations apply at every World Youth Day, but since the cost of travel to Australia was higher than usual, the filtering effect was particularly strong.

The frequency of prayer among those aged 15–34 was distributed as shown in Table 2.3.

Table 2.3   Frequency of prayer alone

		Frequency	Per cent
Valid	0 Never	93	1.1
	1 Once or twice a year	199	2.3
	2 Occasionally, but not as often as once a month	801	9.1
	3 Once or twice a month	833	9.5
	4 About every week	1805	20.6
	5 Usually every day	3568	40.7
	6 Several times a day	1474	16.8
	Total	8773	100.0
Missing	-99 No response	605	
	-98 Not asked	158	
	Total	763	
Total		9536	

Forty-one per cent of the sample claimed to pray usually every day, and a further 17 per cent said that they prayed several times per day. These two groups will be a special focus of interest in what follows.

The young people who attended World Youth Day were markedly different from the general population of Catholic youth in their home countries: they were far more religious than is typical. For example, Mason, Singleton and Webber (2007) found that only 26 per cent of typical young Australian Catholics prayed daily or more often (compared with 58 per cent of the WYD sample); and only 3 per cent prayed more often than once a day (compared with 17 per cent of the WYD sample). Obviously, to conduct research on prayer in the general population in secularised countries would require a very large and expensive sample in order to obtain a sufficient number who engage in the practice.

Targeting an event such as World Youth Day, which attracts relatively more religious youth, secured a much more useful sample.

Data and Methods of Analysis

Form and Content of Prayer

Those who reported praying weekly or more often were asked a set of questions about the form and content of their prayers. Both questions were multiple-response: people could choose more than one answer. Variations in form and content were explored by analysing responses by gender, age-group, country of residence and frequency of prayer.

Frequency of Prayer in Relation to Other Religion Variables

The bivariate relationships between frequency of prayer and a wide range of other variables were explored, showing some strong associations.

Prayer and Civic Engagement

The survey included several indicators of civic engagement, namely how often respondents had engaged in volunteer work in recent times, the approximate amount of money they had given to their church in the previous twelve months, and how much to other organisations and causes. They were also asked about their reasons for engaging in community service activities. Responses to these questions were compared by frequency of prayer.

Influences on Frequency of Prayer

Next, to show the influences shaping frequency of prayer, a multiple regression analysis was performed, using as the dependent variable the self-reported frequency of prayer.

Findings and Discussion

The Form and Content of Prayer

Hypothesis 1
Those who reported praying weekly or more often were asked a set of questions about the form and content of their prayers. Initial results are shown in Table 2.4, with items rearranged in descending order of frequency:

Table 2.4   Preferred form of prayer and content of prayer (% often)[10]

Form of prayer which respondent uses often:

Talk with God in your own words	86.4%
Say prayers you have memorised	59.7%
Spend time quietly thinking about God	42.7%
Read a passage from the Bible and meditate on it	17.5%
Read from a book of prayers	14.7%

Themes which often form the content of respondent's prayer:

Ask God for guidance in making decisions	81.5%
Thank God for blessings	80.6%
Pray for individual people you know	78.3%
Ask God to forgive your sins	70.1%
Express your love for God	54.4%
Pray for the world – e.g. for peace, justice, relief of poverty	40.7%
Ask God for material things you need	21.9%

The form of prayer most commonly used by respondents was that of a spontaneous conversation with God.[11] Memorised prayers were also used often, as was thinking about God. Less frequently used were meditation on a text of the Bible, or recitation of prayers from a prayer book.

Asked what they prayed about, the young people reported that most often they expressed thanks to God for blessings or asked for guidance in making decisions. Almost as common were prayers for other individual people and requests for forgiveness; more than half the respondents favoured simply expressing their love for God; and a large minority often prayed about issues like peace and justice in the world. Far down at the bottom of the list was prayer for material things for oneself. Only 22 per cent said they often prayed for this.

The respondents clearly understand prayer as the key element in a relationship with a personal Other whom they love and trust. Over half of them talk to this Other each day, sometimes often during the day, to share their lives; very rarely to seek tangible benefits for themselves. This finding, although taken for granted in theology and spiritual writing, has rarely been explored sociologically, and runs counter to some of the classic sociological analyses of prayer. But it is well supported by the evidence.

---

[10]   The two sets of response items in this table have each been rearranged in the order of preference of the respondents.

[11]   The social–psychological theories and research of Sundén et al. show how prayer can be 'conversation' rather than 'monologue'. See the discussion in Mason (2013).

Hypothesis 1a) is confirmed: that in this sample of young practising Catholics, the content of prayer, whether regular or occasional, is predominantly not the seeking of worldly advantages, but the expression of a personal relationship with God.

The survey respondents were so numerous that we can mine deeper to explore variation in the form and content of people's prayers by age, gender, nationality and frequency of prayer.

There was very little variation by gender in the form or content of prayer.

The following table compares the form and content of prayer across age-groups.

Table 2.5   Preferred form of prayer and content of prayer by age-group

Age-group	15–18	19–24	25–29	30–34	All 15–34
Form of prayer					
Talk to God	83.3%	87.7%	87.5%	89.5%	86.4%
Memorised prayer	59.6%	59.2%	59.7%	61.3%	59.7%
Think about God	36.8%	41.2%	48.0%	55.6%	42.7%
Meditate on Bible	8.0%	17.1%	26.4%	30.9%	17.5%
Prayer from a book	7.0%	14.5%	22.2%	24.5%	14.7%
Content of prayer					
Ask guidance	77.8%	82.7%	83.6%	84.2%	81.5%
Thank God	74.9%	82.2%	83.3%	87.2%	80.6%
Pray for others	79.9%	78.8%	76.8%	74.5%	78.3%
Ask forgiveness	67.6%	69.8%	73.0%	73.0%	70.1%
Express love for God	46.9%	55.2%	59.1%	65.4%	54.4%
Pray for the world	46.7%	37.0%	36.4%	43.0%	40.7%
Seek material things	20.1%	21.9%	23.8%	23.8%	21.9%

It is remarkable that the *relative* order of preference among various forms and contents of prayer does not change, regardless of the age of the subject. For example, reading from a prayer book remains the least popular form of prayer from youngest to oldest, and asking for material things is by far the lowest priority in the content of prayer for all ages. However a much higher proportion of older than younger respondents do use a book of prayers. While fewer than half the school-age group spend prayer-time 'expressing your love for God', two-thirds of the over-thirties do so. Baesler (2002) found a similar correlation between age and these types of prayer, which he categorised as indicating 'receptive' rather than 'active' forms of prayer.

Does the form and content of prayer differ depending on how intensely and frequently people pray? The next table compares the prayers of those who pray only about once a week with those of respondents who pray more often: daily and more than once a day.

Table 2.6   Preferred form and content of prayer by frequency of prayer – % who often chose each form and content (column %; respondents could choose more than one response)

FORM	How often do you pray just by yourself (not with others or at a religious service)?			
	About every week	Usually every day	Several times a day	Total
1 TALK	86.8%	90.0%	93.8%	90.0%
2 MEMO	53.5%	62.4%	71.1%	62.1%
3 THINK	35.0%	41.3%	63.0%	44.5%
4 BIBLE	8.3%	15.9%	35.2%	18.3%
5 PR BK	6.2%	12.8%	31.6%	15.3%
Total	100.0%	100.0%	100.0%	100.0%

CONTENTS	About every week	Usually every day	Several times a day	Total
1 THANK	75.0%	84.4%	90.7%	83.4%
2 GUIDE	77.1%	85.3%	90.2%	84.3%
3 OTHERS	77.2%	80.3%	86.9%	81.0%
4 FORG	62.7%	72.7%	83.3%	72.5%
5 LOVE	38.7%	56.0%	77.4%	56.3%
6 WORLD	40.4%	40.6%	47.4%	42.1%
7 MATERIAL	17.1%	23.1%	28.0%	22.6%
Total	100.0%	100.0%	100.0%	100.0%

Note: See Table 2.4 for the full text corresponding to these abbreviated headings.

The relative order of preference among forms of prayer remains the same whether people pray weekly or more often: but there are large differences in the proportion of each group using a particular method of prayer. 'Talking with God in your own words' is most favoured across all ages, and Bible meditation and use of a prayer book are least often used: fewer than 10 per cent of those who pray weekly make use of either of these methods, but up to a third of those who pray very frequently do so. 'Just thinking about God' is a frequent choice for only a third of those who pray weekly, but for two-thirds of those who pray several times a day. There are similar variations in content. For those who prayed weekly, prayer for others is the most popular by a small margin; thanksgiving and prayers for guidance are almost equally popular in all groups. The largest difference across these groups is that only about a third of those who pray weekly feel comfortable with 'expressing their love for God', while three-quarters of those who pray more than once a day often pray in this way.

Characteristics of Prayer Across Cultures

How did the form and content of prayer vary by national religious culture? Respondents came from a wide variety of countries, as shown in Table 2.2. The preferred form of prayer followed the pattern we have already seen, and differed very little across countries of residence. Table 2.7 shows the reported content of prayer in the main countries of residence. The rows in bold italic show the range of variation on two items on which regions did differ, from the lowest region (UK/etc.) to the highest (Asia).

Table 2.7   Those who prayed weekly or more: preferred content of prayer by country of residence (% often)

	MAIN COUNTRIES OF RESIDENCE							
	1 Aus	2 NZ	3 USA	4 Can	5 UK/ etc.	6 Asia	7 Other	Total
1 THANK	81.7%	79.0%	84.2%	81.3%	75.5%	90.1%	86.4%	83.4%
2 GUIDE	83.7%	82.3%	85.9%	84.9%	81.7%	86.4%	83.4%	84.3%
3 OTHERS	82.2%	81.7%	86.6%	83.0%	86.3%	74.2%	74.0%	81.0%
4 FORG	*68.1%*	*73.3%*	*74.2%*	*70.9%*	*66.0%*	*81.7%*	*77.6%*	*72.5%*
5 LOVE	*51.5%*	*51.7%*	*63.4%*	*53.9%*	*42.8%*	*63.8%*	*63.2%*	*56.3%*
6 WORLD	44.5%	40.8%	42.6%	36.3%	38.9%	32.8%	47.1%	42.1%
7 MATERIAL	20.2%	24.0%	18.8%	19.3%	18.0%	35.0%	24.8%	22.6%
Total	100.0%	100.0%	100.0%	100.0%	100.0%	100.0%	100.0%	100.0%

As expected, the hierarchy of preference among the themes forming the content of young people's prayers is the same, especially the notably low priority given to prayer of petition for personal material advantages, even across such diverse nationalities as are represented here. However, the proportion of those who report that they often pray in more intimate ways: asking forgiveness for their sins, and expressing love for God, varies considerably across nations, following the same pattern as almost all the other indicators of religiosity in this survey (such as church attendance, acceptance of Catholic beliefs and moral teachings):

Asia and 'Other' share the highest position, followed by USA, Canada, New Zealand, Australia, with UK and Ireland lowest.

We conclude that hypothesis 1b) is confirmed: The form and content of prayer are influenced by age and frequency of prayer and, to a limited extent, by country of residence.

Frequency of Prayer in Relation to Other Aspects of Religiosity

Hypothesis 2

Our second hypothesis was that the frequency of prayer would be positively associated with other religious practices such as attendance at church services and at Reconciliation (Confession), with Catholic identity, Catholic beliefs and moral values, and with a sense of belonging and purpose.

In the review of recent research it was noted that Norris and Inglehart (2004: 107–10) reported a strong negative association between household income (deciles) and the proportion of populations in post-industrial societies who pray daily. Our findings did not support this proposition. In our own data the expected negative relationship between frequency of prayer and a subjective measure of standard of living was negligible (gamma -.034). The relationship between standard of living and how frequently respondents prayed *for material benefit for themselves* was also tested: the gamma of -.036 showed the relationship was extremely weak.

There is a very strong relationship between frequency of prayer and two other key Catholic practices: attendance at Mass[12] and at Reconciliation (Confession).[13] Table 2.8 shows in condensed format the relationship of frequency of prayer with the variables listed in the hypothesis. The percentages are column percentages; the last number in the first row is to be read as indicating that 90.9 per cent of those who pray daily or more often attend Mass every week or more often.

---

[12]   Gamma .62 p <.001
[13]   Gamma .51 p <.001

Table 2.8 Measures of religiosity by frequency of prayer (% of frequency group)

Selected measures of religiosity	Frequency of prayer		
	Never to occasionally	Monthly to weekly	Daily and more
Religious practices			
Attendance at Mass weekly or more often	49.0%	73.2%	90.9%
Friends attend church regularly (% responding 'Most of them do')	26.2%	37.1%	62.7%
Attendance at Reconciliation (Confession) regularly (every 2/3 months or more often)	21.9%	37.8%	66.0%
Catholic beliefs (strongly agree)			
That Jesus was truly God and truly human and was raised bodily from the dead	67.0%	82.0%	95.0%
That Mary was a virgin when she gave birth to Jesus	59.8%	76.0%	91.8%
That Jesus is truly present in the consecrated bread and wine at Mass	49.1%	68.4%	89.1%
After death the soul is reunited with the risen body	12.1%	29.7%	58.2%
It is okay to pick and choose your religious beliefs without having to accept all the basic teachings of your religion as a whole. (Strongly disagree)	12.8%	20.4%	42.7%
Things that make belief hard: issues about the church, beliefs, rules about morality	43.2%	41.5%	28.4%
Strong agreement with Catholic moral teaching			
Morals are relative: there are no definite rights or wrongs for everybody. (Strongly disagree)	14.7%	24.8%	43.3%
The church law that priests must be male and unmarried. (Strongly Agree)	13.2%	21.2%	45.9%
Church teaching on not having sex before marriage	16.3%	25.7%	59.9%

Selected measures of religiosity	Frequency of prayer		
	Never to occasionally	Monthly to weekly	Daily and more
Church teaching opposing the death penalty	44.1%	53.2%	67.3%
Church teaching opposing abortion	34.0%	48.6%	75.5%
Church teaching opposing euthanasia	26.2%	36.6%	64.0%
Church teaching opposing same-sex marriage	20.2%	29.4%	60.1%
Church teaching supporting workers' rights to take industrial action	24.3%	30.9%	45.3%
How influential is faith in shaping your life? (It influences almost everything I do)	11.7%	27.7%	68.4%
Reasons why you attend Mass			
I want to worship and thank God	30.3%	46.4%	73.3%
I get the strength to keep trying to live as a Christian	39.6%	57.8%	78.8%
It's good to be with others who share the same beliefs	52.5%	60.8%	63.5%
I'm fulfilling my obligation to attend (at weekends)	44.1%	44.1%	45.6%
I come away more empowered by the Holy Spirit	22.4%	34.8%	58.1%
I experience Jesus' love for me and express my love for him	29.2%	48.6%	74.3%
Catholic Identity (% strongly agreeing except first question)			
How a person lives is all that matters; being Catholic or not doesn't really matter at all. (Disagree)	23.5%	31.5%	50.4%
Being a Catholic is a very important part of who I am	66.8%	85.8%	93.6%
Catholicism contains a greater share of truth than other religions do. (Agree)	28.5%	41.4%	65.2%
Catholic devotions such as Eucharistic adoration or praying the Rosary are important to me	35.6%	58.0%	82.7%

	Frequency of prayer		
Selected measures of religiosity	Never to occasionally	Monthly to weekly	Daily and more
Attitudes to self and own life			
How close do you feel to God most of the time (% responding 'Very close')	3.9%	5.4%	24.6%
I feel I don't really belong anywhere. (Strongly disagree)	30.4%	37.8%	51.3%
My life has a purpose	27.3%	36.2%	56.4%
My life fits in as part of God's plan	13.7%	28.0%	52.7%

The strong associations between prayer and these other aspects of religion support our contention that prayer is the fundamental religious act: by establishing and maintaining communication with God, it undergirds, supports and strengthens all of these visible expressions of the relationship: religious practices, belief, moral attitudes and identity.

Prayer and Civic Engagement

Hypothesis 3
This hypothesis states our expectation that those who pray more often will also show higher civic engagement in volunteering and charitable giving.

Table 2.9 shows several measures of respondents' civic engagement during the previous year: how often people undertook volunteer work and how much money they donated to the church and to other organisations and causes.

Table 2.9   Forms of, and reasons for, civic engagement by frequency of prayer (% of frequency groups)

	Frequency of prayer		
Volunteering and donations	**Never – occasionally**	**Monthly, weekly**	**Daily and more often**
Frequency of engaging in volunteer work last 12 months: (monthly or more often)	27%	35%	40%
Median amount given to church in last 12 months	$90	$209	$376
Median amount given to other organisations/causes in last 12 months	$85	$115	$265
Reason why you did community service (% Strongly agree)			
Compassion for those in need	30%	40%	56%
A sense of duty, moral obligation	27%	25%	35%
Identifying with people who were suffering	18%	22%	34%
Religious beliefs	12%	20%	41%
To help give disadvantaged people hope and dignity	25%	29%	46%
To make a contribution to my local community	26%	30%	40%
For social reasons, to meet people	10%	13%	15%
To gain new skills and useful experience	22%	26%	28%

All of these measures increased significantly with frequency of prayer. The table also shows a contrast in the motives underlying civic engagement: religious and humane considerations, rather than self-interested concerns, were foremost among the motives of those who prayed more often. These findings show that prayer by no means leads to withdrawal from the world or rejection of the claims made on the believer by others; rather, the reverse is true: prayer sensitises the one who prays, and makes the person more aware that they are responsible for fellow humans, and more responsive to claims for assistance.

Influences on Frequency of Prayer

Hypothesis 4
What influences shape the intensity of the prayer-life of these young Catholics? Specifically, what makes the difference as to whether they will pray only occasionally, or every day / several times a day? We have shown that praying daily or more often is far from rare among young people today, even among those from highly secularised countries like Australia. Table 2.3 above showed the wide variation in frequency of prayer among the youth in our sample.

Some of this variation was associated with age: only 45 per cent of the school-age group (15–18) prayed daily or more often, but this proportion increased with age to 77 per cent of the 30–34 age group. About the same proportion of young men as young women reported praying daily or more than once a day: the bivariate relationship between gender and prayer was negligible.

On the basis of our previous research, we hypothesised that higher frequency of prayer would be explained by:

- Age of the respondent;
- Traditionalism of the Catholic culture in their home country;
- Parents' frequency of attendance and 'enthusiasm for their religion';
- Having friends who attend services regularly;
- Membership in a church group such as a youth group or prayer group;
- Previous religious experiences.

The traditionalism of the Catholic culture varies very greatly across societies, even amongst English speakers: Australia, New Zealand and the UK are highly secularised, the USA less so.[14] But in Asia and particularly in less developed

---

[14]   However, Christian Smith's National Survey of Youth and Religion (2005, 2009) shows significant decline in youth religiousness in the USA.

countries, Christian subcultures tend to be still quite strongly traditional. We expected the differences in country of residence among our respondents to affect the frequency with which people prayed.

The religious context of a person's family of origin is well established as a source of influence on their religious development. Our analysis initially tested measures of the frequency of parents' attendance at church services and the respondent's assessment of how enthusiastic each parent was about their religion, at the time when the respondent was growing up. However, father's attendance and enthusiasm were weaker predictors and did not remain significant when mother's attendance and enthusiasm were controlled, so the final analysis did not use these measures.

The hypothesis was explored using multiple regression analysis. The methodological and statistical details of the procedure are reported in Appendix I.[15] Here we present and discuss the findings.

The dependent variable in the analysis was frequency of prayer. Five cumulative models tested the sets of independent variables listed below.[16] The variables marked with an asterisk are those which retained significance in the fifth model after all controls had been added; the number after the asterisk indicates the relative weight of their influence on frequency of prayer, in order from strongest (1) to weakest (12).[17]

Model 1 commenced with the religious context items entered:

- Catholic traditionalism of home country
- mother's church attendance
- mother's enthusiasm for her religion *8.

Model 2 added peer support elements:
- church attendance of friends *2
- membership of a small group in the church *6.

Model 3 added two 'classic' religious experiences: often felt as strong, dramatic acts of God:
- A clear answer to prayer *4
- Being healed by God's power *7.

---

[15]   Appendix I, not shown here because of limitations of space, can be found on the website: http://dlibrary.acu.edu.au/research/wyd/.

[16]   The method was direct entry of each set of independent variables.

[17]   All of these effects were statistically significant at $p < .001$. The order is based on the relative size of the beta weights.

Model 4 added several 'experiences of the presence of God', occurring in the context of:
- quiet reflection or prayer alone *5
- reading the Bible *9
- personal suffering or sickness *12.

Also added in this model were two often reported responses to an experience of the presence of God, and a measure of how valuable, on reflection, one considered such experiences:

- extraordinary joy without any reason *11
- a moment of truth, of deeper conviction that God was real; God became more important *10
- evaluating one's experiences of the presence or action of God as highly valuable *1.

Model 5, finally, added controls for two demographic factors:
- age *3
- gender (female).

Discussion

The following factors became progressively less significant as more variables were controlled in successive models, and were not retained in the final model:

- mother's church attendance
- Catholic traditionalism of home country.

The analysis used gender as a routine control variable, but it was not expected that it would be a significant influence on frequency of prayer among young people, and the results confirmed that this was so.

Family influence was represented in the final model by mother's 'enthusiasm for her religion', which retained its significance. There was so little variation in mother's church attendance (81 per cent were weekly attenders) that this was a poor predictor and was discarded.

The traditionalism of the Catholic culture of one's home country turned out not to have as strong an influence as expected on frequency of prayer; its significance diminished as other predictors were added.

Age retained the significant association with frequency of prayer evident in the bivariate analysis reported above.

Peer support for one's religious commitment is always very important for contemporary young adults, and emerged as a major influence on frequency of prayer, as also did membership in a church-related small group.

The most striking result that emerged was this: by far the strongest influence on how often a person prayed was the history of significant moments in their relationship with God: whether they had experienced what they believed to be a clear answer to prayer; whether they had felt healed by God's power in body, mind or spirit; whether they had been strongly aware of the presence of God in a moment of quiet reflection or when reading the Bible or in a time of suffering or sickness; and the response that these encounters had drawn from them: extraordinary joy, or a deepening of faith in God; and finally, whether, reflecting afterwards on these events, they still considered them highly valuable.

We had not anticipated this result, and had looked first for influences external to the person, in their family or their society, which would explain why some prayed very often and others rarely. The measures of religious experiences had been collected for a different reason. Yet given that the forms and contents of these young people's prayers were found not to fit the models of magical manipulation or contractual back-scratching, but appeared rather as the expression of a continuing relationship with a divine person, it is easy to understand, in reflection, that the history of that relationship – its pattern of development, its peak experiences – is the strongest influence over the present intensity of the relationship, one manifestation of which is the frequency of prayer.

The results of this multivariate analysis of factors related to frequent prayer provide strong evidence of the basically relational character of prayer for these young people.

Conclusions

1. Amongst young Catholics who pray at least weekly, the *content* of prayer:

- expresses aspects of a personal relationship with God, rarely seeks material assistance
- is more intimate and intense among those who are somewhat older, or pray more frequently.

2. Frequent prayer is strongly and positively associated with other religious practices such as church attendance and attendance at Reconciliation (Confession), with a personal sense of Catholic identity, with the holding of orthodox Catholic beliefs and moral values, and with a sense of personal security and well-being.

3. Compared with those who pray weekly or less, those who pray once or more each day show higher civic engagement in volunteering and charitable giving.

4. Family religious socialisation and current peer support influence how often a person prays, but the strongest influence stems from significant moments in their continuing relationship with God.

In short, for these youth, prayer is relationship.

References

Baesler, E. James (2002). 'Prayer and Relationship with God II: Replication and Extension of the Relational Prayer Model'. *Review of Religious Research*, 44/1: 58–67.

Baker, J.O. (2008). 'An Investigation of the Sociological Patterns of Prayer Frequency and Content'. *Sociology of Religion*, 69/2: 169–75.

Grimes, Ronald L. (1990). 'Victor Turner's Definition, Theory and Sense of Ritual'. In Kathleen M. Ashley (ed.), *Victor Turner and the Construction of Cultural Criticism: Between Literature and Anthropology*, Indiana University Press, 141–6.

Krause, Neal and Linda M. Chatters (2005). 'Exploring Race Differences in a Multidimensional Battery of Prayer Measures Among Older Adults'. *Sociology of Religion*, 66/1: 23–43.

Mason, Michael (2013). 'Prayer: Making the Sacred Real'. In Giuseppe Giordan and Linda Woodhead (eds), *Prayer in Religion and Spirituality*, Annual Review of the Sociology of Religion. Leiden and Boston: Brill, 9–25.

Mason, Michael, Andrew Singleton and Ruth Webber (2007). *The Spirit of Generation Y : Young People's Spirituality in a Changing Australia*. Mulgrave, Vic.: John Garratt Publications.

Mauss, Marcel (2003). *On Prayer*. (W.S.F. Pickering, (ed.)). New York: Durkheim Press / Berghahn Books.

McCullough, Michael E. (1995). 'Prayer and Health: Conceptual Issues, Research Review and Research Agenda'. *Journal of Psychology and Theology*, 23: 15–29.

Norris, Pippa and Ronald Inglehart (2004). *Sacred And Secular : Religion and Politics Worldwide*. Cambridge UK , New York: Cambridge University Press.

Pargament, Kenneth (1997). *The Psychology of Religion and Coping: Theory, Research, Practice*. New York: Guilford Press.

Poloma, Margaret M. and George Gallup (1991). *Varieties of Prayer: A Survey Report*. Philadelphia: Trinity Press International.

Poloma, Margaret M. and Brian E. Pendleton (1989). 'Exploring Types of Prayer and Quality of Life'. *Review of Religious Research*, 31/1: 46–53.

Smith, Christian (2005). *Soul Searching : The Religious And Spiritual Lives of American Teenagers*. Oxford , New York: Oxford University Press.

Smith, Christian (2009). *Souls In Transition : The Religious and Spiritual Lives of Emerging Adults*. Oxford , New York: Oxford University Press.

Stark, Rodney and William S Bainbridge (1996). *A Theory of Religion*. New Brunswick, New Jersey: Rutgers University Press.

Weber, Max. ([1922] 1964). *The Sociology of Religion*. Boston: Beacon Press.

Chapter 3

Pentecostal Prayer as Personal Communication and Invisible Institutional Work

Yannick Fer

In the opening sections of his unfinished thesis on prayer published in 1909, M. Mauss described an historical movement of internalisation and individualisation of prayer, contrasting its ritual, institutional and collective forms with more personal practices: 'At first strictly collective, said in common or at least according to forms rigidly fixed by the religious group (...), prayer becomes the domain of the individual's free converse with God' (Mauss 2003: 24). From his perspective, this evolution was in line with the transformation of the notion of the person into the 'category of the "self"' at the end of the eighteenth century in Europe, a change in which he saw the decisive influence of Protestant 'sectarian movements':

> There it was that were posed the questions regarding individual liberty, regarding the individual conscience and the right to communicate directly with God, to be one's own priest, to have an inner God. The ideas of the Moravian Brothers, the Puritans, the Wesleyans and the Pietists are those which form the basis on which is established the notion: the 'person' (*personne*) equals the 'self' (*moi*) equals consciousness, and is its primordial category'. (Mauss 1985: 21)

This historical transformation echoes a more recent trend towards individual empowerment and a de-legitimisation of institutional regulations, a 'shift in the repository of the truth of belief from the institution to the believer' (Hervieu-Léger 2000: 168). So does contemporary prayer seem all the more free and personal, taking place in a context of de-institutionalisation of religion, with individuals moving away from religious apparatuses of validation and control to build by themselves a 'spiritual but not religious' experience (Roof 1994: 59–60).

A theological filiation links Pentecostalism to the eighteenth century Protestant movements mentioned by M. Mauss – especially the Wesleyan revival. They share a common quest for individual sanctification through a deepening of the personal relationship with God, so that Pentecostalism appears as 'an extension of Methodism and the Evangelical Revivals (or Awakenings) accompanying Anglo-American modernization' (Martin 2002: 7). At the end of the nineteenth century in the southern United States, many Evangelicals worried about the success of theological liberalism and Darwinism joined the Bible schools of the holiness movement to pray for a 'new blessing' (Séguy 1975: 40). For these first Pentecostals, the experience of the 'baptism in the Holy Spirit', or glossolalia, has marked the restoration of the bond between the individual and God, through an 'immediate' communication (without visible mediation) that brought both personal salvation and an 'increased power' into missionary activities. However, the 'emotional' feature and the effervescence of Pentecostal services have driven many sociologists who draw their inspiration from the Weberian theory of modernity to underestimate – or even forget – this dimension of internalisation and individualisation of the relationship with God (Fer 2010a). Caught in a simplistic opposition between emotion and institution, the various dimensions of the Pentecostal prayer have thus been too quickly interpreted in terms of a 'de-modernisation' (Hervieu-Léger 1990). And because this interpretation regards, *a priori*, the 'charismatic' experience as a synonym for de-institutionalisation, it neglects the possibility of a Pentecostal institution able to produce a relatively stable and coherent type of religious sociability based on a specific articulation between a 'spiritual' subjective experience and 'religious' objective control (Fer 2010b).

Drawing mainly on fieldwork conducted since 2000 in the Assemblies of God (AoG) of French Polynesia,[1] I aim to show that in this kind of classical Pentecostalism, the pivotal role that prayer plays in the implementation of an 'enchanted' individualisation should prompt us to reflect further on the reshaping of institutions in these times of 'de-institutionalisation'. Pentecostal prayer is indeed at the core of a well-grounded illusion which proclaims the primacy of personal experience ('personal relationship with God') over the truths of any church, while giving to this same church the responsibility of establishing and

---

[1]   The most recent field data mentioned in this chapter comes from fieldwork conducted in French Polynesia from July to September 2009, in the frame of the research project titled MYSTOU, 'A Mysticism for All. Conception of the Individual and the Conditions of Evangelical Protestantism Emergence, Europe, Maghreb, Arctic, Oceania' (ANR-08-JCJC-0060–01) directed by Christophe Pons (IDEMEC).

maintaining the communication with God, through institutional work destined to remain 'invisible'.

Personal prayer, the most usual and ordinary form of Pentecostal prayer practice, also sheds the brightest light on the Pentecostal apparatus that ensures the progressive integration of specific ethical dispositions, and the acquisition of the cognitive and linguistic patterns that help to identify God's presence, to 'hear God' (Luhrmann et al. 2010: 68): when Pentecostals pray, they 'communicate' with God through a set of 'invisible' mediations that enable them to 'stay online' and to be guided in their everyday life by a 'voice of the Holy Spirit' functioning as a voice of the Pentecostal habitus.

Prayer in tongues represents a second aspect of this Pentecostal system of communication, associating 'a cognitive grasping with an affective capture' (Gonzalez 2009: 214) in an intense moment of 'meta-communication' with God that has no other signification than the certainty – felt both within the body and through a series of empirical sensory experiences – that one is communicating with 'a living intimate God' (Brahinsky 2012: 222).

Finally, the prayer of intercession, especially in those practices inspired by the theology of 'spiritual warfare', is one of the routes by which the individual commitment to an intimate relationship with God is made to serve the church community and collective mobilisations for missionary activities (evangelistic campaigns) or political purposes (prayers for the nations).

Personal Prayer and the 'Voice of the Holy Spirit'

> In the run of a day, we often encounter persons or circumstances that annoy us. In such cases, we can apply the 'Pray ceaselessly' principle with the 'SOS' prayers. And if we have been staying online with God, then we can pray 'Lord, help me to have your attitude towards this person or in these circumstances' and at that moment, God will answer you. (Venditti and Venditti 1996: 127)

This advice comes from lesson 6 ('the well-balanced prayer') of the INSTE[2] programme for discipleship training, published by the Evangelical network of the Open Bible Standard Churches and used by the AoG of French Polynesia for the socialisation of new converts. As T. Luhrmann remarks in her study of Vineyard Churches, prayer was understood by the congregants of these churches to enable the person who prays to develop a dialogic, interactive relationship

---

[2]　Institute of Theology by Extension.

with God. And they perceived this ability to hear God 'speak' as 'a skill, which they needed to learn by repeatedly carrying on inner-voice "conversations" with God during prayer and being attentive to the mental events that could count as God's response' (Luhrmann et al. 2010: 69–70). Until the mid-2000s, this learning was systematically implemented within the AoG of French Polynesia in the INSTE groups, which bring together each week a dozen new church members willing to 'grow in (their) relationship with Jesus-Christ and follow him as a disciple'.[3]

This notion of 'growth' underscores the fact that the decision to join a Pentecostal church is experienced less as a way to establish a needed relationship with God than as the logical consequence of a preliminary appeal, a dialogue initiated by God himself. Through the evocation of 'changed lives', a presentation of the Bible focused on individual psychology, and a preacher who 'allows the social background of his hearers to "put him off"' (Hollenweger 1988: 466), the Pentecostal evangelistic rhetoric indeed aims for personal appropriation of the message it delivers. It aims to convince individuals already engaged in a search for 'solutions' – and therefore more inclined to think that 'God knows their situation' – that a personal communication with God has actually been established, and that it is now up to them to maintain and deepen this communication. 'Jesus is speaking to you tonight, he died for you and wants to save you, are you ready to open your heart to him?', Pentecostal preachers ask.

This representation of the heart as the place of contact with God 'seems to operate as an extension of the love language', P. Gonzalez notes, 'taking God as that great Other that bursts into the faithful's interiority, even to the point of inhabiting and filling it' (Gonzalez 2009: 213–14). The learning of personal prayer in the INSTE groups uses this same symbolic vocabulary to describe a more concrete process of integration and embodiment of Pentecostal ethical norms, ultimately leading converts to experience the voice of God – initially 'heard' as an external appeal – as an inner-voice of conscience, expressing both God's will and their new identity 'in Christ', in an 'intensely participatory sense of God acting in one's mind' (Luhrmann et al. 2010: 69).

So the 'relationship with God' which is established and maintained through personal prayer is not just the enthusiastic experience of an 'emotional' contact with God, it aims more broadly to achieve a biographical invention, as expressed in the INSTE handbook, by use of the notion of discipleship ('follow Jesus') and the search for a 'godly attitude' in everyday interactions.

---

[3]   'Commitment to the Discipleship Training', first day, lesson 1 (Venditti 1996: 8).

The plausibility of this invention first relies on a distinction drawn since the outset of Pentecostal socialisation between who converts are supposed to be, and who they continue to be, in Pentecostal terms, between their 'new identity in Christ' and their 'old nature'. As soon as they join the church, converts have indeed to testify to what God has done in their life, and to demonstrate clear signs of in-depth change. They must attempt to become their 'true' selves as proof to themselves, to other potential converts, and to other church members that the effects of conversion are both 'real' and 'miraculous'. Prayer then becomes a way to submit their relationship to the world and their psychological conflicts (expressed in terms of tensions between the true self and the old nature) to the mediation of God: 'Is that thought from you, Lord?', Pentecostals ask in their prayers, 'are my thoughts, my reactions, my attitude in a given situation really inspired by God?'

Thus prayer takes place within a long-term effort of self-reformation. And rather than an intimate dialogue lived at some distance from religious institution, personal prayer represents the most complete expression of the institutional work of socialisation, training and control which contributes to the subjective enchantment of a 'spiritual', highly personal experience. As M. Mauss noted:

> Even in mental prayer where, according to the formula, Christians abandon themselves to the Spirit (...), this spirit which controls them is the spirit of the Church. The ideas they generate are those of the teachings of their own sect, and the sentiments which they speculate on are in accord with the moral doctrine of their denomination. (Mauss 1985: 33)

In classical Pentecostalism, personal prayer is precisely where the 'spirit of the Church' is to be heard, not in the frame of an absolute domination over individual conscience, but rather a relational paradigm establishing a dialogue between the ethical dispositions instilled by Pentecostalism and the inertia of pre-existing social dispositions. This 'inner-conversation' is based on a system that B. Boutter (drawing from Bateson's work) has defined as a 'system of complementary interactions between the individual and God'. Previously engaged in 'symmetrical relations', the individual had to cope with the limitations of his/her own will and the conflictive nature of ordinary social relations. After conversion, he/she strives to cast off this direct confrontation by establishing a triangular communication in which God intervenes as an omnipresent mediator (Boutter 1999: 251–4). Between the self and others (including this 'other' within him/her), there is now God, who 'answers all prayers'. Ideally, this system of communication contributes to a moderation of personal behaviours (more thoughtful and less reactive, being less directly involved with 'worldly' stakes) which is part of the ethical rationalisation of lives that the Pentecostal conversion promises ('a righteous life before God').

The result of this double process of incorporation of the Pentecostal ethics and appropriation of this specific system of communication is that the 'voice of the Holy Spirit' becomes, as a member of the AoG of French Polynesia explains, 'more than conscience in a life': 'He is there and if you do something that does not conform to the word of God, he will show you, he will warn you, that's not the good way. It's more than conscience, the Holy Spirit in a life'.[4] In fact, this acquired capacity to issue reminders to oneself without any visible mediation other than the practice of prayer points to the progressive incorporation of a Pentecostal habitus (Fer 2010b): the convert who 'stays online' can rely on a set of stable and systematic dispositions in order to transform his/her relationship to the world, and this 'mediation of God' can thus be described in the same terms as the habitus, as 'a principle of real autonomy in relation to the immediate determinations of the "situation"' (Bourdieu 1984: 135). But this Pentecostal habitus can't totally overcome the tensions generated by the lasting presence of the 'former self', or the relative uncertainty of 'God's answers' in some situations, without activating a set of 'invisible' mediations. Such mediations function as an apparatus of both indirect communication (through which part of the 'answers' can be received) and control (through which the institutional authority and the church community objectively intervene within the frame of the 'personal' relationship with God).

So, while personal prayer is experienced as an intimate conversation, associated with the biblical image of the 'upper room' (where the INSTE handbook suggests believers should return to pray), it also involves several 'ratified participants' (Goffman 1981, 9), church members or ministers who get to share personal 'matters of prayer', and to forward answers 'on behalf of God' that they may 'receive' during their own prayers.[5] From the third day of the INSTE programme, a 'partner of spiritual growth' is assigned to each student: 'they shall pray together, sharing their prayer requests as well as their fulfilment', the authors explain (Venditti and Venditti 1996: 15). They also recall the

---

    4   Interview with Marthe in Papeete, 2 April 2001.
    5   In his ethnography of a Catholic charismatic prayer, S. Parasie also uses this concept of 'ratified participants' to specify the different modes of participation implemented by the three actors involved in the prayer's interactions (the speaker, the other participants, the Holy Spirit). For example, during praises, 'the speaker talks directly to the Holy Spirit and indirectly to the other participants in prayer, acting as "ratified participants"' (Parasie 2005: 350).

community dimension of Christian life: 'Your decision to follow Christ is personal, but life in Christ is very relational', as communion within the 'family of God' is a 'means of spiritual growth' (Venditti and Venditti 1996: 237).

Prayers said in common and the sharing of prayer requests, prompted by the conspicuous sympathy of 'brothers and sisters in Christ' and by a duty of transparency, foster the circulation of personal information within the church, thus enabling God to 'answer' individual needs through a kind of community control subjectively experienced as an intimate conversation with God. When this system of 'enchanted' communication fully works, the institutional position of the pastor can itself be interpreted as linked to specific relational competences, those of an 'exhibitor of communication' (*montreur de communication*) who contributes to resolving problems by translating them in terms of 'a lack of information, exchange, listening' (Neveu 2001: 111). It is always God who answers prayers, so it is with God that believers need to reconnect, by distancing themselves from bad influences and their 'old nature', correcting deviant behaviours, wiping out old conflicts, or persevering in prayer and biblical reading.

This Pentecostal 'relational Gospel' attuned to the contemporary ideology of the 'society of communication' (Neveu 2001) states that communication is always the solution, and no conflict can withstand an open and transparent dialogue. Moreover, because personal communication with God is regarded as the core of religious commitment, this 'relational Gospel' also implies moments during which the moderation that personal prayer (through the 'mediation of God') introduces in one's relations with the 'world' gives way to a more direct and emotionally intense communication with God which is an end unto itself, and freed from the constraints of 'the world'.

Prayer in Tongues and Meta-Communication

During services held in the Assemblies of God of French Polynesia, following a series of enthusiastic songs expressing the fighting spirit of a 'victorious' community ('We are the King's Army'), and after the sermon, there is in a more personal tone a 'time of praise', when a torrent of words strives to express the frantic will to communicate to God feelings so intense that they run up against the limits of ordinary language. 'You have blessed us *so many times*', 'you're *so* wonderful', '*how much* your presence does me good', believers say, while the lyrics of the songs play on the same theme: 'Flood my heart, flood my life, come upon me, Spirit of God', 'plunge me into your river of love' (Fer 2005: 307). 'Prayers in tongues', uttered in an unintelligible language, are to be heard during this time of praise, as everyone begins to pray simultaneously in a noisy hubbub.

At first glance, this emotional effervescence may appear as contradicting the processes of internalisation of the religious experience, or the rationalisation of behaviour associated with personal prayer. Thus does this apparently disordered time of prayer in tongues seem to fit the classical scheme wherein a 'primitive' emotional experience is opposed to a more institutionalised and developed form of religion, dominated by the 'modern primacy of reason' (Hervieu-Léger 1990: 229). The Pentecostal rhetoric, which rejects intellectualism, proclaims that salvation is a matter of 'heart', advocating 'a return to the source' of Christianity through the palpable experience of God's presence. This would seem to explicitly include Pentecostalism among the 'emotional religiosities' that M. Weber described: from his perspective, such religiosities seeking 'the integration of one's pattern of life in subjective states and in an inner reliance upon god, rather than in the consciousness of one's continued ethical probation', must have 'a completely anti-rational effect upon the conduct of life' (Weber 1978: 571). In this way Pentecostal services, being distant heirs of the 'whining cadence' of Moravian Pietism evoked by M. Weber (Weber 1978: 571), should be considered as a religiosity of immediacy, naturally unstable and without any durable impact on the rationality of individual behaviour.

J.-P. Willaime suggests a more subtle approach through the notion of a Pentecostal 'ambivalence', generated by the coexistence of 'the emotion of the believing community' on one hand, and a 'Pentecostal ethical qualification fostering (...) upward social mobility and access to positions of responsibility' on the other (Willaime 1999: 13, 23). But he still implicitly considers these two dimensions (emotional and ethical) as opposed and deriving from the unique perspective of individual integration into an encompassing community, leaving unexplored the articulation between subjective individualisation and institutional control: emotion is seen as an inherently collective fact, and it is through a 'reshaping of community belonging in the context of a destabilised traditional socio-economic order' (Willaime 1999: 20) that the convert manages to reform his/her life.

This kind of theoretical opposition between body, emotion and community on one hand and spirit, reason and the individual on the other tends in fact to hinder a full understanding of the emotional contents expressed during prayers in tongues; such an understanding would require an approach to religious emotions not as some universal, raw material but rather as 'embodied thoughts' shaped by specific socialisation processes (Fer 2010a). The following example, collected in 2000 during a service at the AoG in Faa'a (Tahiti), helps to identify the thoughts and feelings that these prayers in tongues contain by re-situating them within the continuity of praise offered in intelligible language:

> Thank you Lord, your presence does us so much good, we celebrate you, we exalt you, thank you for your goodness, your fidelity, thank you because you love us just as we are, receive all the recognition of my heart, you touched my heart, you saved me, you are everything I have, Lord, *I can't find words*, you're so wonderful, your immense, incomparable love [followed by a prayer in tongues].

In this moment of collective effervescence, during which the emotions shared by the church community are subjectively perceived as one sign of the immediate presence of God, prayer in tongues comes as the expression of a set of incorporated beliefs and dispositions focused on the intimate, individual relationship with God. Here, as M. Rosaldo wrote regarding the substantive relations between emotion and thought:[6]

> what distinguishes thought and affect, differentiating a 'cold' cognition from a 'hot', is fundamentally a sense of the engagement of the actor's self. Emotions are thoughts somehow 'felt' in flushes, pulses, 'movements' of our livers, minds, hearts, stomach, skin. They are *embodied* thoughts, thoughts steeped with the apprehension that 'I am involved' (Rosaldo 1984: 143).

Thoughts and feelings, expressed to the extent of overflowing the limits of ordinary language, show the personal involvement of the convert engaged in intense and transparent communication with God, as well as the will to tell God everything, within a ritual frame where 'God is there' and 'is acting' more than ever. So the same system of communication encompasses the seemingly contradictory dimensions of Pentecostal experience, the ethical moderation introduced through personal prayer and the emotional intensity of prayer in tongues. This prayer in tongues doesn't use a system of complementary interactions, made necessary by the presence of a 'third' actor (the 'world' or the 'old nature'), but rather a meta-communication between two actors. The establishment of 'verified' communication with God then becomes an end unto itself, and the most important message, beyond what is actually said:[7]

---

[6]   She regarded as a crucial point 'that feeling is forever given shape through thought and that thought is laden with emotional meaning' (Rosaldo 1984: 143).

[7]   This meta-communication, Winkin explains, is based on the fact that 'when A communicates with B, the simple act of communicating can include the implicit statement:

> In your prayer, when you don't know what to say [a pastor from the AoG of
> French Polynesia explains], 'those of you who are baptised in the Holy Spirit, just
> speak in tongues, and the Holy Spirit will speak for you. (...) When you're in
> adoration, you don't know which words to use, pray in tongues, the Holy Spirit
> will raise unspeakable words to God.[8]

This exhortation underlines the fact that 'for most people, glossolalia does not
come easily, and improves greatly with practice' (Wolfram 1974: 128; Samarin
1972: 44–72). In the AoG of French Polynesia, as in many other classical
Pentecostal churches, the ability to speak in tongues comes less from spontaneous
disposition than from a learning process implying argumentation, theological
convictions and sensory work (Brahinsky 2012: 223–4). In this regard, Pentecostal
practices of speaking in tongues are similar to the necessary emotions described
by M. Mauss (1969: 269–79), as the acquisition of this specific skill marks an
important step in the evolution of an individual's status within the church. The
experience officially recognised by Pentecostal institutions as 'baptism in the
Holy Spirit' indeed demonstrates a personal capacity to fully hear the 'voice of
God'; it therefore opens access to church positions of responsibility.

In her PhD dissertation on charismatic Christianity in Reunion Island,
V. Aubourg mentions the analysis developed by F.A. Sullivan, who describes a
mental attitude consisting of allowing sounds to be formed on a subconscious
level, close to a daydream, in which believers express their will to 'let go' (Sullivan
1988: 235, quoted by Aubourg 2010: 409–10). Anna, a member of the AoG of
French Polynesia who had to wait for five years after her water baptism before
she managed to speak in tongues, uses a similar expression to explain her own
experience: 'One side of me was stuck with these things (...) I was afraid, for a
long time I had this fear', she says, until she 'understood the importance of it'
and decided that 'I should be open to the Holy Spirit. Before, I was afraid, I
didn't feel the need, I didn't know how to let go.'[9] This 'letting go' shows a will
to open oneself to God, including – as P. Gonzalez notes – a radical acceptance
of God's touch, of sensory capture in continuation of the move first made by
converts when they accepted the reception of 'God in their heart'. Prayer in
tongues can thus be considered in terms of an 'intimate conviction', pointing out
to 'two dimensions which are intimacy, interiority, on one hand, and conviction,

---

"we are communicating". In fact, this statement can be the most important message sent and
received' (Winkin 2001: 60).

  8   Pasteur L. Levant, service at the AoG of Papeete (Tahiti), 27 March 2001.
  9   Interview with Anna in Bora Bora, 6 December 2000.

understood as a commitment inseparable from a certainty, on the other hand' (Gonzalez 2009: 214).

Prayer of Intercession and Spiritual Warfare

Because Pentecostals largely see religious commitment as a 'self-surrender' to God, they tend to correlate the degrees of personal involvement with parallel variations of 'God's presence'. A 'strong' presence of God (indicated by 'evident' acts of the Holy Spirit, such as healing and prophecies) logically corresponds to an equivalent personal involvement/surrender, and vice versa: during the service, the emotions shared by the church members (who express a high degree of involvement) are thus perceived as one of the signs of 'God's presence'. Following this same circular reasoning, in the prayer of intercession, individual dispositions nurtured by a particularly intense involvement with God are *in fine* made to serve as collective 'spiritual warfare'. There are indeed circumstances in which it seems evident to Pentecostals that a struggle between Good and Evil is taking place (for example, during evangelistic campaigns). But there are also personal experiences whose particular intensity testifies to an ongoing struggle, taking place in a higher spiritual dimension accessible only to believers endowed with a specific 'gift'.

Therefore, the observation of practices associated with this 'gift of interceding' throws light on the Pentecostal elaboration of a commitment to others, based on the subjective experience of an intimate relationship with God. 'The key for intercession', the INSTE handbook explains, 'is to acknowledge responsibility for fighting the enemy of our souls' (Venditti and Venditti 1996: 138). And the mechanisms through which at some point individuals or church communities endorse this responsibility indicate how this shift from personal concerns towards collective mobilisations occurs, notably through the prayer of intercession.

The first of these mechanisms is the Pentecostal system of distribution of 'gifts' and 'ministries', an orientation process which progressively determines the 'mission' of each church member, through a constant interaction between (on the one hand) social distinctions 'enchanted' by the religious discourse on equal dignity of all 'gifts and talents', and (on the other) a relative liberation from social determinations based on the accumulation of religious capital (rewarding faithfulness to the institution) and/or spiritual capital (the strength of a personal 'testimony') (Fer 2010b: 166). Depending on his/her personal dispositions, each convert (called to be 'witness of God in the world') is given a role both in the

Pentecostal missionary enterprise and within the field of church positions. The position of intercessor acknowledges a specific and personal ability to intervene with God in the interests of others, and offers to the most disadvantaged converts (in terms of social, cultural and economic capital) the opportunity to access highly respected positions on the basis of 'spiritual' capital.

Hinano, working in Moorea hotels as a housekeeper, owes her 'ministry of intercession' within the AoG of French Polynesia to an episode of 'healing' attributed to the Holy Spirit – she stopped taking pills that were prescribed for life against the effects of serious obesity – and also to a 'vision' she received during a heart attack. During the surgical operation, her heart 'gave up' and she 'found herself upstairs', walking in a garden along with 'an angel aged about 30, he wore a white tunic, I know it was Jesus':

> The mission I have consists – she says – in interceding for lost souls. Sometimes, I wake up in the night and I pray, I pray and then a name gets out of my mouth. He puts names and figures in front of me, I just intercede. (...) Now I know that, when there is an evangelistic campaign, it's my duty to go with God's servants and to pray for lost souls, I have to go with them and it's my greater pleasure, my greater joy.[10]

In her case, the physical evidence of the heart attack marks her accession to a spiritual dimension that remains invisible to others and where the salvation of 'lost souls' is at stake. Drawing on this foundational event, she can legitimise her position within the church missionary apparatus ('with God's servants', meaning with the pastors) by the equation posited between a total personal commitment (night and day) and a strong presence of God. Thus intercession finally situates her intimate experience within the frame of an action for others 'wanted by God', an aspect of 'God's plan' encompassing her individual destiny.

Evangelistic campaigns, in which Hinano participates, constitute a second mechanism leading Pentecostal converts from their personal relationship with God towards collective mobilisations. These campaigns dramatise the struggle between Good and Evil around the salvation of souls, in a way immediately understandable to any church member, with a unity of time and place: this struggle takes place here and now. Their organisation by the AoG of French Polynesia, with the installation of a marquee on private or public land, underlines the territorial dimension of this struggle: 'Evangelisation is an incursion into enemy territory' (Gonzalez 2008: 47), into the world outside the church walls.

---

10   Interview with Hinano, 24 December 2000, in Moorea.

Prayers of intercession contribute to this dramatisation, while they also proclaim through a call for divine protection the solidarity that unites the 'brothers and sisters in Christ' in this confrontation with evil forces (which is inseparably a confrontation with the dominant society's gaze on converts).

In July 2009, the small AoG assembly of Moorea held a one-week open-air evangelistic campaign. Each evening, a group of four to six people was formed to intercede 'from the beginning of the preaching until the final call'.[11] They gathered under the small marquee of the refreshment stall, a few metres from the main marquee, and formed a small circle, praying with closed eyes. Thus they symbolically set up a spiritual protection whose efficiency depends on the state of relations amongst church members, as the pastor in charge of this campaign warned: in this 'spiritual warfare', division is the best weapon of 'the enemy'[12].

An evangelistic campaign organised on a larger scale – as in July 2001 when the AoG of Tahiti sent fifteen people to Nuku Hiva (in the Marquesas Islands, a distant archipelago where Catholicism is dominant) for a three-week campaign – implies a more complex 'strategy of prayer', including a series of intersecting prayers of intercession from the local level to the whole of French Polynesia:

> During these three weeks, I divided the group in five groups of ten people. (...) I developed a strategy of prayer for the city. I sent five people, half of a group, to the diocese, in the cathedral of Taiohae, some of them went to the diocese and the cathedral to pray. Another group stood on the hill over the bay of Taiohae, in order to intercede towards the hospital, which is a key symbol, representing illness, death, etc. So everyday, during two hours, people have interceded, interceded. It even happened that some people interceded during the night, several hours during the night. And from my point of view, this enabled the spirit of God to work into the hearts and it enabled us to have an open sky, that's an important point. (...) We also had the support from all the assemblies over here (in Tahiti) and all the assemblies in French Polynesia, and that's very important, everyday they interceded for us. From my point of view, this contributed to the good outcomes.[13]

Such territorialisation of religious imaginary draws its inspiration from the vocabulary and practices spread since the end of the 1980s by the charismatic theology of spiritual warfare, which has theorised a change in the scale of

---

11   AoG of Moorea, preparatory meeting with Pastor E. Barber, 13 July 2009.
12   Ibidem.
13   Interview with Pastor E. Barber, 24 September 2001, in Tahiti.

religious commitment, from the torments of the individual soul to a spiritual war against the guardian spirits of cities and nations. The growing influence of this movement amongst Evangelicals contributes to a shift from individuals towards territories, from a 'spiritual' experience towards political–religious activism. These new forms of commitment originate from the sense of a declining influence of Christianity over secularised Western societies and urban territories of 'inhuman' size fostering a fragmentation of social life. This is what F. McClung (an international leader of the charismatic missionary network Youth With a Mission) explains:

> Demonic bondage is normally associated with individuals, but the moral disintegration of our society makes the possibility of large-scale spiritual warfare against entire cities or nations seem possible. (...) If we have a view of sin that is limited to personal choices, we will miss an important truth, Cities and nations take spiritual characters and lives of their own. (McClung 1991: 29–31)

The personification of territorial entities helps Evangelicals to conceptualise the sense of a resistance to Christianity beyond individual consciences. It prompts converts to situate their personal experience, initially focused on an inner confrontation between Good ('the new identity') and Evil (the 'old nature'), in the frame of a broader spiritual warfare requiring a collective effort: converts need to become 'warriors of prayer' to take part in this struggle, in which God himself is involved and where the salvation of souls is at stake. These practices of intercession articulate several levels of action, from local 'targeted' prayers to the World Prayer Centre founded by the main theologian of spiritual warfare, Peter C. Wagner (described by one of his admirers as 'a spiritual version of the Pentagon' (Jorgensen 2005: 447)), including the intermediary level of the prayers for the nation. Nations, symbolised by their emblems and flags and understood in terms of an ontological bond between a people and a territory, today indeed crystallise a new charismatic political imaginary (Gonzalez 2008), inspiring a combination of prayers of intercession and political commitment in order to 'cast the demons out of the structures (and) get structures back to their role, their vocation, the kingdom of God'.[14]

---

[14]   Tom Marshall, undated video recording (VHS), 'lesson 2', personal archives of Chris Marshall, viewed in December 2007 (Victoria University in Wellington, Religious Studies Department).

Conclusion

The historical internalisation and individualisation of prayer that M. Mauss described as a rather linear process in fact includes a more ambivalent reconfiguration of religious experience. The observation of Pentecostal practices of prayer – understood as a personal communication with God – shows that the individualisation of subjective experience does not systematically imply (as Mauss believed) a concomitant decline in institutional or collective practices and controls. By enjoining individuals to 'become themselves' through free and voluntary choices, distancing themselves from any compulsory destiny or obedience to institutional authorities (Ehrenberg 2000: 156), the Pentecostal rhetoric is in line with an historical process of de-legitimisation of institutional constraints. But it produces a kind of biographical invention which is not merely a synonym for religious dis-belonging. Converts are convinced that they need to take responsibility for their own lives and find in their constant and transparent communication with God a mediation enabling them to symbolically achieve their independence, while this mediation objectively relies on an 'invisible' institutional apparatus of control.

This communication with God is lived as an intimate conviction, felt in bodies and 'verified' through a set of inculcated evidences ('the manifestations of the Holy Spirit'). It nurtures a sense of personal commitment to God which finally leads to collective mobilisations, where 'God calls' on his followers to take part in the confrontation with spiritual forces that govern the world, endowing them with 'spiritual gifts' and exposing them to circumstances which 'require' an activist involvement. So the distance between the most intimate prayer (when, in their 'upper room', converts call to God to struggle against the inherited dispositions of their 'old nature') and collective prayers, inspired by the theology of spiritual warfare, is not the same distance that M. Mauss observed between 'elementary' forms of religion and the more developed expressions of modern individualisation. Rather, it points out that prayer 'is always, basically, an instrument of action' (Mauss 2003: 22) and underlines the existence of a continuum connecting the contemporary personalisation of religious experience to new forms of commitment for others.

References

Aubourg, V. (2010). *L'église à l'épreuve du pentecôtisme, L'expérience religieuse à l'île de la Réunion*. PhD Dissertation in Anthropology, University of Reunion Island.

Bourdieu, P. (1984). *Questions de sociologie*. Paris: éditions de minuit.

Boutter, B. (1999). *La mission Salut et Guérison à l'île de la Réunion. Contribution à une anthropologie du pentecôtisme dans les sociétés en mutation*. Strasbourg, PhD Dissertation in Ethnology, University Strasbourg II.

Brahinsky, J. (2012). 'Pentecostal Body Logics, Cultivating a Modern Sensorium', *Cultural Anthropology* 27(2).

Ehrenberg, A. (2000). *La fatigue d'être soi, Dépression et société*. Paris: Odile Jacob.

Fer, Y. (2005). *Pentecôtisme en Polynésie française, l'évangile relationnel*. Geneva: Labor et Fides.

Fer, Y. (2010a). 'Emotion', in *Dictionnaire des faits religieux*, edited by R. Azria and D. Hervieu-Léger. Paris: PUF, 312–16.

Fer, Y. (2010b). 'The Holy Spirit and the Pentecostal Habitus, Elements for a sociology of institution in classical Pentecostalism', *Nordic Journal of Religion and Society* 2, 157–76.

Goffman, E. (1981). *Forms of Talk*. Philadelphia: University of Pennsylvania Press.

Gonzalez, P. (2008). 'Lutter contre l'emprise démoniaque, Les politiques du combat spirituel évangélique', *Terrain* 50, 44–61.

Gonzalez, P. (2009). Voix des textes, voies des corps, Une sociologie du protestantisme évangélique. PhD Dissertation in Social Sciences, University of Fribourg (Switzerland) and EHESS (Paris).

Hervieu-Léger, D. (1990). 'Renouveaux émotionnels contemporains. Fin de la secularisation ou fin de la religion?'. In *De l'émotion en religion, renouveaux et traditions* edited by F. Champion and D. Hervieu-Léger. Paris: Centurion, 217–48.

Hervieu-Léger, D. (2000). *Religion as a chain of memory*. New Brunswick: Rutgers University Press.

Hollenweger, W.J. (1988). *The Pentecostals*. Peabody: Hendrickson Publishers.

Jorgensen, D. (2005). 'Third Wave Evangelism and the Politics of the Global in Papua New Guinea, Spiritual Warfare and the Recreation of Place in Telefomin', *Oceania* 75(4), 444–61.

Luhrmann, T., Nusbaum, H. and Thisted, R. (2010). 'The Absorption Hypothesis, Learning to Hear God in Evangelical Christianity', *American Anthropologist* 112(1), 66–78.

Martin, D. (2002). *Pentecostalism, The World Their Parish*. Oxford: Blackwell.

Mauss, M. (1921, 1969). « L'expression obligatoire des sentiments (rituels oraux funéraires australiens) » (1921), in *Oeuvres 3. Cohésion sociale et division de la sociologie,* Paris: Les Éditions de Minuit, 1969, 269–78.

Mauss, M. (1985). 'A category of the human mind, the notion of person; the notion of self', in *The category of the person. Anthropology, philosophy, history,* edited by M. Carrithers, S. Collins and S. Lukes. Cambridge: Cambridge University Press, 1–25.

Mauss, M. (2003). *On Prayer.* New York: Berghahn Books.

McClung, F. (1991). *Seeing the City with the Eyes of God, How Christians can rise to the urban challenge.* New York: Chosen Books.

Neveu, E. (2001). *Une société de communication?* Paris: Montchrétien.

Parasie, S. (2005). 'Rendre présent l'« Esprit-Saint ». Ethnographie d'une prière charismatique', *Ethnologie française* 25(2), 347–54.

Roof, W.C. (1994). *A Generation of Seekers. The Spiritual Journeys of the Baby Boom Generation.* New York: HarperCollins.

Rosaldo M.Z. (1984). 'Toward an Anthropology of Self and Feeling', in *Culture Theory, Essays on Mind, Self and Emotion,* edited by R.A. Schweder and R.A. Le Vine. Cambridge: Cambridge University Press, 137–57.

Samarin W. (1972). *Tongues of men and angels, the religious language of Pentecostalism.* New York: Macmillan.

Séguy, J. (1975). 'Situation socio-historique du pentecôtisme', *Lumière et Vie* 125, 33–58.

Sullivan, F.A. (1988). *Charismes et Renouveau charismatique, Une étude biblique et théologique.* Nouan-le-Fuzelier: éditions du Lion de Juda.

Venditti, L. and Venditti N. (1996). *Formation du disciple. En suivant Jésus dans un service fidèle, INSTE first lever, 'préparation au service'.* Des Moines, Open Bible Standard Churches/Departement of International Ministries.

Weber, M. (1978). *Economy and society, an outline of interpretive sociology, Volume 2.* Berkeley: University of California Press.

Willaime, J.-P. (1999). 'Le pentecôtisme, contours et paradoxes d'un protestantisme émotionnel', *Archives des sciences sociales des religions* 105, 5–28.

Winkin, Y. (2001). *Anthropologie de la communication. De la théorie au terrain.* Paris: De Boeck Université/Seuil.

Wolfram, W. (1974). 'Review of Samarin, W. 1972', *Language in Society* 3(1), 126–31.

Chapter 4

Transcendence and Immanence in Public and Private Prayer

Martin Stringer

Two Women at Prayer

Over the last twelve years I have written two books based on detailed ethnographic studies of people who could be said to have been at prayer. The first focused on those who were firmly within the churches and looked at the way individuals derived meaning from the worship of the church (Stringer 1999). The second looked primarily at those on the edges of Christian congregations and looked at the way in which they engaged with what I described as the 'non-empirical' (Stringer 2008). While there was clearly something about prayer in both books, I am sure that the word itself was not used in either text. Part of this is a matter of definitions, and it is not my purpose in this paper to engage in the definitional question. Part of it was a desire to try and focus on a range of specific practices and/or relationships without predetermining the reader's response to those practices through given terminology. So, for example, I problematized 'worship' in the first book (1999: 21–42) and I questioned the nature of 'belief' in the second (2008: 37–53), although I could not ultimately do without either of those terms. I could, however, explore what I needed to explore without reference to 'prayer' and that might be an interesting finding in relation to the wider themes of this particular book. That, of course, does not mean that something that could be called 'prayer' did not exist within the field, or within my own analysis. As I have already suggested, there was clearly something about 'prayer' in both books.

In order to identify what I might, in other contexts, have called 'prayer', and in order to set out the terms of the present discussion, I want to draw on two examples from the second book. In chapter four on sacred space I drew attention to the activities of two women. The first was an older lady who had lived a very troubled life in a deprived inner-city neighbourhood of Birmingham and who came to the church every week to clean (2008: 54–5). She told one of my students that it was in the act of cleaning, as she worked around the altar and close to the tabernacle where the elements of the Eucharist were reserved, that she chatted to God, shared her problems with him and took comfort in the conversation (Schofield 1999: 179). The second woman is typical of a group of mainly women who lived in a mining village north of Coventry and had been part of that community all her life (Stringer 2008: 59–61). She had witnessed the close of the mine, the unemployment that followed and the rapid decline of her village. She had no connection to the church but most days, she told another of my students, she would visit the grave of her grandmother in the graveyard surrounding the Anglican church, or she would find time to sit in her kitchen, light up a cigarette, and chat to her grandmother who had died some years before (Kimber 2001: 118). Again, as with the woman in the church, she would share her troubles and gain comfort from the conversations.

The points I made about these conversations in the book were twofold. The first was to note the structural equivalence between the two situations (Stringer 2008: 62). Both women were engaged in conversations with a non-empirical other. The fact that one was thought of as 'God' and the other as a dead grandmother was structurally irrelevant. Both women, I could have said, were engaged in 'prayer'. The second point was that both women actually constructed that 'other', in their recounting of the situation, in exactly the same way (2008: 63). The mode of communication was informal, and I used the mining woman's word 'chatting' to highlight this very informal register. The nature of the relationship was also intimate. This is probably obvious in the case of the woman from the mining village and her grandmother. She had known this woman when she was alive, had probably grown up with her as a child, and the relationship was close and very intimate even after death. What came through very strongly, however, in the way that the woman from the Birmingham church talked, was that her construction of the God that she chatted to while cleaning the sanctuary drew on exactly the same kind of language and was presented as being equally as intimate as the mining woman and her gran. What I derived from this was the assertion that for many people the other is seldom constructed as 'transcendent', as assumed by many previous definitions of religion, and that our definition of religion has to begin with an understanding of the other that is not transcendent, although I purposefully avoided the suggestion that the other is therefore 'immanent'.

When I go back, however, and match this against the findings of the first book, on the meanings derived from formal Christian worship, there appears to be a contradiction. I was very careful in that book not to specify what meanings individuals derived from their worship. Rather, I aimed to outline the process by which meanings were generated (1999: 199–220). However, what is clear, from the texts used within the worship, both of formal liturgies as well as within hymns, choruses, informal interjections, sermons and so on, is that the normative construction of the 'other' within this worship was clearly that of a transcendent other, an other that is far from the intimate, immanent other of the conversations outlined in the second book. In these terms it is interesting to note that the woman from Birmingham actually found it very difficult to engage with God through the formal liturgy of the church, there were too many people around, it was too 'other', or perhaps we could say that the other it assumed was too 'transcendent' (2008: 55). She preferred the intimate isolation of the cleaning on a midweek morning. In terms of this paper, however, I want to explore this contradiction, the immanent other of the individual women at prayer versus the transcendent other of formal worship, with reference to wider literature and other contexts where I, or other ethnographers, have experienced 'prayer', or engagement with non-empirical others, in the field.

In this paper, therefore, I want to develop a possible sociology of prayer that recognizes the role of the 'other', the recipient of the prayer or the 'conversation partner' to pick up the imagery of chatting, as one of the social actors. To that end I wish to begin with the concepts of immanence and intimacy as developed in the examples that I have already given and move out towards the more transcendent assumptions of the formal liturgies. I want to ask what kind of constructions of the other take place in different forms of prayer and whether the nature of the other, immanent or transcendent, or the kind of relationship that is assumed to exist between the other and the one (or more) praying have any impact on these constructions. In other words, is it the intimate nature of horizontal relations (human to human) that determines the immanence of the 'other', or vice versa, or is there something much more complex happening within these situations?

God, Saints and Grannies

When talking about the question of intimacy at the end of the chapter where the stories of the two women were outlined I argued that 'for many Christians their relationship with God, or Jesus, or the saints takes a similar form to the intimate chatting to the dead described by others. The language of Jesus as friend, or Mary as an intimate companion and guide, has a similar structure' (2008: 66). I also made reference to a previous book in which I had outlined the theory that within Christianity there was a constant need to engage with the intimate other whenever the other of the official church became too transcendent (Stringer 2005: 20–21). This is a standard theoretical model that exists in the study of devotion within the Christian, or more specifically Catholic, world and that has, at times, been applied to a number of other situations (Christian 1981). There are many examples I could choose from to explore these ideas, but for the purposes of this paper I am going to use an example from the work of Max Harris on the celebration of saint's days, Corpus Christi and carnivals as this brings the idea into the contemporary world (2003). In looking at the popular Christian festivals, primarily of Spain, the Caribbean and Latin America, Harris notes the way in which each festival has a dominant message, as upheld and supported by the church hierarchy and the political leaders, and an alternative, radical message, which is often difficult to identify from written texts, but which becomes clear primarily in the performance of the festival along with its processions, dances, drinking and general disorderliness. Drawing on the work of James Scott, Harris therefore distinguishes between the public and the hidden transcripts within each festival (Harris 2003: 9–10; Scott 1990).

In one festival, the celebration of the patron saint of Sariñena, a small town in Aragon, Northern Spain, Harris draws attention to the distinction between the statue of the saint which is carried by the revellers, and which witnesses the street processions, the dances and other activities within the town, and the static image of Christ in Majesty within the town church that looks out over the heads of the congregation in something approaching disdain and disapproval (2003: 24–5). The identification of the statue of the saint with the people in Sariñena is reinforced by the fact that he is given a local diminutive name, Antolín, and he is allowed to wear the same uniform of red and green sashes and checked bandana as the principle dancers from the town (2003: 22). The saint is one of the people and it is easy to have a close, intimate relationship with him. Prayer to the saint most probably takes the same structural form as that of the two women in my first examples. On the other hand the Christ in Majesty of the town church is distant, transcendent and beyond reach. As Harris says of the statue of the Christ figure situated above the high altar, 'not only could we not bring him flowers or pat his feet, we could not even make eye contact with him' (2003: 24). The saint is, therefore, of the people, while the Christ figure, as portrayed within the official discourse of the church, is distant and unapproachable. This, Harris argues, is common to most, if not all the festivals that he has studied, and he develops the principle that 'fiestas afford a fertile opportunity for the insinuation of a hidden transcript of folk theology into the public transcript of formal Catholic devotion. Such hidden theological transcripts, visible in performance rather than in text, offer a corrective to the public theology of church ritual, preaching and art, especially where the latter have been largely shaped by those in power' (2003: 29).

As Harris suggests, this is a common interpretation of popular devotions within Christianity, especially within the medieval period, and can even be said to be inherent within the Christian message itself. God is seen to be too distant and unapproachable by ordinary human beings. Within the Old Testament it is impossible to look God in the face and live, and the distance between God and humanity is seen to be too great for any kind of reconciliation. God therefore sends his son, a humble, ordinary human person, to reach out to, and to mediate for, the ordinary people of the world. Over time, however, as Jesus is in turn appropriated by an increasingly powerful church, he is portrayed within the official discourse, and in Christian art, as becoming increasingly more distant, more regal and more transcendent. At this point devotion to Mary takes over as the means by which ordinary Christians can engage in intimate relations with the divine, as Mary, the mother of us all, intercedes with her, now distant, son. As Mary also becomes more distant, virginal or queenly, so local saints come in to take on that human, immanent, mediating role. 'If the exalted Virgin Mary still seems somewhat out of reach', Harris suggests, 'the folk turn to a saint' (2003: 27). Within such a construction the Reformation, and later evangelical revivals, could be seen to be, in part, about bringing Jesus back down to the human level and re-establishing that close, personal, relationship with Jesus that negates the need for other local intermediaries. As the popular hymn proclaims 'what a friend we have in Jesus'. Pentecostalism, therefore, may only be the latest phase in a similar dynamic with the Holy Spirit, now seen as the intimate other, being the latest in a long line of mediators with the transcendent God.

This all seems very plausible and has been used in many different ways in the analysis of Christian prayer and devotion. Harris is just one of many who have developed similar ideas, although it is interesting to see that the only reference he makes to the wider literature is to Peter Brown's classic work on the origins of the cult of the saints (Brown 1981). He quotes Brown as saying 'Mediterranean men and women, from the late fourth century onwards, turned with increasing explicitness for friendship, inspiration and protection in this life and beyond the grave, to invisible beings who were fellow human beings and whom they could invest with the precise and palpable features of beloved and powerful figures in their own society' (Brown 1981: 50). Brown, however, was talking of the fourth century, and the problem with all these approaches is that history does not always support the theory. In historical terms, the devotion to the saints pre-dated, and was in official contexts, superseded by devotion to Mary which, in turn, was supplanted by devotion to the very human Jesus of the late medieval imagination, along with all the images of the suffering Christ that predominated in the fourteenth and fifteenth centuries (Christian 1981). The Reformation in this view, is simply an extension of the focus on the very human nature of Jesus within the context of communal, often lay-led, local devotional societies, what I have referred to elsewhere as the monasticisation of the city (2005: 176). This is not, however, to deny Harris's specific analysis of the feast of Saint Antolin in Sariñena and similar events, it is simply to question the historical narrative that implicitly underpins it.

From the point of view of this paper, however, the question is focused not so much on history but on the apparent need, within Christian devotion, and potentially on a global scale, for human beings to engage in conversations with, or prayer to, an other that is constructed as being on the same scale and social level as the individual themselves, that the relationship of prayer is essentially one of intimacy. Whether this is a human universal is, as I suggest in my book on the definition of religion, something that still needs to be investigated (2008: 114). However, there are many other examples from a very wide range of different global contexts. Just to take one very local example, Chris Baker and Justin Beaumont quote the following from a member of a Muslim study circle in the Northwest of England: 'I found that a lot of my friends who are not religious don't understand praying. I tell them that it is my little moment with God ... you sit there and you talk to him and say everything that is going on in life ... it's a relief ... when you pray, you are unloading your problems' (2011: 43). The construction here is exactly the same as those of the women I began with in this paper and with the villagers in Sariñena, and while the nature of the other is not expressed, the intimate relationship with that other comes through very clearly.

In all these situations, therefore, what is important is the idea of intimacy. The question, however, is whether the intimate relationship necessarily implies an immanent other? The quote from the Muslim study circle probably throws this into the most stark relief as it is difficult to imagine any construction of God within Islamic thinking that constructs that God as immanent. Is it necessary, therefore, when talking about prayer, to maintain a relationship between intimacy and immanence? Can we maintain the intimacy of the relationship without necessarily implying an immanent construction of the other?

Pentecostal Traditions: Immanence and Intimacy

Another way of looking at the whole question of intimacy and immanence, therefore, comes from a reflection on 'prayer' within the Pentecostal tradition.

Here there is no real question that the other that is being engaged with is of a transcendent nature. The God of Pentecostal religion is a God of power. This is a God who can heal, who can perform miracles, who can enter into the lives of individuals and transform them, who can sweep through a congregation with the power of wind and fire. A simple analysis of the language of many Pentecostal prayers, whether sung in chorus fashion or spontaneous outbursts within the congregation, shows that the construction of the other, of God, whether as Father or as Spirit, is one of transcendence and power. The relationship that is constructed with that other, however, is not entirely one of awe and wonder, although there is clearly a strand of this within many Pentecostal traditions. The core of Pentecostal practice is the willingness to welcome that transcendental power into the very heart of our beings, to be washed with the spirit, to immerse ourselves in that power and to be transformed. The relationship is one of immense emotional fervour and ultimate intimacy and it is this that characterizes so much of Pentecostal prayer and provides its appeal to so many people in contemporary society.

Thomas Csordas, in his study of Catholic Charismatic groups in the States, quotes a woman who speaks of the presence of the Lord: 'it is "like He's right in the room". This is an "immediate thing", not a physical presence and yet more than "something in your head"' (1997: 175). There is a sense of familiarity here as there is in many of the other quotes offered by Csordas. The Lord is, perhaps, part of the group at prayer, one of the community despite the power and glory that is ascribed to him. It is not, however, what Csordas defines as 'prayer', 'an everyday life activity' (1997: 175), that is perhaps what we think of as most typical of Charismatic or Pentecostal engagement with God. Csordas sees this primarily in the act of prophecy and devotes a whole chapter to the detailed analysis of the language of prophecy (1997: 202–46). Daniel Albrecht distinguishes a number of 'modes of Pentecostal ritual sensibility' and identifies modes of celebration, transcendental efficacy, contemplation, penitence and transcendental ecstasy (1999: 180–86). All of these stress the transcendental nature of the other, but Albrecht is also keen to emphasize the way in which such ritual modes work to create a sense of community, and once again, a community that implicitly includes the other as an intimate member of the group.

Danièle Hervieu-Léger argues that in contemporary society, with its particular emphasis on the individual, the growth of emotional religion is, if not inevitable, at least clearly in tune with the times (2000). With the collapse of tradition and the bonds of community and family that held society together in pre-modern times, or so Hervieu-Léger argues, the individual is left isolated and in need of alternative models of belonging and community. This leads, in turn, to constructions of community that are built on common interests, so called 'elective fraternities' (Hervieu-Léger 2000: 149–56). In the absence of strong familial ties these elective fraternities develop significant emotional bonds for their members. The close intimate relationships that exist between individuals who see themselves as sharing a common goal are the fundamental basis for the elective fraternity. They are 'uniquely founded on the act of the choice by one of another and [they] depend on the strength of emotional ties that unite the individual members' (2000: 152).

The example that Hervieu-Léger uses to illustrate this emotional community is the body of fans that developed around the lead singer of The Doors, Jim Morrison, particularly after his death (2000: 153–5). She explains how the strong emotional bonds, established through celebrity, between the fan and the singer, were continued beyond death: 'circles of his followers in North America, Europe and elsewhere gather to read his texts or come to chant and recite them at his grave in Père Lachaise, which is now a place of pilgrimage throughout the year' (2000: 154). In its own way this is probably another kind of prayer, although the 'presence' of the other in this case may be less certain as it is not clear whether the relationship that is established is entirely between members of the community or whether there is an implied relationship with the dead rock star as well. There is, however, something of the transcendent and the intimate about this 'other' as there is in Pentecostal worship, and it is as a different, perhaps more 'modern', kind of charisma that Hervieu-Léger introduces it into her text. It is the emotional tie that binds a particular community together through their own individual relationships with an, arguably, transcendent other. Emotion is seen to be essential for the 'modern' construction of elective fraternities of this kind.

In many Pentecostal churches, along with other contemporary evangelical traditions, the emotional element of the relationship with the other, the level of intimacy that I have been talking about, is often sustained through the use of small groups or 'cells'. It is within this safe and close environment that the intimate relationship with the other can most clearly be expressed. This, however, raises two distinct questions. The first asks about the commonly-stated distinction between horizontal and vertical relationships within worship, the other relates to the relationship between intimacy and immanence that I have been exploring within this paper. In answer to the first issue, given my starting point of treating the other as a social actor within the relationships under discussion, the distinction between a vertical relationship with the non-human other, as opposed to a horizontal relationship with human others, does not really make sense. If we accept Hervieu-Léger's understanding of the emotional content of elective fraternities, it could easily be argued that the intimate relationship with the human others in the group leads, almost inevitably, or at least not surprisingly, to an intimate relationship with the non-human other who becomes a full member of the group. The other becomes a part of the emotional structure of the group, a friend, a sharer with the human others in the intimate emotionalism of the relationship. Does this, therefore, mean that the construction of the non-human other inevitably moves from the transcendent to the immanent?

Robert Wuthnow, in his study of small groups, arguably believes that this is so (1994). Drawing on a wide range of empirical evidence from the States, Wuthnow suggests that the development of small groups, or we could say elective fraternities, leads to an emphasis on the mundane. Their members tend to look in on themselves and focus on the daily lives and the many little problems shared within the group (1994: 173–82). This in turn, according to Wuthnow, leads to a position where prayer is focused on the smaller, everyday aspects of life; help to find a parking space, care for a sick child, help with a squabble at work and so on (1994: 239–42). This leads, by turns, to an understanding of God as one who is concerned primarily with the mundane and the everyday, a God who, in Wuthnow's terms, becomes 'domesticated' (1994: 255). In the terms I am developing the other becomes very immanent, and probably very intimate also. The experience of Pentecostal worship, and perhaps the gathering of fans at the graveside of Jim Morrison, suggests that this is not always the case. In order to explore this further I want to move from my second to my first book.

Back to Worship

This question, therefore, takes me back to the analysis of liturgy and the situations outlined in my first book, *On the Perception of Worship* (1999). Here I was looking very specifically at the situation of worship within four very particular congregations in Manchester. I did not focus on the words of the texts, almost deliberately so, as I was arguing that, as an observer, I could not determine in advance which words, actions or images would actually trigger meaning for the members of the congregations within any one act of worship. Many of the worshippers I spoke to clearly only ever remembered a very small part of the whole, and the part that was remembered was usually very personal to them. That aside, however, it is clear that many of the words, in all the acts of worship that I observed, assumed a transcendent other, as did the structure and form of the worship itself. There was no sense of a small intimate group in any of the congregations, no gathering with an immanent other and sharing together in their intimacy. If anything I might want to argue that the attempt to retain the transcendence of the other was one of the factors that made many of these acts of worship relatively dull, although there were certain aspects of all four churches that I have to say were far from dull.

In looking at this further I want to focus, not on any of the specific acts of worship from my book, they all took place in the 1980s, but on two forms of worship that are clearly growing in popularity in the contemporary church. The first is the kind of praise and worship service associated with many contemporary evangelical churches, and perhaps best typified by the music and activities of an organization such as Hillsong, a global brand of Christian praise and worship. The other is the increasing popularity of Cathedral worship, and particularly choral evensong, which is recognized to be one of the most successful forms of worship in the Church of England when measured by the increase in numbers attending. At first sight these two forms of worship may appear to have very little in common, and both are a long way from the intimate, informal conversation with the immanent other as expressed in the discussion of the two women mentioned at the beginning of this paper.

If these two forms of worship share anything, I would suggest, it is a clear sense of the transcendent other. Whether we are singing of a Jesus who is Lord and ruler of all, through the medium of the contemporary rock band, or proclaiming the words of the Psalms set to the choral music of previous centuries, the other that is being recognized as the focus for that worship is undoubtedly transcendent, above and beyond the human realm. It is also difficult to see either activity as intimate in any real sense. There is no immediate relationship with other individuals within the group engaging in the worship. All horizontal contact is mediated through the music; that is through the band, or the choir, who is leading the worship. The congregation stands, or sits, shoulder to shoulder focused on the source of the music. At no point are they asked to communicate with each other. However, it is not as distinct individuals that the members of the congregation are expected to engage with the worship. The uniqueness of the individual is submerged within the wider congregation; they become a crowd. In both cases, therefore, the individual is invited to enter into the worship, and perhaps to lose the self within the community, to lose the self, albeit in very different ways, within the music of the worship. There is a strong sense of communitas within both forms of worship, a levelling of the congregation to the role of spectator, however fully involved those spectators feel themselves to be (Turner 1969).

Central to this sense of communitas, I would argue, is the transcendence of the other. It is that relationship, in prayer, of the group, the community and the overarching other that is central. This is mediated through the music and the language of transcendence within the texts and is felt by each individual in their own unique way. What is more there is nothing of the conversational about this form of prayer. This is praise; the glorifying of the other and the expression of total submission, both to the event and the other that the event is focused on. Again we may have a definitional problem in that this kind of praise is actually very different in form and structure from the intimate conversations of the women I mentioned earlier, but both, I would suggest, should still be considered as forms of prayer. What is more each of these two examples can also be seen, like the examples of the two women, as structural equivalents in the analysis of prayer. In this case the conception of the other is very similar, if not identical (although that might be an interesting theological question), and the congregations are also very similar, at least in structural terms. What differs is, of course, the medium through which the experience of prayer is mediated: Christian rock or Anglican chant. What I am suggesting, however, is that these media may not be as different as we might imagine, at least, not in the sense of the form of prayer that they encapsulate.

If we cannot use 'immanence' of these situations, therefore, or even 'intimacy', I could perhaps suggest a further 'i' that may make sense of these acts of worship. These events, I would argue, both involve very 'intense' experiences. This is something that they may, or may not, share with some of the other examples that I have already discussed, Pentecostal worship for example, or the fans gathering at the tomb of the rock star. It may not, however, be true of the more conversational prayer of the two women with whom I began this paper. This sense of intensity, however, also fits with Hervieu-Léger's theories of the place of the individual in the modern world, the sense that the individual is encouraged to seek out intense experiences to make sense of their lives where tradition and the mundane ordinariness of everyday life no longer suffice (2000: 57–61). Such intensity can be found in drugs or alcohol, in rock concerts, raves or festivals, in football matches or other sporting fixtures, or even in the following of reality television (2000: 53–7). The shared intensity, or the memory of such intensity, provides the basis for conversation and shared intimacy at other times, but the intensity itself is often individual, even when it is experienced as part of a crowd. Choral evensong or the Hillsong praise and worship event is not so very different from other concerts, whether of classical or popular music, with the added intensity of being experienced within the presence of, and for the pleasure of, a transcendent other. This, arguably, raises the level of intensity beyond that of the normal event and adds a new dimension that can only come from these collective forms of prayer.

Talk of intensity also introduces another element into this discussion. Throughout the paper I have talked about the emotional element of prayer, or of the group that gathers for prayer, and words such as 'intimacy' and 'intensity' imply a certain emotional content. We could, however, turn to another body of analysis and describe both of these not only as emotional but also as embodied (McGuire 2007). These forms of prayer are not simply intellectual activities, an assumption that I certainly made in the analysis of worship in my first book, and a valid criticism of that analysis. These forms of prayer are 'embodied'. Being embodied they engage the individual, or the group, in a very particular way, they demand something more than intellectual assent. Using the language of my analysis of worship, we could note that in each case the 'experience' is one that is set aside from the everyday; it is 'significant'. In its own way the experience is all encompassing, but it is also part of a sequence of such experiences that are 'repeated' and cumulative in their effects. Finally it is an experience that sends the individual back into the world with a powerful new 'memory' (1999: 212–13). There is, however, one last point to note in terms of embodiment before I begin to draw this discussion to a close. We often think of the powerful, significant, emotions of intensity and intimacy as embodied because they take emotional, and often physical, energy. However, the relaxed, conversational, prayer of the two women that I began with is also embodied, not in a powerful, life-changing and dramatic way, but in a quiet, relaxed, and we could almost say 'refreshing' or 'renewing' way. This is certainly the way in which the women, in the midst of their own difficult lives, expressed it to my students.

A Possible Classification

How then do I draw a conclusion from all these examples? First I hope that I have shown that there is no obvious and deterministic relationship between prayer that is intimate and an other that is immanent. The different contexts that I have discussed raise different kinds of relationship between intimacy, immanence (or transcendence) and intensity. There is no easy relationship between them. It is possible, however, I would suggest, to see how they might be brought together into a single model.

I am not a great fan of classifications and neat forms of categorization. Nothing is ever quite as cut and dried as this kind of analysis tends to assume. I am, however, going to attempt to draw this discussion together within a possible three-dimensional grid, a series of interlinked continua. This is certainly not meant to be seen as the last word on these events, or an alternative to future detailed ethnographic work. What strikes me, however, within all these examples, and the analysis that I have offered of each one, is first the importance of emotion or embodiment within each context, and the way in which that points to a deep and often very significant underlying relationship with the other that I would argue must sit at the heart of all prayer. A 'sociology of prayer' cannot exist, therefore, without recognizing the place of the other as one of the social actors. Beyond this, however, there is, as I have suggested, a clear distinction between a number of different axes along which it is possible to develop a continuum in relation to the way in which the other, and the prayers' relationship to the other, can be mapped.

I want to suggest three distinct axes, and hence a three-dimensional model. The three axes are 'immanence versus transcendence', 'intimacy versus distance' and 'intensity versus whatever we might think the opposite of intensity might be, perhaps casualness, or relaxation'. These axes, I am suggesting, can each function independently and are not necessarily related to each other. That is important as I want to move away from an analysis that suggests that intimacy inevitably leads to immanence, or that transcendence implies intensity and so on. These are different features of the relationship with the other within prayer and can, so I am arguing, function independently of each other within any one situation. The situation of the two women from my second book both represent prayer that sits within the immanent, intimate and non-intense sector of the model. Pentecostal prayer is often transcendent, intimate and intense, as is the 'chanting' of the fans at the grave, while that of the villagers in Sariñena is possibly immanent, intimate and intense, at least during times of festival. The prayer of Wuthnow's small groups might be immanent, intimate and more or less intense, and the example of Hillsong and choral evensong is often transcendent, distant and intense. Of course, others will quibble with the specific designations, and that is one reason why I find such classifications unhelpful in a general sense. The specific points I am trying to make, however, are (a) that we need to recognize that the nature of the relationship with the other in prayer is complex, (b) that this can work along a number of different axes, (c) that each of these axes probably acts independently and (d) that it is only in the detailed ethnographic exploration of each specific context that any full understanding of prayer within any one situation can be developed.

References

Albrecht, Daniel E. (1999). *Rites in the Spirit: A Ritual Approach to Pentecostal/ Charismatic Spirituality*. Sheffield: Sheffield Academic Press.

Baker, Christopher and Justin Beaumont (eds) (2011). *Postsecular Cities; Space, Theory and Practice*. London: Continuum.

Brown, Peter (1981). *The Cult of the Saints*. Chicago: Chicago University Press.

Christian, William A. (1981). *Local Religion in Sixteenth Century Spain*. Princeton: Princeton University Press.

Csordas, Thomas J. (1997). *Language, Charisma and Creativity: The Ritual Life of a Religious Movement*. Berkeley: University of California Press.

Harris, Max (2003). *Carnival and Other Christian Festivals: Folk Theology and Folk Performance*. Austin: University of Texas Press.

Hervieu-Léger, Danièle (2000). *Religion as a Chain of Memory*. Cambridge: Polity Press.

Kimber, Geoff F. (2001). *An Investigation into the Attitude of a Warwickshire Mining Community to Church and Spirituality*. Unpublished MPhil thesis, University of Birmingham.

McGuire, Meredith (2007). 'Embodied Practices: Negotiation and Resistance', in Nancy Ammerman (ed.), *Everyday Religion: Observing Modern Religious Lives*. Oxford: Oxford University Press, 187–200.

Schofield, Sarah (1999). *What is the Role of Worship, and the Decisions Made About It in the Lives of Those Living in Urban Priority Areas, with Particular Reference to the Experience of Power and Powerlessness*. Unpublished MPhil thesis, University of Birmingham.

Scott, James C. (1990). *Domination and the Arts of Resistance*. New Haven: Yale University Press.

Stringer, Martin D. (1999). *On the Perception of Worship: The Ethnography of Worship in Four Christian Congregations in Manchester*. Birmingham: Birmingham University Press.

Stringer, Martin D. (2005). *A Sociological History of Christian Worship*. Cambridge: Cambridge University Press.

Stringer, Martin D. (2008). *Contemporary Western Ethnography and the Definition of Religion*. London: Continuum.

Turner, Victor W. (1969). *The Ritual Process: Structure and Antistructure*. Harmondsworth: Penguin.

Wuthnow, Robert (1994). *Sharing the Journey: Support Groups and America's New Quest for Community*. New York: The Free Press.

Chapter 5
Prayer as a Tool in Swedish Pentecostalism

Emir Mahieddin

Introduction

Although Sweden is renowned as one of the most secularised societies in the world, the region of Småland, in the south of the country, is a space of strong Christian religiosity (Åberg 2007). It is thus considered as the Swedish 'Bible belt'. Jönköping, with its 84,000 inhabitants, is the capital of the region and is sometimes called 'Sweden's Jerusalem' or 'Småland's Jerusalem'. In 1861 the Jönköping Evangelical Association (*Jönköpings missionsförening*) was founded. This new religious association based on pietistic Christian principles attracted to town many inhabitants from the county of Jönköping and from the whole region. For many decades lines of believers would have crossed the landscape four times in a year, singing psalms and songs of praise, to reach Jönköping for celebrations, calling to mind the Hebrews wandering in the desert, walking to Jerusalem on the important days of the Jewish calendar. In 1897, a journalist wrote in a local newspaper entitled *Sanningsvittnet*: 'Something comparable to what used to happen in olden times in Jerusalem attracts people to the four annual meetings [...] of the association in Jönköping', hence the now famous nickname of the town (quoted by Oredsson 2007: 42). This sobriquet, which is not appreciated by all, still points to its significant proportion of Christian believers and 'free churches' (*frikyrkor*).[1] In the Nordic religious landscape, the latter category refers to Protestant denominations which constituted themselves as assemblies that were autonomous from the State Evangelical Lutheran Churches. The congregations affiliated to the Pentecostal movement, on which I will centre this paper, are part of this category of churches, and it is from this context that I investigate prayer.

---

[1]   Although they are not always accurate, statistics can serve as relevant indicators here – knowing the limits one can notice in the definition of belonging to a religious group. On a national scale, depending on the level of engagement, born-again Christians represent from 1 per cent to 2 per cent of the whole Swedish population. In Småland, the free churches would gather around 10 per cent of the population (see Åberg 2007).

In the first part of the paper I will explore ethnographic data I have gathered concerning the stylistic variations observed in Swedish Pentecostal prayer at different moments of religious life. These variations point to a sharp contrast between two spaces of Christians lives which were symbolically constructed as a public space on the one hand, when it comes to Sunday services; and, on the other hand, as a private space, when it comes to the so called 'cell groups' and individual prayers. In the second part, I propose an analysis of these contrasted behaviours, referring to contextual data and to individual and collective discourse, which allows understanding and/or explaining, at least partially, what appears at first sight as a sort of *'decharismatization'* of Swedish Pentecostalism, starting three decades ago. Finally, in the third and last part, I try to demonstrate how a socio-anthropological study of prayer permits us to draw a certain set of conclusions on the dynamics of symbolic production in the Swedish evangelical milieu, and, at the same time, to have a general idea of what praying means to the religious subject, in the frame of his/her relationship to an invisible being – in this case Jesus Christ. In brief, my aim is to investigate contemporary mutations of prayer in Swedish Pentecostalism. In what way did it change? On what sorts of mechanisms are these mutations based? What sense do they have in their cultural configuration of emergence? What can the observation of prayer teach us about the Swedish context? And above all, as it is our concern in this volume, what can the analysis of the mentioned mutations, and of the existential posture of the praying subject, teach us about prayer itself, as a social and cultural fact?

The Swedish Pentecostals: Joshua's Generation

Pentecostalism – or 'Pentecostalisms', if one is allowed to put the word in a plural form, as it was suggested by André Corten and André Mary (2000) – is renowned for its focus on the bodily experience of the Holy Spirit while praying, giving space to the manifestation of charismata (spiritual gifts) during services. Prophecies, visions, healing and speaking in tongues are gifts from the Spirit, as described in the second chapter of the Acts of the Apostles, and specific features of Pentecostal liturgy. Thus, Pentecostal Christians often pray in tongues, or glossolalia, this 'tongue of fire' – or 'tongue of the Spirit' – which allows worshippers to communicate with God in an ideal order of ineffability. Thus the Swedish Pentecostal movement had been called in its early days in the 1910s 'tongue movement' (*tungotalrörelse*) and its followers were often referred to by their detractors as 'tongue speakers' (*tungotalare*). From the language of words to body language, Pentecostals are also famous for their ecstatic corporal manifestations throughout their meetings and collective prayer moments. During these, some individuals see their body shivering under the power of the Spirit striking them. And as they were called 'tongue speakers', they were also referred to by the deprecatory term 'shakers' (*skakare*).[2] The effusion of charismata leads some worshippers to 'fall into the Spirit', as the expression says, which literally means that individuals tumble to the ground during an intercession prayer, overwhelmed by the Holy Ghost. Many ethnographic descriptions of Pentecostal worship mention these facts all over the world (see among others Hollenweger 1972; Cox 2001; Corten and Mary, *op.cit.*; Corten and Marshall-Fratani 2001).

It is therefore surprising that one cannot observe these things in the Swedish Pentecostal assemblies, either the classical movement or the more recent charismatic forms, including the Vineyard movement – even though the latter is famous for having given birth to the Toronto blessing in 1994 which initiated new spiritual manifestations such as laughing out loud, crying, or even shouting animal sounds, and several moments of collective effervescence characterised by an intense exteriorisation of religious emotions.[3] Indeed, a Sunday worship visitor in a Swedish church will be struck by the absence of such charismatic demonstrations, though they are supposed to be proper to the Churches claiming to be Pentecostal. Prayers are often led by the pastor, or by an elder, in front of a surprisingly calm audience, in which only certain individuals dare express themselves 'out loud', though in a cautious whisper, with contained and controlled bodily gestures.

It is more often in the prayer cell groups,[4] which slowly became the private sphere of Pentecostalism because of their constitution out of mutual affinities, that charismata find a fuller expression. Sometimes, it is in the privacy of a conversation with a friend that one shares prophecies and visions, or in the context of an intercessory prayer that a person feels the Spirit invading him/ her powerfully. Beyond that, some Christians will only speak in tongues in the intimacy of a personal exchange with God, in the solitary presence of the Lord, while praying in their bedroom or driving their car.

Swedish Pentecostalism has not always been like it is today. During the coffee time or during meetings, I often heard Christians referring, in a nostalgic tone

---

[2]   The movement was also referred to as 'The new revival' (*den nya väckelsen*), about this see Sundstedt 1969.

[3]   Note that the church of Toronto was excluded from the Vineyard movement because of the controversial dimension of these manifestations.

[4]   For a detailed history of cell groups, see David Hunsicker (1996). 'John Wesley: Father of Today's Small Group Concept?'. In *Wesleyan Theological Journal* 31/1: 192–211.

or not, to a period when prophecies popped out here and there in the assembly, people spoke in tongues, and miracles were common. Nowadays, some of them regret that the meetings became 'boring', lacking surprise or divine presence. They wish to go back to the 'good old time'. Among these nostalgic people is Patrick, a young enthusiastic Pentecostal I met in a prayer group, who converted at the end of adolescence. The first time I saw him, he was warning his fellows against the routine they settled into in their relationship with God. In prophetic terms, he calls his generation 'Joshua's generation'. According to him, his generation of Pentecostals is the third since the first awakening at the beginning of the century in 1906, and it 'has not known the founding moments like the first converts', which he compares to Moses' generation, when the Hebrews fled from Egypt. The third generation consists of the people who will remain after all the non-believers of the second generation leave because of their lack of faith, subsequent to their involvement in a church motivated by tradition. 'They practice because of their parents but do not know what it really is to believe', says Patrick. He adds: 'these will soon leave the church of their parents, as the sons of the first Hebrews in the desert who preferred being devoted to the Golden Calf, and only the chosen ones will remain'. Patrick interprets this calm in the contemporary Swedish Pentecostal liturgy as a lack of enthusiasm in faith of the second generation of Pentecostals, a calm that will soon be over.

But how did Swedish Pentecostalism get to this situation? How was this 'second generation' born, to refer to the terms used by Patrick? And what led it to change the liturgical aspects of the Pentecostal church? To answer these questions, I will mainly refer to national elements of historical and political context. Indeed, Pentecostalism observed in other contexts, including Africa or Latin America, offers the classical features of a Pentecostal or Charismatic Church. Its liturgy is even sometimes characterised as 'violent' by anthropologists (see Mary 2000), and public healing, prophesy or speaking in tongues is still common.

The Reasons for a 'Decharismatization'

It is difficult to date precisely the beginning of the 'decharismatization' (the progressive disappearance of charismata) of Sunday worship in Sweden. It is a result of a long process that probably extends throughout the whole second half of the twentieth century. But we can note a breaking point which started an acceleration of that process at the beginning of the 1980s with the emergence of the Faith movement, a trans-denominational movement influenced by the Gospel of prosperity, of which the famous Word of Life (*Livets Ord*), studied by the British anthropologist Simon Coleman (2007),[5] was an organisational manifestation (see Aronsson 2005). Very present, active and expert in the use of media technology, this assembly, and its leader Ulf Ekman, quickly attracted public opinion, which expressed its disapprobation through terms characteristic of allegations against so-called 'sectarian movements' (brainwashing, money extortion from believers who are victims of their own naivety, blind trust in a charismatic leader). This disapproval was also rooted in the effervescence of the Word of Life worship where the believers, as well as the preachers, expressed themselves in tongues and were slain in the Spirit.

Nowadays, even if the Word of Life remains the most charismatic denomination in the Swedish religious marketplace – we still hear speaking in tongues and can observe a few individuals shaking and jumping on the spot as they used to in the past – their liturgical style has 'cooled down', experiencing a similar process to the one experienced by classical Pentecostalism in Sweden, although it happened within a much shorter period of time. But because of the bad reputation of Word of Life in its early years and up to the 1990s, some 'classical' Pentecostals told me they felt compelled to act with discretion to avoid being related to Ulf Ekman's controversial movement by public opinion. This effect was made stronger because of the double affiliation of many followers, who still occasionally visited the Sunday services in their more classical Pentecostal church of origin (*Pingstkyrkan*).[6]

But why was Swedish opinion disturbed by the charismatic practices, and why did the Pentecostals react as they did, deciding not to deploy as much charismata as they used to and 'disciplining' their bodies during the Sunday service? Was the appearance of a more charismatic dissident church in the religious landscape the only reason? Or did it just highlight broader dynamics?

The explanation is probably related to the specificity of the Swedish religious configuration, dominated over centuries, and still today, by the Evangelical Lutheran Church, which was the state Church up to 1 January 2000. The salience of this type of Church in the Nordic countries is well recognised by sociologists of religion. It is the main provider of all the rites of passage in life, and a majority of Swedes (around 70 per cent in 2010)[7] remain members of a Church, even when declaring themselves non-believers. Many are still baptised (50 per cent of all newborn children in 2010), confirmed, married and buried in accordance

---

5   See also Coleman 1989, 1996, 2006 and Gifford 2001.

6   See Coleman 2007, who explains he met Pentecostals who still went to both groups (*ibid.*: 188). The author describes as well how the bodily practices of « Word of Lifers » betrayed the double belonging of these believers, generally among youngsters.

7   Svenska kyrkans medlemutveckling år 1972–2010. www.svenskakyrkan.se.

with Christian ritual. This seems to be an illustration of the 'belonging without believing' which is one of the main characteristics of Nordic religiosity. Thus, although a lot of Swedes claim to be non-believers,[8] a large majority of them benefit from a socialisation into Lutheran religiosity (when they are themselves involved in the ritual of course, but mostly as spectators of rituals; from their early years to the last day of their life).

Thus the style of such state-church religiosity, renowned for its sobriety and its silence, contributes directly to a public representation of what is 'religiously correct' in Sweden. Besides, inspired by a liberal and 'rationalising' theology (clergymen contributed to excising magical or supernatural content from Christian practices), national Lutheranism contrasts, in its dogma and liturgy, with the religious offer of its Pentecostal competitors. More than defining the prevalent frame of religious socialisation in the country, the Lutheran Church was also, over a long period, a major political institution that played an important part in education for all the inhabitants of Sweden, notably through the national schooling system. Indeed, the oldest Pentecostals I have met remembered praying every morning before class and following religious teaching at school during their childhood. As a result, the evangelical-Lutheran Church of Sweden acts as a centripetal force that still influences the religious field by its magnetism, still benefitting from a monopolistic situation from which pertained until recently in the national history.

Swedish Pentecostals themselves seldom speak of the 'supernatural'[9] during the Sunday service, and appear to be a somewhat liberal movement compared to their counterparts in other countries. Similarly, female ministry is an accepted fact and the management of sin does not follow repressive and communitarian logics anymore – in contrast to what could have been adopted earlier, namely before the turn of the 1960–70s (evoked elsewhere as a major shift for all the European societies). This repressive approach could lead to some worshippers accused of sinning (consuming tobacco or alcohol, divorcing, etc. according to the metaphorical 'catalogue of sins'[10] as Pentecostals call it) to be expelled from their congregation. Nowadays this part of the Pentecostal history is harshly criticised by a major part of Swedish Pentecostals and by the direction of the church, with regret expressed that their predecessors had failed in understanding and truly applying the message of the Gospels. The latter are broadly considered nowadays in the movement as a message of love and forgiveness, as demonstrated

---

[8]   According to the surveys, only 10 per cent of Swedes claim to believe in a personal God (source: www.eurel.info).

[9]   *Det övernaturliga* in Swedish. This notion is used by the actors themselves.

[10]   *Syndakatologen* in Swedish.

by Christ Himself towards sinners. Christians are instructed to act as a 'little Christ', to quote an expression used by Simon Coleman (2007), and to adopt towards their fellows the attitude that the Messiah had towards His. The first concern is that anyone should feel warmly welcome because everyone has a place close to God. Thus, it is often said in sermons that the 'Lord used sinners to do His will, from Jacob who lied to his own father, to Moses who went as far as committing a homicide'. The idea is that everyone can represent Christ to one's fellows through *examplification* (see Piette 1999: 76–7). The aim is to accomplish the worldly work of God (Tonda 2002), whose social mediators are the Christians and their community.[11]

It is because everyone ought to feel welcome in Church that the Sunday service progressively turned into a public space in which anyone, that is to say non-believers as well, could be expected. One piece of evidence for this is the particular attention given to the prospective visitor, who hears him or herself addressed in the same words every Sunday: 'May the people who are here for the first time feel warmly welcome and live with us a glad moment of worship!'. Sometimes, I also heard people telling me that they did not want to speak in tongues out loud on Sunday as it might frighten the potential newcomers who are not familiar with the gifts of the Spirit.

Recent state policies have also established new relationships between free churches and political institutions, setting new elements which implicitly encouraged the latter to change. In 2000, the parliament implemented separation between the state and the Lutheran church. At the same time, a law was passed which gave a new status to free churches, all of which were considered religious associations, thus earning the right to receive public funds (see Harry 2010). The fund is distributed in accordance with the size of the denomination. As such, the Pentecostal movement received around seven million Swedish crowns in 2010.[12] The amount is not a lot compared with the actual finances of the Pentecostal movement,[13] but it changed the logic of the churches' relation to

---

[11]   The use of this expression, suggested by the anthropologist Joseph Tonda (2002), could be seen as a new surrender by social scientist to the demon of analogy, thus comparing religion to a work, but Christians use this expression themselves (they also speak about the 'workers of God'). Tonda defines this Work of God as a process of transformation of a whole 'culture' or the 'society', a set of physical, linguistic and material practices which aim at producing and reproducing symbolic goods.

[12]   See H. Boström's article in the Swedish Christian newspaper *Dagen*: 'Så mycket får samfunden i statsbidrag', 11 May, pp. 6–7.

[13]   In 2010, the donations of the adherents went up to 335,285,311 Swedish crowns (statistics produced by the church, document online http://www.pingst.se/viewNavMenu. do?menuID=71). The Pentecostals also get State funding through their organisation *PMU*

the state and to surrounding society. It gave a new legitimacy to observing and criticising what happens, what is said, and what is thought in the churches (as a financial contributor). The mixture of this new relation to the Swedish state and the increasing media sphere since the beginning of the 1980s, combined with the concern of Pentecostals to gain credibility, has therefore resulted in powerful constraints causing the progressive disappearance of charismata in favour of a calmer way to signify the presence of the Lord in public. In private, however, the gaze of outside society being absent, glossolalia and other charismata can be uttered without any problem.[14]

Another sociological phenomenon reinforces this situation: the experiment of glossolalia as a spiritual impulse. If speaking in tongues is the result of a process of religious socialisation, that is to say a learning process, it does not imply that one can fully control it.[15] 'We cannot speak in tongues on command, it just comes out!' a worshipper told me. Another one explained that he felt a sort of 'need' to speak in tongues, an 'urge' he almost experienced as a necessity during prayer. Managing this spiritual gift, unequally distributed between private and public spheres, thus appears to be part of a kind of economy of impulses, to quote the sociologist Norbert Elias (1973). One could even think of it as taking place in an economy of affects given the emotional dimension of its manifestation. Therefore, it is relevant to analyse its deployment by interpreting it according to its socio-cultural context of inscription.

This dimension emerges clearly in the comparative work conducted by the sociologist Flavio Munhoz Sofiati, who observed contrasting behaviours concerning the manifestation of the Spirit, thus differentiating French and Brazilian charismatic Catholic styles of worship. The first favour a corporal form of meeting with the Spirit in their prayer group, while the second prefer to

---

Interlife in order to achieve development programmes in the Third World and in Eastern Europe.

[14]   The cell groups which constitute the private sphere are not always a place where one can observe the utterance of glossolalia. Jenny, a Pentecostal lady, told me they had stopped speaking in tongues in prayer when receiving new believers who had not experienced baptism in the Spirit yet.

[15]   Everybody might not agree on the possibility to learn glossolalia but some pastors inside the Pentecostal movement assert that it can be taught and learnt (see Cox 2001). For my part, I met Pentecostals telling that they *practised* speaking in tongues (once they had been baptised in the Spirit) in their car, or, for the case of one woman who was frightened by her own utterances, on her bike, so that the wind blowing on her ears would prevent her from hearing what she was saying. The statements can seem contradictory, that speaking can be trained and that it is an impulse, but maybe this kind of training could be compared to laughing yoga, where the impulse is provoked by repetitive tries to start laughing.

manifest their meeting with God verbally through glossolalia.[16] Both constitute different manners of expressing the presence of God through a given state of the bodies or a modification of language, thus expressing two types of sensitivity.

Similarly, the depiction of Polynesian Pentecostals by the anthropologist Yannick Fer tends to present the latter as developing an inverse model to the Swedish one, privileging glossolalia in public and silent devotion in the intimacy of private prayers. More than an impulse, this tongue of prayer (*bönespråk*) given by God is the expression of the deepest spiritual individuality of the believer; the one in which the ineffable is communicated, the unspeakable request can be transmitted, and through which one builds one's personal relationship to the Lord. Such a manifestation is thus relegated behind the curtains of privacy as if it were impudent to show the deep 'inside' of the self.

Considering this emotional dimension of charismata does not imply that we must think of them as primal utterances of given natural impulses. The product of socialisation, the emotional dimension – and even its impulsive dimension – is the result of a social construction (which does not mean it is not real). In this sense, we can think of this 'decharismatization' process as an observable change of relations between the Pentecostals and the national society, through a series of minor and major events that progressively transformed the social frame in which the believers were rooted, defining new connections and influences in the Swedish Pentecostal regime of emotion (see Riis and Woodhead 2010). This regime of emotion is not Swedish per se, as a result of a pre-existing, and supposedly everlasting, reified culture. It is the result of the historical, institutional work of the Lutheran Church which disciplined the bodies in their churches for centuries. As one of my interlocutors stated very correctly, if one can be scared when observing the manifestation of deep emotions at church in Sweden, nobody seems to be affected by the same exhibitions during a football game in the same country. In other words, it is a *religious* 'Swedish' regime of emotion which was probably implemented in relation to questions of power, the Holy Spirit, in its subversive policy (see Laurent 2000), being able to dismantle the political unity of the State church and the legitimacy of its priests. Prayer, in its emotional dimension, and especially when it comes to the manifestation of the emotions it implies, is thus a political and institutional issue.

---

[16]   Munhoz-Sofiati, F., 'Comment prient les nouveaux charismatiques?'. Workshop Sociology of Prayer, ISSR congress, Aix-en-Provence, 2 July 2011.

The Aesthetics of Prayer: an Inverted Symmetric Relationship

Besides its potentially political dimension, prayer structures the intimate and emotional relationship to the divine and is part of a work of self-fashioning. The latter work aims at fashioning the believer in its attempt to make God present, thus choosing among a finite range of mediations enabling 'externalization' (objects, know-hows, gestures, words).[17] As we saw, the style of the Pentecostal prayer is the result of an articulation between the importance given to the charismatic gifts and the expectations of the surrounding socio cultural environment.

After emphasising the relationship of the believer to this environment, it is interesting to question the modalities of the relationship to the Spirit as it is experienced by Pentecostal believers. Not only is it partly culturally determined, but it is also an interesting case of bonding with supernatural entities (see Pons 2011a). The Holy Spirit (and its Trinitarian corollaries, God and Jesus) acts as a highly effective subjectivation power accompanying Pentecostals in their daily lives. Speaking through them while they speak in tongues, the Spirit appears, at the same time, as a tool and an interlocutor. I intend to illustrate the type of relationship that is experienced with a supernatural entity through developing an example I chose from my fieldwork from among many others.

Bosse is a sexagenarian entrepreneur who started his own company as an electrician in 1972. Since the 1990s, in a parallel of his business activity, he is involved in an NGO named *Östhjälpen* (literally, 'East help') that he helped to found in Romania, some months after the fall of Ceaușescu's regime. He considers this activity as a responsibility 'God has put in his heart'. His first visit in the country was subsequent to a prophecy uttered by the pastor of his church, who was married to a Romanian woman, a few weeks before the Revolution. According to Bosse, the Lord enjoined them to go to Romania as the 'man of Darkness was about to fall' (referring to Ceaușescu). He then evoked his first visit to the country as the answer to a prayer made by Romanian religious fellows eager to meet Western Christians. During his second journey there, he and an ecumenical group of Swedish Christians met the mayor of Deva, the capital of the region they intended to work in, in order to learn about their needs. The mayor wanted a new orphanage for handicapped kids to be built, according to Swedish standards. A Lutheran priest, who had travelled with the group, refused, stating that it would be impossible to gather enough funds to lead such a project. At

---

[17]   Here I rely on the work of Albert Piette (1999, 2003) according to whom ethnography can say that God is present in a situation as attached to reality by a range of mediations set by humans in a chain, or a network of actions, know-hows, objects, etc.

most, they could help with a new heating system in the existing orphanage. Bosse got out of the meeting with a resentful feeling of disappointment. He wanted to help the Romanians and make things change in a radical way although he thought the priest was right not to promise something they could not guarantee. He sat on a pavement in the streets of Deva to pray and was moved by the Spirit in a really strong way, as he says, thus transforming his doubts and frustration into strong conviction: 'the orphanage had to be built; it was the will of God', he says. On the way back to Sweden, he tried to convince the priest that they had to do it. He prayed that the Spirit would touch him as well, which eventually happened, right before they took the ferry to cross the Baltic Sea.

The group succeeded in finding a prefabricated building in Gothenburg. They bought it on the cheap and moved it, one piece at a time, to Romania. A real estate agent wanted to sell it for one million Swedish crowns. But Bosse refused, considering the price to be excessive. But 'the Spirit was at work' says Bosse, and they could eventually buy it for 300,000 crowns, because the building was about to be expropriated and demolished by the city hall for a renovation project. To finance the NGO and his multiple trips to Romania, Bosse contributed to the construction of a second-hand store in his hometown in Sweden, Pärtille. The store was a success and fifteen jobs were created and given to unemployed people whose income is guaranteed by the city hall. Bosse sees that as well as the achievement of God's will. In parallel, twenty-eight jobs were created around *Östhjälpen* activities in Romania and distributed to local unemployed women.

In the Pentecostal church of Jönköping, Bosse leads the morning prayer group which gathers ten to twenty persons from eight to nine every week day. He is there every single morning and is absent only when duty calls him back to Romania where he has helped plant more than twenty churches. When evoking his engagement and his assiduity in prayer he says: 'I am just a person observing what God wants to do, I am commanded and I do, and one of the reasons why I come to church every day is the burden the Lord put on my shoulder, on the one hand for the handicapped kids for whom I am responsible, but also for the twenty-eight employees there, for whose needs I have to provide every month and for all the other tasks the Lord gave me ... I have to bend on my knees every morning to stand there to observe the Lord work as he does, through me [...], I am just a little tool in all that. The Lord has got several persons for different tasks and he wants to use us all in different manners'.

As we see in this example, if believers transform the way they pray to construct the presence of a Christ corresponding to the anticipations of the hosting society (hence the 'decharismatization'), by a dialectical logic they also try, by the means of prayer, to transform their society. A weapon in the spiritual warfare between Good and Evil, as Yannick Fer put it,[18] prayer is also, on a more ordinary level, a tool in the work of God (see Tonda 2002). It helps to transform the self on a daily basis as well as transforming the world as it is experienced by the subject. One might pray for a parking place, for the achievement of divine will in the Arab revolutions or, as Bosse, for help in a development programme in Eastern Europe; in all these cases, prayer appears to the believer as an instrument delivered by God to humans in order to work on their world by representing Him the best they can. Consequently, I would define prayer as the primary *tool* (or step) with which the Christian works in a process of transformation of the world, in the daily labour of production and reproduction of the symbolic goods of God. 'Culture' and 'society' thus appear as the raw material in need of transformation, analogically to the way the capitalist workers transform material into goods in the industrial working process (Tonda, *op. cit.*).

In this labour process, the Spirit is a tool invested with an autonomous agency by the believer, which results in an inverted symmetric relationship in which the Christian himself/herself appears as a tool to be used by the Spirit, as Bosse's words illustrate. Prayer is thus comparable to an aesthetic experience; that of human beings who become spectators of their own actions; observing a supernatural entity working through them and just appreciating the beauty of the result. Pentecostals settle around them a collective, material, symbolic and linguistic dispositive to presentify God. This disposition allows them to supervene in their actions; as active subjects they are able to influence their own destiny through prayer, and as passive subjects, they are actor-spectators of a world led by the Almighty. There, neither paradox nor contradiction, they find in their interaction with non-visible, immaterial beings a solution of continuity to assume both positions simultaneously. It is in this double existential posture – that of an instrument being at the same time active and passive – that prayer is experienced and narrated.[19] Accordingly, the repeated prayers and their answers,

---

[18]   See Fer, in this volume.

[19]   Pascal Boyer (1997), suggesting a cognitivist approach to religious phenomena, considers counterintuitive assertions, leading to interpretive difficulties when one considers the consequences as being the first feature of religious discourse. The anthropologist Albert Piette (1999) suggested that indeed Christianity was full of these types of utterances, starting with the Christian kerygma. This type of articulation between passive and active existential postures in prayer through the mediation of an invisible entity can be considered as taking place in the assertions Pascal Boyer identified as lying at the ground of religions. Besides, the invisibility of the entity, or its immateriality, might be a resourceful feature to subsume potential contradictions. Indeed, being invisible and immaterial, it can be as plastic as one wishes and adopt a priori 'contradictory' (they are only contradictory in our thought) traits without being endangered in its foundation.

if there are any, constitute a means to draw an aestheticised style of life, in the sense this expression is used by Foucault (1994: 535), an initiative of the self to transform the self. Here the transformation is made through an invisible entity, as we saw in the case of Bosse when the intervention of the Spirit he invoked himself transformed his ethics of responsibility into ethics of conviction on the question of the construction of a new orphanage.

Conclusion

Pentecostals are nothing but lovers. Through hearing testimonies and sermons, daily conversations and pieces of advice given to one another, the ethnographer carrying out Pentecostal fieldwork will be struck by the fact he is observing people involved in a love relationship with an absent being: God. Harvey Cox even sees there the ground of what he calls a 'Pentecostal theology' – even though some scholars might consider this expression to be a sort of oxymoron – in which the Lord appears to be a lover playing the game of what Salvatore Cucchiari named a 'soteriological romance' (1990), in which God tries to court a human being and is 'broken-hearted' when the latter does not reply to his advance (see Cox 2001: 201). As a mere love relationship between two empirical beings is not expressed in the same way in every society, so is it for the relationship to the Almighty. In the Swedish case, the language of love that glossolalia appears to be requires intimacy to be expressed.

More than teaching us a little bit more on the nature of prayer, the Swedish example, parallel to other 'Pentecostalisms', reminds us of the plasticity of this transnational religion which changes at the rhythm of its travels through national boundaries and with the symbolic work of the actors carrying it out and experiencing it in their daily life. As the anthropologist Christophe Pons, a specialist of the Icelandic religious context, stated, one should consider the contemporary revival movements in a cultural perspective as symbolic productions – whereas they are often perceived as 'things apart remaining at the limen of cultures without really entering them, because their proper space would be the non-places of a globalization without attachments' (Pons 2011b: 26).[20] Prayer appears here as a heuristic object, which reveals some of the idiosyncratic features of a given society. Indeed, the manifestation of the Spirit in its utterance is the result of a work of symbolic production in which the subjects involved take into account the constraints imposed by the political and socio-historical

---

[20]   The translation from French is mine.

context in which they are inscribed to draw a temporary and always emerging regime of religious emotion that will help them to be accepted in their society – as well as allowing them to accept a supernatural entity in their daily lives. As the Swedish Pentecostals say, the goal is 'to experience the supernatural in a natural way' (*uppleva det övernaturliga på naturligt sätt*), that is to say that it has to be experienced in a way that corresponds to the constraints and negotiated margins of freedom they have vis-à-vis their national ('cultural Lutheran') fellows.

The relationship to the Spirit is constructed relative to a given environment in an interpretive labour process, producing sense around the self from which results a particular style of spiritual manifestation. This process helps define the style of prayer, whilst the latter contributes to the transformation of the self and of the world as a communication tool with the divine. Through praying, one observes human existence reduced to its passive form, for at least a moment, however active human beings can be.

References

Aronsson, Torbjörn (2005). *Guds eld över Sverige. Svensk väckelsehistoria efter 1945*. Uppsala: Livets Ord Förlag.

Boyer, Pascal (1997). *La religion comme phénomène naturel*. Paris: Bayard.

Coleman, Simon (1989). 'Controversy and the Social Order: Response to a Religious Group in Sweden'. PhD thesis. University of Cambridge.

Coleman, Simon (1996). 'The Charismatic Gift', *Journal of the Royal Anthropological Institute* 10: 421–42.

Coleman, Simon (2006). 'When Silence isn't Golden: Charismatic Speech and the Limits of Literalism', in Engelke, Matthew and Tomlinson, Matt (eds), *The Limits of Meaning, Case Studies in the Anthropology of Christianity*. Oxford: Oxford University Press, 39–63.

Coleman, Simon (2007 [2000]). *The Globalisation of Charismatic Christianity. Spreading the Gospel of Prosperity*. New York: Cambridge University Press.

Corten, André and Mary, André (2000). 'Introduction', in Corten, André and Mary, André (eds), *Imaginaires politiques et pentecôtismes. Afrique/Amérique latine*. Paris: Karthala, 11–33.

Corten, André and Marshall-Fratani, Ruth (2001). *Between Babel and Pentecost. Transnational Pentecostalism in Africa and Latin America*. Bloomington and Indianapolis: Indiana University Press.

Cox, Harvey (2001 [1995]). *Fire from Heaven. The Rise of Pentecostal Spirituality and the Reshaping of Religion in the Twenty-First Century.* Cambridge, MA: Da Capo Press.

Cucchiari, Salvatore (1990). 'Between Shame and Sanctification: Patriarchy and Its Transformation in Sicilian Pentecostalism', *American Ethnologist* 17: 687–707.

Elias, Norbert (1973 [1969]). *La civilisation des mœurs.* Paris: Calmann-Levy.

Foucault, Michel (1994). *Dits et écrits, vol. IV.* Paris: Gallimard.

Gifford, Paul (2001). 'The Complex Provenance of Some Elements of African Pentecostal Theology', in Corten, André and Marshall-Fratani, Ruth (eds), *Between Babel and Pentecost. Transnational Pentecostalism in Africa and Latin America.* Bloomington and Indianapolis: Indiana University Press, 62–79.

Harry, Frédérique (2010). 'Les mutations du protestantisme militant en Scandinavie. Du mouvement populaire au rencoforcement convictionnel : transformaiton structurelle et idéologique des organisations missionnaires et des antennes de jeunesse en Norvège et en Suède de 2000 à 2010'. Thèse de doctorat. Paris: Université de la Sorbonne.

Hollenweger, Walter J. (1978). *The Pentecostals.* Minneapolis: Augsburg Publishing House.

Hunsicker, David (1996). 'John Wesley: Father of Today's Small Group Concept?', *Wesleyan Theological Journal* 31/1: 192–211.

Laurent, Pierre-Joseph (2000). 'Diabolisation de l'autre et ruses de l'Esprit : les Assemblées de Dieu du Burkina Faso', in Corten, André and Mary, André. (eds), *Imaginaires politiques et pentecôtismes. Afrique/Amérique latine.* Paris: Karthala, 61–80.

Mary, André (2000). 'La violence symbolique de la Pentecôte gabonaise', in Corten, André and Mary, André (dir.), *Imaginaires politiques et pentecôtismes.* Paris: Karthala, 143–63.

Oredsson, Sverker (2007). 'Vad hände före 1971?', in Oredsson, Sverker (ed.), *Jönköpings kommuns historia. De första 35 åren.* Lund: Historiska Media, 13–49.

Piette, Albert (1999). *La religion de près. L'activité religieuse en train de se faire.* Paris: Métailié.

Piette, Albert (2003). *Le fait religieux. Une théorie de la religion ordinaire.* Paris: Economica.

Pons, Christophe (2011a). 'Jésus aux îles Féroé, ou comment se réinvente la relation au divin', in Houdart, Sophie and Thiery, Oliver (eds), *Humains, non-humains. Comment repeupler les sciences sociales.* Paris: La Découverte, 339–49.

Pons, Christophe (2011b). *Les liaisons surnaturelles. Une anthropologie du médiumnisme dans l'Islande contemporaine*. Paris: Editions CNRS.

Riis, Ole and Woodhead, Linda (2010). *A Sociology of Religious Emotions*. Oxford: Oxford University Press.

Sundstedt, Alfred (1969). *Pingstväckelsen – dess uppkomst och första utvecklingsskede*. Stockholm: Normans Förlag.

Tonda, Joseph (2002). *La guérison divine en Afrique centrale (Congo, Gabon)*. Brazzaville: Karthala.

Åberg, Göran (2007). 'Kyrkor och Samfund', in Oredsson, S. (ed.), *Jönköpings kommuns historia. De första 35 åren*. Lund: Historiska Media, 277–311.

Chapter 6

Contrasting Regimes of Sufi Prayer and Emotion Work in the Indonesian Islamic Revival

Julia Day Howell

This chapter examines contrasting usages of a core Sufi ritual, 'remembrance' of God using repetitive litanies[1] (*dzikr*). These litanies are composed of phrases from the Qur'an and are deployed with the intention of bringing God more and more constantly to mind, and in so doing 'cleansing' the 'heart' of base desires.[2] In Islam, the use of these litanies has been perennially associated with the heroic quest for mystical awareness of God. However, *dzikr* litanies are also recited simply as modest efforts at enriching the obligatory five daily prayers (*sholat wajib*)[3] with a deeper inward focus and sense of intimacy with God.[4]

Dzikr and other Sufi practices have ancient lineages (their advocates say going back to the Prophet himself), but of interest here are the places they have found in Indonesia's Islamic revival of the last thirty to forty years, and the different ways in which they work to support religious recommitment, which, as Bayat (2007) has shown, is the hallmark of Islamic revival around the world. Recommitment, in the revivalist contexts studied by Bayat in Egypt and Iran and also evident in Indonesia (Howell 2008), is not simply a matter of rationally

---

[1]   Here 'litany' is used in the loose sense of prayers in the form of short phrases or sentences, repeated many times, as an act of piety, even if not explicitly to supplicate divine intervention in a particular matter or done as a series of responses, as in some Christian prayers.

[2]   This phrase renders the Arabic 'tazkiya an nafs' which refers to the work of purification (*tazkiya*) of the spiritual body (focused on the heart or *qolbu*) of base passions (*nafs*).

[3]   *Sholat sunnah* are discretionary prayers that are not obligatory (in contrast to the *sholat wajib*) but may be appended to the obligatory prayers.

[4]   *Khusyu* is a highly valued condition of heartfelt engagement in a religious practice, as when one feels fully absorbed in prayer or in a Qur'anic recitation and thereby intimate with God (cf. Gade 2004: 214–15).

re-evaluating one's past and conventional religiosity, finding it lacking, and deciding to do better. Rather, it manifests in programmes of practice aimed at personal development that are themselves emotionally coloured and shaped using the various vocabularies of the sectors of the revival movement with which individuals engage.

Since modernist Islamic reform movements like the Muslim Brotherhood and traditionalist Wahhabi-inspired (neo-Salafist) movements have driven much of the Sunni Islamic revival in the twentieth and twenty-first centuries, contemporary Islamic revival is generally perceived as scripturalist,[5] that is, narrowly legalistic and hostile to expressive, often emotionally intense, Sufi practices.[6] Nonetheless, there is growing recognition of persistent interest in the Sufi heritage around the world, even amongst urban sophisticates, and we see, in urban environments especially, considerable innovation in Sufi practice (Hoffman 1995; Sirriyeh 1999; Howell and Bruinessen 2007).

In Indonesia, too, interest in Islam's Sufi heritage has been a prominent part of the country's Islamic revival (Azra 2012; Darmadi 2001; Hoesterey 2011; Howell 2001, 2007). The traditional Sufi orders (A. *tariqa*, I. *tarekat*) have catered to some of the new interest in Sufi spirituality (now popularly named with the loan word 'spiritualitas') evident in the last several decades. But the desire to cultivate an intensely personal, inwardly focused and emotionally rich religious life using the Sufi heritage is not confined to the *tarekat*. Elements of the Sufi heritage are being explored and practised in new institutional settings, ranging from purely private, individual reading and reflection at home, to salons and mosque-based study groups (*majelis taklim*), and even to commercial courses and televised ministries. While in some of these settings people only study ideas about spiritual life, in others they collectively practise rituals like the *dzikr* litanies and *shalawat* (praise songs and prayers for blessings on the Prophet and his family) that are associated with Sufism.

Our focus here is on those contemporary settings in which people use Sufi litanies (*dzikr*) as important components of their striving to become better Muslims. Like Muslims in general, people who join in *dzikr* groups also are concerned to properly observe *syariah* (religious law, including performing

---

   5   Clifford Geertz (1968) and Ernst Gellner (1981) have used the term 'scripturalist' to describe styles of Islamic religiosity that are narrowly focused on correct observance of the law and reject the Sufi devotional and mystical heritage. It is largely a product of twentieth century reform movements.

   6   For much of the twentieth century scripturalist reformers (both modernist and Wahhabi) have denigrated *dzikr* rituals and other practices associated with the Sufi orders as heretical innovations (*bid'ah*).

the obligatory ritual duties), but they appreciate the Sufi prayers for the ways they help a person 'feel closer to God'. That phrase is actually a common refrain throughout the revival movement, even in scripturalist settings, but is especially salient in groups drawing on Sufi themes and rituals. Of particular interest in this chapter will be the ways the litanies themselves are incorporated in a larger service or performance, how this shapes emotional states associated with 'closeness to God', and how the value of litany recitation is framed by different kinds of groups that promote its use.

Descriptions of conventional Sufi orders commonly detail the litanies that are given to aspirants on their initiation. The particular verses, the multiples in which they are used, the voicing of a litany or silent repetition of it, postures adopted and directions faced are also richly documented, showing a range of variation from one order to another in how *dzikr* rituals are performed. That range, however, is reasonably narrow, insofar as a limited repertoire of verses is used in the orders. But more importantly, both collective and private performance of the *dzikr* in Sufi orders inevitably involves long series of repetitions of the verses. In contemporary, non-*tarekat* settings this is often not the case. That variability in how *dzikr* litanies are, as it were, orchestrated within larger ritual and performance contexts, and the kinds of emotional regimes encouraged in these different contexts, form the central issues that will be explored in the pages that follow.

In order to grasp how the different orchestrations of *dzikr* litanies work to shape regimes of religious emotion and qualities of religious experience, it will be necessary to call not only upon recent re-evaluations of the relationship between thought and emotion, mind and body, but upon the psychology literature that problematises the relationship between thought and mind, thinking and awareness. Riis and Woodhead (2010: 14–17) have argued that the sociology of religious emotion needs to incorporate a more nuanced understanding of the interplay between emotion and thought than allowed by common-sense formulations of emotion as bodily and irrational and of thought as reflective and potentially rational. They urge that we build on the now substantial literature showing how emotion shapes and partly constitutes ostensibly rational thought processes, just as understanding and evaluative concepts can channel and modulate emotion.

Similarly, I argue that the sociology of religious emotion, where it deals with rituals ideally focused on mystical states, needs to assimilate what anthropological studies of those rituals show about their performance structure. We also need to be informed by insights into the cognitive shaping of subjective states emergent in such rituals modelled by psychologists from ethnographic studies and directly elicited practitioner reports. Particularly helpful is the distinction Deikman (1969) has drawn between discursive and non-discursive thought, signalling the important recognition that not all forms of awareness (or mentation) consist in what we ordinarily mean by 'thought', i.e., talking to ourselves and others. In Deikman's model of qualities of awareness, meditative states are characterised by a radical diminution in discursive thought and, significantly, are facilitated by practices that disrupt ordinary discursive consciousness. This disruption, as Fischer (1971) has shown, may be accomplished by using practices that generate 'hyperarousal' (repetitive bodily actions that stimulate heartbeat and breathing) which disrupt streams of thought by persistently interrupting them (as in trance dances and drumming rituals) or by 'hypoarousal' techniques, which dampen down bodily arousal and substitute for chatty thoughts a single object of thought that may collapse into non-discursive awareness. With the diminution, and possibly even cessation of discursive thought, construction of the self as an 'I', in contrast to an other, may no longer be sustainable, potentially opening 'the doors of [non-ordinary] perception'. It is this kind of consciousness transformation that the metaphysical literature on Sufi gnosis envisions, describing a condition called 'fana' (loss of self-awareness in the presence of God). Extended *dzikr* practice can be seen to work to disrupt discursive thought, as in Deikman's model, through the rhythmic, ongoing repetition of the short phrases of the litanies, which relentlessly push aside streams of distracted thought.

While this matter need not be engaged in the study of emotions associated with many rituals, it is called for in any examination of rituals orchestrated in such a way as to facilitate transformations in states of awareness (or ASCs). This is generally not the case with *dzikr* rituals performed outside the Sufi orders as part of feast day celebrations or life-crisis rituals, where only very short braces of litanies are used. But it has always been the ideal purpose of *dzikr* recitations in Sufi orders where they have been one of the essential methods (along with disciplines of self-control guided by ethical reflection) used to achieve spiritual perfection and mystical knowing (*hakikat* and *makrifat*).

Recently some new types of groups have emerged in Indonesia outside the Sufi orders that make *dzikr* recitation a central feature: the so called 'majelis dzikr' and 'majelis shalawat'. 'Majelis' (I.) means 'assembly' or 'meeting', so a *majelis dzikr* is a group that meets to recite *dzikr* and a *majelis shalawat* is one that gathers to perform *shalawat* prayers to praise and ask blessings on the Prophet Muhammad and his family. *Majelis shalawat* always include *dzikr* litanies in their programmes, although groups called *majelis dzikr* may not include the *shalawat*. Several of the *majelis dzikr* and *majelis shalawat* have mass audiences mobilised in live rallies of thousands and reached through the mass media via the internet and television. Here I will compare the orchestrations of *dzikr* litanies in a conventional Sufi order now popular with Indonesian national elites as well as with ordinary citizens, the Tarekat Qodiriyyah Naqsyabandiyah Suryalaya, with *dzikr* practice used in two examples of the *majelis dzikr* and *shalawat*. The two *majelis* are the Majelis Shalawat and Dzikr Nurul Mustafa founded by Al-Habib Hasan bin Ja'far Assegaf, and Majelis Zikir Az Zikra led by Arifin Ilham. The primary public presence the Majelis Nurul Mustafa is in mass prayer rallies, which regularly crowd up to 10,000 people into stadiums, fields or a kilometre or so of Jakarta streets blocked off from late afternoon until after midnight. Arifin Ilham, still a popular revival preacher (*da'i*), was for much of the first decade of the twenty-first century one of the highest-rating celebrity televangelists; he also regularly conducts live mass services that spill out onto the streets from mosques around Jakarta and elsewhere in the country.

This comparison will illustrate the diversity in usages of *dzikr* litanies by *tarekat* and non-*tarekat* groups and the 'emotion regimes' (see Riis and Woodhead 2010: 10–12) commonly associated with them. I will show that in the mass rally and mass-media ministries where *dzikr* is used, the patterning of litany recitations and their rhetorical framings serve to amplify emotions drawn from everyday life experience, refocusing them upon the religious object (the Prophet and his family, and ultimately, Allah). In contrast, in the more intimate settings of the traditional Sufi order examined, the patterning of the litany recitations and the instructions framing them offer practitioners the possibility of moving beyond everyday emotions of remorse, repentance and love (such as known from family and romantic experience) into non-ordinary subjective states where (as the classical *tasawuf* literature leads us to expect) self-awareness is muted or effaced and ordinary emotion words, in retrospect, less often seem applicable. The words of the litany, then, are used to transcend words, sometimes successfully.

As *dzikr* practice in the Sufi orders has so strongly shaped scholarly understandings of how the ritual should be used (if at all) in pursuit of mystical union with God, I will begin with an account of Tarekat Qodiriyyah Naqsyabandiyah, Pesantren Suryalaya, the Sufi order that I have spent the most time studying, first in the 1990s in Yogyakarta and Tegal (in central Java) and then from 2003–06 in Jakarta.[7]

---

[7]   Where not otherwise specified, the material in this section is based on my fieldwork with TQN Suryalaya starting in the 1990s when I did participant observation with groups in Yogyakarta and Tegal and visited Pesanteren Suryalaya in West Java. I worked together with MA Subandi in carrying out time series surveys of members of TQN Suryalaya on their demographic profiles and also interviews with selected members on their experiences in

Dzikr Litanies in the Spiritual Practice of a Sufi Order: Tarekat Qodiriyyah Naqsyabandiyah, Pesantren Suryalaya

The Qodiriyyah Naqsyabandiyah Sufi order (*tarekat*) was established together with its associated religious boarding school, Pesantren Suryalaya in 1905 in the mountains of West Java by Syeikh H. Abdullah Mubarok bin Noor Muhammad. It is probably the Sufi order best known for attracting and accommodating the new Muslim middle class that grew rapidly along with New Order economic development from the 1980s. Not coincidentally, this was about the same time that the national press began carrying stories about a 'rush to the *tarekat*' (*Amanah* 36 [1987]: cover and 6–10) and my own surveys from two central Java regional branches of the TQN Suryalaya showed substantial growth in numbers, including highly educated urbanites, and a more diverse gender and age profile than had been typical of Sufi orders in the past (Howell, Subandi and Nelson 2001). In a later study of privileged Jakartans who had taken university-style adult religious education courses, including one on *tasawuf*, at the progressive Muslim think tank, the Paramadina Foundation,[8] I found that many had joined in weekend excursions to Suryalaya, organised by the Foundation, to become acquainted with actual Sufi practice (Howell 2007). Several lecturers for the Paramadina courses were authorised spiritual guides (*wakil talqin*) for TQN Suryalaya. The order had also attracted national attention for the pioneering drug rehabilitation programme it established, Inabah, using the order's spiritual disciplines, and treating, amongst others, several children of wealthy elites from the nation's capital, Jakarta.

Many people close to TQN Suryalaya have attributed its flourishing during the New Order, and particularly its socially and politically significant patronage by national elites, to the enlightened direction of the order and its school by the founder's son and successor, Kyai H.A. Shohibul Wafa Tajul Arifin, familiarly called Abah Anom ('the Young Father').[9] Not only did Abah Anom sponsor a number of community aid programmes in agriculture and health not commonly undertaken by *pesantren* at the time, but he conducted the *tarekat* in a relatively open and approachable manner that allayed the anxieties of many urbanities about the supposedly secretive and authoritarian Sufi orders.

---

performing *dzikr*. Some of that material was analysed by Subandi and reported in Subandi 2005. In visits to Jakarta from 2003–05 I also interviewed people associated with Paramadina Foundation who were involved with TQN Suryalaya.

[8]   The Paramadina Foundation was founded by leading liberal Muslim intellectual Nurcholish Majdid in 1986.

[9]   Abah Anom passed away in 2011.

Nonetheless, Tarekat Qodiriyyah Naqsyabandiyah, under Abah Anom's direction, continued to offer guidance in the classic pursuit of spiritual perfection and gnosis, to the extent that initiates were prepared to undertake that. A prayer used by initiates after waking for the recommended night vigil prayer (*sholat tahajud*) enunciates this goal:

> Oh God, only You do I strive for and it is only your mercy that I seek. Enable me to love and be joined (*makrifat*) with You.[10]

This did not mean that people necessarily joined the order with spiritual union and gnosis (*makrifat*) as their personal objective, or even that Abah Anom and his spiritual deputies (his *wakil talqin*) cast the pursuit of higher spiritual states (*hakikat* and *makrifat*) as the primary goals of *dzikr* practice. To the contrary, TQN Suryalaya offers initiates instruction in the order's distinctive method of *dzikr* practice to assist with achieving aims that all Muslims would ideally share. Subandi[11] has set these out in a commemorative book on TQN Suryalaya *dzikr* published on the hundredth anniversary of the founding of the order. As he explained: 'The objective of *dzikr* practice is to elevate faith and piety as well as to bring oneself closer to the presence of Allah swt' (2005: 124).

Still, *dzikr* practice in TQN Suryalaya is framed as part of a path of spiritual purification that proceeds in stages towards transcendence of everyday awareness. Initiates learn from their initiating guide (the *syeikh*, or one of his spiritual deputies, a 'wakil talqin') to expect to become aware as they practise their *dzikr* of powerful, unusual sensations, first in the spiritual centre (*latifah*) called the *qolbu* ('heart'). This is located, like the physical heart, slightly below the left breast. Its precise location is learned at the outset of an initiate's tutelage, since it is one of the places on the body to which one must direct one's attention in the sequence of head movements and inhalations and exhalations that accompany the pronunciation of the syllables of the prescribed litany (in this order, the *tahlil: laa ilaa ha illallah*, the profession of God's oneness). In each recitation of that phrase, the spiritual focus is meant to shift from one part of the body to another, each associated with a *latifah* (seven in all), while successive syllables of the phrase are pronounced.[12] Spiritual advancement is

---

[10]   See Subandi (2005).

[11]   Note that the author, Subandi, is a member of the Qodiriyyah Naqsyabandiyah, Suryalaya, order.

[12]   The seven *latifah* are: the Qolbi, located below the left breast; the Ruhi, below the right breast; the Sirri, just above the left breast; the Khofi, just above the right breast; the Akhfa, in the centre of the chest; the Nafsi on the brow between the eyes; and the Jasad or

marked by the 'opening' of successive *latifah*. Practitioners report what they think are activations or openings of the *latifah* to their spiritual directors, who then authenticate each opening and thus the commencement of a new state (*maqaam*) of spiritual development.

Not only is the *dzikr* practised in this *tarekat* framed as a path of sequential spiritual development (a coming to awareness through non-ordinary feelings and legitimated by one's guide), but it is framed as radically psychologically transformative. This is evident from the way that the *dzikr* practice itself is pictured. Thus senior TQN deputy Kyai H. Abdul Gaus describes the first part of the enunciation of the phrase used for the *dzikr*, that is, voicing the syllable *laa* while drawing the breath up from below the belly to the forehead, as 'splitting open' the torso lengthwise, as it were, with a 'laser' (playing on the combined imagery of light, with its spiritual resonance, and a knife) (Subandi 2005: 38). The following moment of the phrase, that where the attention moves to the heart while voicing the segment 'illa', is commonly described by TQN Suryalaya practitioners as like pounding on a stone: breaking the heart open so that through God's grace negative emotions like jealousy, hate, pride and resentment can be drawn out. The classic Sufi understanding of the need for 'purification of the lesser impulses' (*tazkiya an nafs*) here is pictured as being accomplished through powerful gestures and a dramatic excision of entrenched patterns of negative behaviour.

This characterisation of the way spiritual guides in TQN Suryalaya frame expectations for the way *dzikr* practice will work upon them and towards what goals it propels them, already shows much of the form of litany recitation: its use (by speaking out) of a single, axiomatic phrase (the profession of God's oneness); its emphatic recitation, accompanied by particular movements of the head, inhalations and exhalations, and visualisations (or rather imaginatively projecting the soundings of the syllables into the different parts of the body). As in other Sufi orders, initiates are instructed to repeat the phrase of their litany a specified number of times. In TQN Pesantren Suryalaya, practitioners are to do 165 repetitions, unless there are extenuating circumstances, in which case they may substitute a set of just three. Many people (especially men) chant this *dzikr* quite loudly, particularly as the number of repetitions mounts, and although people perform it in a sitting position, the movements of the head, if vigorous, can start to carry the whole chest in swinging movements, generating a feeling of great intensity in a communal performance.

Latiful Qolab that is actually the whole body in its esoteric form. The activation of the Qolab, initiates learn, is experienced as each cell of the body constantly sounding the name 'Allah'.

The full picture of the orchestration of TQN Suryalaya *dzikr*, however, needs further elaboration. The spoken *dzikr* already described (called 'dzikr jahar' or 'loud' *dzikr*) actually forms only one phase of the complete practice. As a discretionary form of prayer, in both group meetings and in individual practice, *dzikr* is meant to follow obligatory prayers (*sholat sunnah*).[13] And in TQN Suryalaya, the 'loud' *dzikr* described above is followed by another form of *dzikr*, a *dzikr khofi*, which is silent (literally 'hidden' or 'secret'). In some other orders a silent *dzikr* is used to the exclusion of loud *dzikr*. In TQN Suryalaya the silent *dzikr khofi* follows directly on from the performance of the 'loud' *dzikr jahar*, and consists of the repetition 'in the heart' of just one word, 'Allah'. The silent *dzikr*, like the loud *dzikr*, is done in a sitting position.

When performed at a regular weekly meeting of a chapter of the order, the *dzikr* recitation, including both its loud and silent segments, makes up most of the meeting time, other than announcements and socialising after the prayers over food provided by the hosts. At larger gatherings, the *dzikr* will be of similar length, but is prefaced or followed by longer prayers, sermons and, depending on the occasion, by instructional addresses or a reading of the hagiography[14] of the founder of the order.

Viewed from a comparative perspective, using Fischer's typology of practices associated with changed states of awareness, it is evident that the Qodiriyyah Naqsyabandiyah order somewhat surprisingly combines a practice likely to stimulate hyperarousal (visibly heavy breathing and rhythmic body movements sustained in a constant pattern over a long period of time, most likely accompanied by somewhat increased rate of heartbeat) with another practice that is conducive to hypoarousal. The long duration of the loud *dzikr*, and the intricate patterning of both breathing and mental focus, plus, in private practice, tracking the number of repetitions with prayer beads (*tasbih*), work against sustaining ordinary discursive thought by persistently interrupting it in an unyielding rhythm with a single short phrase. The silent *dzikr* appended to the loud *dzikr*, in contrast, involves near physical immobility, but it too, as it were, erodes discursive thought by focusing on a single religiously significant

---

[13]   As for all Muslims, the obligatory prayers are to be performed five times a day, at set times, and using an invariant text in Qur'anic Arabic with accompanying prescribed body movements. TQN Suryalaya also enjoins *sholat tahajud*, that is, waking at two in the morning for prayers, including both the required *sholat wajib* and *dzikr*, after a full body ablution (shower). Many traditional Muslims (those culturally associated with the Nahdlatul Ulama) also commonly do this *sholat tahajud*.

[14]   On ritual reading the hagiography of Abdul Qadir Al-Jaelani in TQN Suryalaya and wider practices of such ritual readings in West Java see Millie (2009).

word. The silent *dzikr* clearly resembles one-pointed meditation practised in other traditions.

However surprising this combination of hypoarousal and hyperarousal practices, this ritual structure does for many practitioners work personal transformations. As reported by Subandi (2005: 125–53), these include mildly altered feeling states like 'ketenangan' (calm); disruptions in perceptions of time; changed perspectives of the person's own dispositions; and, in a few cases, beatific experiences of dissolution of self-awareness. Subandi emphasises in his analysis of the reports the respondents' comments about the way they feel they have changed, not only in their dedication to diligent performance of the obligations of the faith, but in recognising and eschewing their former egotism or narrowly instrumental (occultist)[15] approaches to spirituality.

Dzikr Litanies in the Majelis Shalawat Nurul Mustafa and the Majelis Zikir Az Zikra

Majelis Nurul Mustafa.

Since the turn of the century, the Majelis Nurul Mustafa has become one of the most popular of the *majelis shalawat* and *dzikr*. This new type of group builds on the institutional framework of a *majelis taklim* (a lay religious study group), itself a relatively recent social form very similar to what people used to call simply a 'pengajian'. *Pengajian* are informal religious instruction classes offered by a person recognised for his or her religious learning (such as an *ulama* trained in a *pesantren*), and given individually or in small groups at the invitation of the learner or their parents. *Majelis taklim* draw on the spirit of religious revival, and particularly on the value placed on lay initiative in 'calling' others to religious renewal (*dakwah*), traceable to the early years of the Muslim Brotherhood in Egypt. They are often formed by groups of laypeople associated with a particular mosque, or by those who have come to appreciate a particular teacher, who may himself seek to rouse the public to form such groups to support his ministry. Such lay-initiated *majelis taklim*, common in big cities, have attracted considerable public notice since the 1990s. An older generation of *majelis taklim* (perhaps only retrospectively identified as such and otherwise known simply as

---

15 In Central Java especially it is common for people to take an initiation in a Sufi order in hopes of acquiring supernatural power. One such person in the interviews reported came to see his interest in such powers as narrowly egotistical and undesirable after practicing the TQN *dzikr* for some time.

pengajian) were formed by senior figures in *pesantren* (for example, the wives of the *pesantren* master) as charitable contributions to the religious lives of people living nearby their schools (Winn 2012; Srimulyani 2007).

Today's *majelis shalawat* and *dzikr* seem to have arisen from *majelis taklim* by including among their outreach activities and featuring in their programmes *dzikr* litanies and *shalawat* prayers and recitations. This is illustrated in the story of the formation of Majelis Nurul Mustafa. As the story reveals, Habib Hasan introduced the *dzikr* and *shalawat* rituals to enhance the appeal of his ministry, which previously had been entirely didactic, focusing on correct understanding of basic religious obligations. With that approach, he did not get the public response for which he had hoped. His enormous popularity developed after he began using the *dzikr* and *shalawat* rituals.[16]

Habib Hasan's success with Majelis Nurul Mustafa also exemplifies the current appeal in Indonesia of Hadhrami preachers descended from the Prophet Muhammad. Called 'habib' (A. 'beloved'; pl. *habaib*) they are especially revered in Jakarta among the Batawi 'natives' of the city. Expectations that *habaib* are endowed with special spiritual qualities by virtue of their descent from the Prophet have evidently helped Habib Hasan and a number of other *habaib* to become popular, and even to achieve success as religious teachers relatively early in life, unlike *ulama* of previous generations. In the past, the usual expectation was that a person would be ready to start his own teaching establishment only after spending his entire youth in formal religious education, thereafter waiting, perhaps many years, to receive spiritual authority (*ijazah*) from his teacher.

Habib Hasan was only twenty three when he founded the Majelis Nurul Mustafa in Jakarta. Born in 1977 into a Hadhrami family living in Bogor, near Jakarta, he was strongly formed by his religious education in the Indonesian Arab community. His early religious education came through private study with his father, who was a respected *ulama*, and from other local scholars with whom the family was connected. For formal religious education his father sent him to Malang in East Java where for three years he attended *pesantren* established by *ulama* of Arab descent and patronised substantially by members of the Indonesian Arab community (Pesantren Al-Faqihiyah and Darut Tauhid). From there he went on to tertiary studies at the State Institute of Islamic Studies (IAIN) Sunan Ampel (still in Malang), where he took his degree in the Tarbiyah Faculty. With these substantial qualifications, but still very young

---

[16] Unless otherwise specified, the material in this section is based on material from the Nurul Mustafa website, from observations made by the author of a *majelis* rally in February 2012, and on interviews conducted by Dr Arif Zamhari and reported in Zamhari and Howell (2012).

(only twenty one), he returned to the Jakarta–Bogor area and began his career as a religious teacher.

He made his start in 1998 by receiving pupils in small rented quarters. Already apparently thinking of his pupils as the core of some kind of group, he styled what most people would have called simply a *pengajian* a 'majelis taklim', dubbing it Majelis Taklim Al-Irfan. Still, at this time, Habib Hasan was strongly focused on his own spiritual life, hardly venturing out except to visit the grave of his grandfather, Habib Abdullah bin Muhsin Alattas. It was only after a year of these pilgrimages and graveside vigils that an extraordinary dream propelled him into a new phase of more active ministry. He dreamed that the well-known *habib* Ahmad bin Alwi Al-Haddad appeared to him, telling him that he must move to Jakarta and undertake an active religious outreach.

Following the directions received in that dream, Habib Hasan moved straight away to Ciganjur in South Jakarta and started small lecture circles (*halaqah*), making particular efforts to reach the youth in the area. But before long he sensed that religious instruction by itself was not drawing much enthusiasm. To remedy this he introduced into his classes recitations of a litany, the Ratib al-Attas, which is popular among Hadhramis, and then added other *shalawat* prayers and some *dzikr* litanies. The new format proved popular. The numbers coming to his gatherings grew, and people in other neighbourhoods invited him to establish circles for them. By 2000 the numbers had grown to such an extent, and the groups had become so spread out, that he had arranged for a large mosque in one of the neighbourhoods to host a gathering open to people from all over the city. At this point, he recognised that the scale of his following merited a name. For this he turned to two already widely revered *habaib*, Al Habib Umar bin Muhammad bin Hafidz, from Yemen, and Al Habib Anis bin Alwi Al Habsyi from Surakarta, in Central Java. They chose the name 'Nurul Mustafa', incorporating an epithet for the Prophet Muhammad, 'al-Mustafa'. We can see the bestowal of a name for the *majelis* as a kind of spiritual authorisation (*ijazah*), which, together with his own lineage and modern tertiary religious studies, compensated for his youth and helped secure his credibility as a religious guide.

Majelis Shalawat and Dzikr Nurul Mustafa now has neighbourhood groups attached to over 250 mosques around Jakarta and surrounding urban areas. Thousands attend the central Saturday meeting every week, arriving in rented cars and buses and on motorcycles. Major events, held in stadiums, or on commandeered city streets or fields, draw as many as ten thousand, according to Majelis organisers. The larger meetings are publicly advertised over the Majelis website and also with big banners strung across city streets or along the roadside.

The programmes themselves are highly produced so as to engage the audience for two-and-a-half to three hours. The Nurul Mustafa staff often arrange to have fireworks set off before the meeting begins, drawing in people from the surrounding area who do not yet know about the event and creating a festive atmosphere. For events held in a field or on blocked-off city streets, the *majelis* spread out plastic sheet flooring, and where that gives out, people spread their own mats or pieces of newspaper bought from enterprising followers. Those who arrive early enough to be near the front may see Habib Hasan's police escort arrive, followed by the Habib's car and vehicles carrying other speakers, including male family members and special guest preachers who will help give religious instruction talks. The guest speakers may be either locals or perhaps a Yemeni visitor close to the Habib's family. Behind them come phalanxes of young people in Nurul Mustafa jackets riding motorbikes and brandishing *majelis* banners while chanting the *tahlil* (the profession of God's oneness, *laa ilaa ha illallah*). While they mill about with enthusiasm, the Habib and the other speakers are conducted to the temporary stage and are welcomed by other ordinary participants (*jema'ah*) singing Arabic praise poems (*kasidah*) recollecting the arrival of the Prophet Muhammad in Madina after his flight from Mecca. Those who arrive later and find themselves in the middle or back of the crowd will be able to see Habib Hasan and the other speakers on projection screens strategically erected around the field or down the long street. These later arrivals would have missed the cavalcade but would have enjoyed the market stalls they passed on arrival.

The tone becomes more sober as the prayer programme proper begins, and yet it changes many times during the long ceremony, from sombre to celebratory, from deeply reflective to ponderously and then giddily inspiring. There will be an opening reading from the Qur'an, followed by several of a number of collectively spoken *dzikr* litanies recited while seated and without attention to the direction of head movements or the inner gaze, nor with any particular patterning of breathing. Nonetheless the murmured words sound quietly reflective. That initial brace of *dzikr* does not last very long – perhaps just around ten minutes. After that, Habib Hasan leads the brighter singing of popular *shalawat* prayers for the Prophet, accompanied by drums and tambourines. Recitations of short passages from elegantly composed *maulid* books[17] follow. The passages are sung

---

[17]   Maulid books like the Barzanjiy, the Diba' and the Simtudduror consist of lengthy hagiographies of the Prophet and longer praise poems written in Arabic in literary forms admired for their beauty. They are commonly excerpted by traditionalist Muslims in Indonesia, including Hadhramis, for use in ceremonies celebrating the birth of the Prophet (Maulid al-Nabi), at commemorations of the death of an important religious figure (a *kyai*

over and over again in rotation for the better part of a half an hour. People who know the passages well become deeply absorbed in keeping up with the cycles; others work at making out the words from books they have brought to the prayer meeting. Then follows a section of the programme with more overt instructional content: recitations of verses from the Aqidatul Awam on the doctrines of the faith, written by the eighteenth century scholar Ahmad Al-Marzuqi Al-Maliki Al-Makki and used for basic instruction in *pesantren*. In between the verses, the Habib explains their meaning.

Thereafter comes the section of the programme given over to *tausiyah* (religious guidance) by the several preachers who have come for the event. Each speaks for about ten minutes, followed by Habib Hasan, who gives the final address. These talks are kept lively by the variation in the topics the speakers choose, by the different rhetorical styles they adopt, and by differences in their personal appeal, whether as a member of Habib Hasan's family, as a local celebrity preacher or as a distinguished scholar visiting from the Hadhrmaut. Despite the common purpose of providing religious guidance on doctrines of the faith, a recurring theme in the talks is the unique privilege the *jema'ah* (the community of followers) have of drawing close, through the *majelis*, to the Prophet via his own 'grandchildren', i.e., Habib Hasan and the brothers who assist him. Emotion surrounding this idea is built up by some speakers through the use of dramatically modulated voice registers, volume and pacing, building from low, steadily repeated warm evocations of love for the Habib to more excited and higher pitched phrases, and rapidly flashing images of how the *jema'ah* are connected through love of the Habib to his saintly forebears in the holy land. From there the *jema'ah* are projected into the very family circle of the Prophet himself, along with the *habaib*.

Reviewing this rally format, it is evident that the *dzikr* and *shalawat* are orchestrated in quite different ways from the *dzikr* used in the Qodiriyyah Naqsyabandiyah Sufi order associated with Pesantren Suryalaya. Majelis Nurul Mustafa uses both *dzikr* and *shalawat* in repetitive sequences, but none are deployed so as to disrupt discursive thought, as in TQN Suryalaya prayer gatherings. The Majelis uses one of a number of popular, very short *dzikr* phrases drawn from the Qur'an, but in its prayer meetings the *dzikr* phrases are not repeated long enough to drive a shift from ordinary discursive consciousness to non-discursive altered states. Not only are the braces of *dzikr* short, but no

---

or *habib*), and at life crisis rituals. Muslims outside *pesantren* circles tend to think of both popular, short *shalawat* prayers for the Prophet and passages taken from the *maulid* books as *shalawat*.

detailed instructions are given that might serve, as in the Sufi order, to trammel attention as each successive segment of the chosen *dzikr* phrase is enunciated. In total, the *dzikr* litanies do not make up a large part of the Majelis ceremonies. They do, however, provide interludes in which the participants can withdraw into a more inward focus.

The *shalawat* prayers and praises for the Prophet take up more than half of the smaller prayer meetings of the Majelis, but in the huge rallies, with multiple invited speakers they clearly represent a smaller portion of the whole event. Nonetheless, even in the big rallies far more time is devoted to *shalawat* of one sort or another than to *dzikr*. It is therefore important to consider the structure of the *shalawat*, some of which are relatively short and do have repetitive elements.

Some of the *shalawat* prayers, as we have seen, are relatively short and have repetitive refrains, or are themselves repeated for as long as an hour. They nonetheless consist of sequences of full sentences, so they are actually richly discursive, firing the imagination with images of life with the noble founders of the faith. The accompanying music helps colour the song-like recitations with a vibrant warmth. The recitations also display the example the Prophet provides for a correct Muslim life, and evoke a pleasing solidarity among the *jema'ah* and between the *jema'ah*, the *habaib* and the Prophet. The longer 'shalawat' passages, drawn from the *maulid* books, work as pieces of literature. Being less familiar, more demanding linguistically, and lengthy (even in their shortened forms) they inspire admiration and love for the Prophet, but support a quieter mood of reflection.

The sermons play a key role, not only in delivering religious instruction, but in projecting the distinctive role of the *majelis* leader and his family in helping the *jema'ah* to become closer to God. They frame the way the participants are to understand that spiritual fulfilment and help the ritual do its work of evoking gratifying emotions associated with that kind of fulfilment. Thus the talks build on the already existing expectations of many Jakarta Muslims, particularly the less privileged Betawi-descent Jakartans, that learned *habaib* are likely to have special spiritual gifts and to be favoured by the Prophet because of their family connection. Further, being close to the *habaib* means being close, along with them, to the Prophet and thence to God. The sermons elaborate this theme, some with great rhetorical power. The whole occasion of the rally is framed as a celebration of family closeness, with the *habaib* and with the Prophet, which is a way of becoming close to God.

The Majelis rallies and local prayer meetings do picture a path of spiritual perfection that people work on. It is trodden by learning how to be a good Muslim. The learning is mostly through stories about the life of the Prophet rather than through the study of bald rules. However, perfection seems to be quite a distant goal with sincere effort to improve one's everyday behaviour an acceptable proximate goal. Habib Hasan does see himself as a spiritual director for people keen on spiritual improvement, but he does not give initiations. The *majelis* does not even record memberships. Thus the structure of the Majelis is quite loose. It is really little more than a network of community groups loosely coordinated by Habib Hasan's staff. Nonetheless, he discourages those who regard him as their guide to become the pupil of another spiritual guide at the same time.

Majelis Zikir Az Zikra.

The Majelis Zikir Az Zikra grew out of the ministry of one of Indonesia's highest rating televangelists of the early twenty-first century, M. Arifin Ilham. He is not a *habib*, like so many principals of *majelis shalawat* and *majelis dzikr*, but like Habib Hasan he was relatively young by Indonesian standards when audiences of millions started looking to him for spiritual advice. Born in the South Kalimantan city of Banjarmasin in 1969, he rocketed to national fame in 2001 when he accepted an invitation to conduct a nationally broadcast service in the beautiful At-Tin mosque in South Jakarta before a live audience of 7,000 people. He had attracted the mosque committee's attention for the distinctive format of services he had been conducting in smaller mosques around the city, and for his personal magnetism as an orator and prayer leader. He had begun introducing *dzikr* litanies into the services he led, combining the litanies with what he called *muraqabah*. These were guided reflections, which he spoke for the audience, on the shortcomings people ought to be thinking about as they faced God.

Crucial to the impact of the *dzikr* and the *muraqabah* were the soulful tones in which Ilham rehearsed those shortcomings, modelling wrenching repentance so powerfully that his audiences (like those of another celebrity televangelist of the day, Abdullah Gymnastiar) were moved to tears. The key features of that service at At-Tin, namely the enormous scale and beauty of the occasion, and the deeply regretful repentance he evoked, lent to his ministry the two names by which it subsequently became known: 'Dzikr Akbar' ('Great Dzikr', that is, a collective *dzikr* on unprecedented scale with high production values in televised events) and 'Dzikr Taubat' ('The Dzikr of Repentance').

Given Arifin Ilham's upbringing, he was an unlikely young man to use *dzikr* litanies, much less to start promoting them. His father was active in the Modernist Muslim Muhammadiyah organisation known for its disapproval of the litanies, considering them without Qur'anic precedents (*bid'ah*) and in any case likely to encourage distasteful irrationality. Young Arifin shared that vigorously disapproving attitude towards *dzikr* with his father, and while in high school developed a talent for religious oratory that promoted an entirely scripturalist religiosity. By the time he finished university in Jakarta in 1995 (he had majored in International Relations at the secular Universitas Nasional) he had won prizes for his oratory, both in Indonesia and in Singapore, and had enough preaching engagements to consider himself launched on a career as a *'da'i'* (a revivalist preacher).

That was before his near death from snake bite. Weakly struggling for survival, he experienced a number of dreams, in the most crucial of which he saw himself saving Muslim souls from Satan by conducting *dzikr* prayer services. Upon his recovery he felt impelled to follow the direction of those dreams. His ministry developed rapidly from there.

Ilham has written several books[18] to defend his use of *dzikr* and map out a path of spiritual development using *dzikr*. He sees it not only as a permissible supplement to the required prayers, but, in fact, as a vital motivation for strictly following religious law. In his *Indonesia Berzikir*, he warns that Muslims are in danger of being spiritually corrupted by materialism, and intellectually seduced by Western science. Moreover, Islam is not responding to this adequately, because the contemporary preoccupation with strict adherence to the obligatory prayer regime alone is experienced by too many people as arid and spiritually unsatisfying. In doing *muraqabah* and practising *dzikr*, on the other hand, the believer becomes deeply aware of the work of Satan, regrets his acquiescence in it, is impelled to true repentance, and then actually can feel the pleasure (*kenikmatan*) of being close to God. Moreover, *dzikr* is urgently needed not just by individuals to save their souls, but to save Indonesia, since with this stronger religious motivation Indonesian Muslims will resist Western secularisation, renounce debilitating corruption and forefend God's wrath that otherwise will be visited on the nation.

Elsewhere, in his *Indonesia Berzikir*, Ilham does mention a less socially and politically urgent goal toward which people might aim when they adopt regular *dzikr* practice: the possibility of achieving gnosis. Thus he lists *makrifat* as one of sixty boons God may give to those who do the practice intently. But his primary preoccupation is with repentance and a return to religiously lawful behaviour.

These writings and his sermons frame the emotional tone of the *dzikr* performed in his collective Dzikr Akbar. That *dzikr*, paired with his free-form

---

[18]   See Ilham 2004 and Ilham and Yakin 2004. On Arifin Ilham see also Mujtaba 2004, Syadzili 2005 and Howell 2010.

commentary on the kinds of sins people need to consider in their hearts (his *muraqabah*) is primarily an occasion for regret, repentance and yearning for forgiveness. These sentiments are coupled with a fearful hope for that forgiveness. The *jema'ah* are also led to expect that the *dzikr* will help attain a deeper spiritual focus (*khusyuk*), which will be pleasurable and sustaining. That sweet intimacy, however, has a serious religious purpose: to motivate 'obedience' to the laws of the faith, and thereby defend it and the country as a nation of Muslim believers. And, considering the orchestration of the *dzikr* within the Dzikr Akbar, the programme actually offers little opportunity for people to move beyond the words of the ritual into extended non-discursive meditative states, such as have lifted the veils of mystical perception and gnosis for Sufis in the religious orders.

Conclusions

In all three contemporary settings examined, *dzikr* litanies are proving attractive to Indonesian Muslims, despite ongoing pressures from scripturalist wings of the Islamic revival to do away with them. For several decades now the Sufi order TQN Suryalaya, which has arisen from the traditionalist Islamic community and guides initiates in litany practice, has been attracting urbanites who have been undertaking their *own* religious renewal but appreciate guidance in spiritual development from a classically authorised Sufi master. And the inspired young lay preachers who have formed *majelis dzikr* and *shalawat* (new loosely structured organisational frameworks for religious outreach or *dakwah*) are going after their complacent fellows with revival messages, hoping to inspire in them religious recommitment. Both the *majelis* preachers introduced here found that their ministries were much more effective after they started including the *dzikr* rituals. As in other parts of the world, there is an appetite for experiential religiosity.

However, as we have also seen, not everyone who starts convening rituals that include *dzikr* litanies is actually programming them in such a way as to make use of the psycho-physiological potential most likely realised when very short phrases are repeated for considerable periods of time, as in the Qodiriyyah Naqsyabandiyah order discussed above. Both of the newer format devotional groups, the Majelis Nurul Mustafa and Majelis Zikir Az Zikra, use *dzikr* only in short braces, interrupted by other ritual forms (mostly the *shalawat* in the case of Majelis Nurul Mustafa and the *muraqabah* in the case of Az Zikra), giving little opportunity for practitioners to shift from discursive (chatty) to non-discursive awareness and so into the classic mystical states described in the *tasawuf* (Sufi) metaphysical literature.

Even though there are hints in these newer groups that the great mystical ideal of union with God (*makrifat*) is desirable, actually very little in the teaching and ritual programmes of the groups impels practitioners towards that goal. In Nurul Mustafa, happy closeness in the prayer meetings with the Habib and the expectation that blessings (including a welcome in the immediate family circle of the Prophet) will flow from that seem to take the place of striving to ascend to toward gnosis through individual spiritual disciplines. Arifin Ilham does very much emphasise that *dzikr* should bring an awareness of God's presence that is palpably pleasurable, and he quotes a well-known listing of benefits of doing *dzikr* that includes 'makrifat', but his interest on behalf of his *jema'ah* in spiritual experience is largely instrumental: to motivate solidarity of the Muslim community and strict conformity to its rules. This does anticipate a change in behaviour of practitioners, but it is hardly transformative, in the sense of precipitating a re-evaluation of one's way of being in the world and what one values, such as has happened with some of the Qodiriyyah Naqsyabandiyah initiates whose experiences were described by Subandi.

This consideration of the relative importance or otherwise of gnosis in different *dzikr* groups has already brought forward the strong contrasts in the emotional colouring given to the devotional programmes in which their *dzikr* is performed. In the case of Habib Hasan's *shalawat* group, as we have seen, hopeful projection of family love and solidarity is the most constant refrain. Interestingly this is evidently quite an open 'family' as the Habib does not actually require that the *jema'ah* be Muslims. On the other hand, Arifin Ilham, who is often pictured overwrought with regretful emotion and who is known for bringing his audiences to tears of regret, makes not only repentance but obedience the dominant stances of his ministry.

While much attention has been given here to the orchestration of *dzikr*, considering how its length and placement in a prayer programme may affect its impact, and how the framing of devotions by speakers shapes the emotional tone carried away from the meetings, further consideration should probably be given to the capacity of the differently structured groups to work with people aspiring to spiritual development. The personal psychological transformations that Subandi reports from the use of the TQN *dzikr*, may owe as much to the close monitoring of spiritual work that goes on in that *tarekat* and the opportunities it gives for reflection as to the formal features of the litany and prayer programmes themselves.

Acknowledgements

The author gratefully acknowledges funding support from the Australian Research Council and from the School of Social Sciences and Psychology at the University of Western Sydney for the research upon which this chapter draws.

References

Azra, Azyumardi (2012). 'The Dynamics of Sufism in Indonesian Islam: Islamic Spirituality in an Age of Secularism', a paper presented to the Biennial Conference of the Australian Association of Asian Studies, held at the University of Western Sydney, Sydney 11–13 July 2012.

Bayat, Asef (2007). *Making Islam Democratic.* Stanford, CA: Stanford University Press.

Darmadi, D. (2001). 'Urban Sufism: The New Flourishing Vivacity of Contemporary Indonesian Islam'. *Studia Islamika*, 8(1): 205–7.

Deikman, Arthur J. (1969). 'Deautomatization and the Mystic Experience'. In *Altered States of Consciousness, A Book of Readings*, (ed.) Charles Tart. New York: John Wiley.

Fischer, Roland (1971). 'A Cartography of Ecstatic and Meditative States'. *Science* 174, 4012: 897–904.

Gade, Anna M. (2004). *Perfection Makes Practice: Learning, Emotion and the Recited Qur'an in Indonesia.* Honolulu: University of Hawaii Press.

Geertz, Clifford (1968). *Islam Observed. Religious Development in Morocco and Indonesia.* Chicago: University of Chicago Press.

Gellner, Ernest (1981). *Muslim Society.* Cambridge: Cambridge University Press.

Hoesterey, James (2011). *Sufis and Self-Help Gurus: Islamic Psychology, Religious Authority, and Muslim Subjectivity in Contemporary Indonesia.* Proquest: UMI.

Hoffman, Valerie (1995). *Sufism, Mystics and Saints in Modern Egypt.* Columbia, SC: University of South Carolina Press.

Howell, Julia Day (2001). 'Sufism and the Indonesian Islamic Revival'. *Journal of Asian Studies* 60(3):701–29.

Howell, Julia Day (2007). 'Modernity and the Borderlands of Islamic Spirituality in Indonesia's New Sufi Networks'. In *Sufism and the 'Modern' in Islam*, edited by Martin van Bruinessen and Julia Day Howell. London: IB Tauris, pp. 217–41.

Howell, Julia Day (2008). 'Modulations of Active Piety: Professors and Televangelists as Promoters of Indonesian "Sufisme"'. In *Expressing Islam: Religious Life and Politics in Indonesia*, (ed.) Greg Fealy and Sally White. Singapore: ISEAS Press, pp. 40–62.

Howell, Julia Day (2010). 'Indonesia's Salafist Sufis'. *Modern Asian Studies* (Cambridge, UK) 44(5): 1029–51.

Howell, Julia Day and Martin van Bruinessen (2007). 'Sufism and the "Modern" in Islam'. In *Sufism and the 'Modern' in Islam*, edited by Martin van Bruinessen and Julia Day Howell. London: IB Tauris.

Howell, Julia Day, Subandi and Peter L. Nelson (2001). 'New Faces of Indonesian Sufism: A Demographic Profile of Tarekat Qodiriyyah-Naqsyabandiyyah, Pesantren Suryalaya in the 1990s'. *Review of Indonesian and Malaysian Affairs* 35(2): 33–60.

Ilham, M. Arifin (2004). *Hakikat Zikir, Jalan Taat Menuju Allah*, rev. ed. Depok: Intuisi Press.

Ilham, M. Arifin and Syamsul Yakin (2004). *Indonesia Berzikir: Risalah Anak Bangsa untuk Negeri Tercinta* [Indonesia Joins in *Zikir*: The Story of a Child of the Nation for his Beloved Country]. Depok: Intuisi Press.

Millie, Julian (2009). *Splashed by the Saint, Ritual Reading and Islamic Sanctity in West Java*. Leiden: KITLV Press.

Mujtaba, Achmad Nawawi (ed.) (2004). *Menggapai Kenikmatan Zikir: Fenomena Muhammad Arifin Ilham dan Majelis Zikir Az-Zikra* [Attaining the Gifts of *Zikir*: The Phenomenon of Muhammad Arifin Ilham and the *Zikir* Group Az Zikra], Mizan, Jakarta.

Riis, Ole and Linda Woodhead (2010). *A Sociology of Religious Emotion*. Oxford, UK: Oxford University Press.

Sirriyeh, Elizabeth (1999). *Sufis and Anti-Sufis, the Defense, Rethinking and Rejection of Sufism in the Modern World*. Richmond, Surrey: Curzon.

Srimulyani, Eka (2007). 'Muslim Women and Education in Indonesia: The pondok pesantren experience'. *Asia Pacific Journal of Education* 27(1): 85–99.

Subandi, M.A. (2005). *Dimensi Sosial Psikologis Dzikir Pembelah Dada*. Yogyakarta: Campus Press.

Syadzily, Tb. Ace Hasan (2005). *Arifin Ilham, Dai Kota Penabur Kedamaian Jiwa* [Arifin Ilham, the City Preacher Who Spreads Spiritual Tranquility]. Jakarta: Hikmah.

Winn, Phillip (2012). 'Women's *majelis taklim* and gendered religious practice in northern Ambon'. *Intersections: Gender and Sexuality in Asia and the Pacific*, 30 (November). http://intersections.anu.edu.au/issue30/winn.htm accessed 15 May 2013.

Zamhari, Arif and Julia Day Howell (2012). 'Taking Sufism to the Streets: Majelis Zikir and Majelis Shalawat as New Venues for Popular Islamic Piety in Indonesia'. *Review of Indonesian and Malaysian Affairs*, 46(2): 47–75.

Chapter 7

A Socio-Anthropological Analysis of Forms of Prayer Among the Amish

Andrea Borella

'And when you pray, do not keep on babbling like pagans, for they think they will be heard because of their many words. Do not be like them, for your Father knows what you need before you ask him'.

Matthew 6:7–8, King James Version

Introduction

In this chapter, which is based on anthropological research in the field conducted over ~~four~~ seven years, I maintain that the different forms of prayer among the Old Order Amish – spoken, silent, sung, communitarian or personal – relate to a deep emotional trope of Amish religiosity, which can be summed up with a single concept: *Gelassenheit*. This is a term in Pennsylvania Dutch, the language of the Amish, which can be translated as humility, submission and abandonment to the will of God. As well as shaping individual sensibilities and internal social hierarchies, this ethos – fostered through public silent prayer – helps maintain Amish distinctiveness and underline the boundary with non-Amish society. In the American imagination this stance and the accompanying way of life are often seen as a 'cage for human potential', fostering a regressive existence that deliberately fetters individuality and imagination. According to this view, the Amish have 'sacrificed freedom in a blind submission to traditional social arrangements and the use of antique contrivances' (Olshan 1994: 231). I hope to show, however, that the silent prayer which is so central to Amish practice can serve to support the autonomy and independence of Amish men and women, despite the appearance of the submission of individuality.

Background

In order to embark upon an anthropological analysis of forms of prayers among the Old Order Amish, it is first necessary to consider the religious background of the Amish church, and to place Amish theology in its wider cultural frame (Oosterbaan 1997). Amish belong to the religious universe of 'Plain People', members of Christian denominations characterized by simple living, plain dress and a certain level of separation from the world – where 'world' is to be understood in its biblical sense as the 'realm of men', as opposed to the 'kingdom of God'.

Historically, the Amish are a Christian church born as an offshoot of an Anabaptist movement, the Swiss Brethren, following a schism that took place in Alsace in 1693 (Nolt 2003). The early Anabaptists believed that the community of the real followers of Jesus Christ had to be based on three principles:

- Separation of Church and state;
- Adult believers' baptism;
- Absolute non-resistance.

The Amish try to live according to these values, respecting a set of rules known as *Ordnung*, a word in Pennsylvania Dutch,[1] the language of the Amish, which broadly means 'ordinance, discipline'. Sociologist Donald B. Kraybill (2001: 112) points out that for the Amish the *Ordnung*, which is normally unwritten and transmitted through the elders' example, is 'the blueprint for expected behaviour ... a code of conduct that the church maintains by tradition rather than systematic rules'. The *Ordnung* contains instructions about how to pray. As is common in many Christian denominations, the Amish utilize different forms of prayer, depending on diverse situations: silent, sung and said; private and communitarian. However, in the Amish view, there is a common ground of every form of devotion which is captured by the ancient Christian hymn which says that 'prayer is the soul's sincere desire, unuttered or expressed'.[2]

Besides the Bible, the Amish have three other major religious texts, the *Martyr's Mirror*, the *Ausbund* and *Die Ernsthafte Christenpflicht* (Luthy 1981). The *Martyr's Mirror* is a seminal work of some 1,330 pages, written in the sixteenth century by Tieleman Jansz van Braght, an elder of the Flemish

---

[1]   Here the term 'Dutch' is an archaism for German.

[2]   'Prayer Is the Soul's Sincere Desire', by Scottish poet James Montgomery (1771–1854).

Mennonite congregation in Dordrecht.[3] It is such an important source for the Amish that it is common to find a copy beside the Bible in every household. The book features the accounts of Anabaptist and other Christian martyrs who lost their lives for the sake of the '*sequela Christi*'. Such figures reveal the real meaning of *Gelassenheit*, complete surrender to the will of God, even to death. The *Ausbund* is the book of hymns used by the Amish during the Sunday service, composed in the sixteenth century in Europe by Anabaptists imprisoned for their faith. The hymns are particularly slow and sad, and appeal to martyrdom for the glory of God, as in the following example:

> Listen all you Christians who have been born again! God's Son from the Kingdom of Heaven died on the cross and suffered death and shame. Let us follow him! Let us take up our cross! The blood of Jesus washes away the sins of those who leave all to follow him, and who believe on God alone – even though they have sinned much. The Holy Spirit is given to those who believe and are baptized, if they follow Christ. With the Spirit they kill the flesh and find peace with God. Those who are washed and made free from sin with the blood of Christ walk in the Spirit with broken hearts. The Spirit rules them and shows them the way. Therefore, purified children of God – born again – keep yourselves pure! Let no man deceive you! The one who does right is right. The one who sins is a slave to sin. Those of us who have been washed with the blood of Christ and made free from sin, are tied together in our hearts. We now walk in the Spirit who shows us the right way and who rules in us. The Spirit rules in our sinful bodies, that are now dead. And in Christ we become members of his body, and buried with him through baptism in his death. Now we live for him and keep his commandments.

> Ausbund: Hymn 114 – 1:3

In this as in many other hymns there is a clear appeal to complete sacrifice in the name of Christ, a pressing call for being a real disciple of Jesus, to the extent of dying as a martyr.

A final source of Amish liturgy is the German Mennonite prayer book *Die Ernsthafte Christenpflicht*, written by the 'Swiss' Mennonites in South Germany, in the early eighteenth century. The first edition was dated 1739, and contained thirty-six prayers, for a total of more than 300 pages. In America there have

---

3   Dordrecht is a town of the greatest importance for the history of the Anabaptists. Indeed, it was in Dordrecht where was written, in the year 1632, the Confession of faith which is still in use among the Amish.

been many re-editions, with the addition of new hymns, until *Die Ernsthafte Christenpflicht* eventually became the main prayer book of the Amish.

All the religious books adopted by the Amish are written in the so-called German of Luther. This remains the idiom spoken inside congregational boundaries which draws a line between the community and the mainstream society, the sacred boundary.

Prayer and *Gelassenheit*

As affirmed by anthropologist John Hostetler (1993: 306): 'Amish stress the Anabaptist theme of *Gelassenheit* with its many meanings: resignation, calmness of mind, composure, staidness, conquest of selfishness, long-suffering, collectedness, silence of the soul, tranquility, inner surrender, yieldedness, equanimity, and detachment'. Kraybill underlines the relationship between tradition and *Gelassenheit*, writing that 'the spirit of *Gelassenheit* calls for yielding to tradition' (Kraybill 2001: 50).

Among the Amish prayer is one of the cornerstones of faith. And it is a cornerstone carved in tradition. As Kraybill (2001: 140) puts it: 'Amish rites of redemption and purification have stood the test of time and show few, if any, traces of erosion. They symbolize, rehearse, and communicate the essence of Amish culture. Kneeling for the rites of baptism, prayer, ordination, footwashing, and confession portrays the humble stance of *Gelassenheit*'. The ultimate goal of Amish prayers is to remain steadfast in faith, rather than modify an adverse destiny.

Since the Amish approach to religious matters is very practical, the *Ordnung* contains few regulations about prayer, and Amish people have rarely written directly on the issue. It is more common to find plain statements about the centrality of prayer for achieving Christian sanctity than substantial instruction concerning how, when and where to pray (Blank 2009: 59).

The Amish recognize that personal prayer is very private in nature and can 'include intimate burdens of [the] heart' (Kauffman 1992). If, following the example of Jesus, public prayers are not discouraged, it is essential to avoid showing off. To pray in order to be heard by men would be completely against the spirit of *Gelassenheit*. Here the Amish believe that the teachings of Christ were clear and incontrovertible: 'But thou, when thou prayest, enter into thy closet, and when thou hast shut thy door, pray to thy Father which is in secret; and thy Father which seeth in secret shall reward thee openly' (Matthew 6:6, KJV). Amish believe that on some occasions, especially during public meetings, written forms of prayer may be suitable. Jesus himself gave his disciples a standard prayer: 'And he said unto them: When ye pray, say, "Our Father ..."' (Luke 11:2, KJV).

Even if the Bible does not state a prescribed number of times for praying, in a booklet that can be viewed as a sort of catechism of Amish faith, entitled '1001 questions and answers on Christian life', the author Daniel Kauffman (1992) advises people to 'pray at least twice a day, in the morning and in the evening'. Normally these prayers should be held during the two main meals of the day. However, since the New Testament clearly instructs to 'pray without ceasing' (I Thess. 5:17, KJV), praying must be considered a habit and an ethos rather than an occasional duty. In typical Protestant fashion, the Amish address their pleas and thanksgivings only to God, in the name of Jesus Christ. In matters of devotion, there is no role for the Virgin Mary, the Saints, or other human beings.

As regards the physical position in which a Christian should pray, the Amish believe that the Holy Scriptures offer useful indications. Jesus in the garden of Gethsemane knelt for praying, as did many other biblical characters (Wight 1953). The custom to kneel for praying traces its root to the very beginning of the Anabaptism, since it probably originated in Switzerland and South Germany and was later brought to Pennsylvania, where it became the universal practice among Amish and other Anabaptist groups of that territorial background. Nevertheless, it has been dropped, over the years, by the progressive factions, while the Amish, as well as other traditional Anabaptist communities, have kept this practice alive, as a symbol of modesty and humbleness (J.P.R. 1996). Kneeling is viewed as a posture which allows people to become as little as possible in the eyes of God. Yet, here again, it was Jesus himself (John 4:24) who taught the Samaritan woman that it is the inner desire of the heart, and not the outward, which is decisive in praying (Kauffman 1992). As for the reasons for prayer, although the Bible gives many reasons, in '1001 questions and answers on Christian life', the dominant motifs are asking God for salvation and forgiveness of sins; invoking the coming of the Holy Spirit; and receiving wisdom, mercy and grace. Kauffman (1992: 89) also instructs that, following Scriptural exhortations, Amish should pray for the government (I Tim. 2:2), for labourers in the harvest (Luke 10:2), for the 'saints' (the saved) (Eph. 6:18), for their persecutors (Matthew 5:44) and for fellow believers experiencing trials (Acts 12:5). As for the attitude of prayer, according to the Holy Book, a Christian must address God with faith and thankfulness, in spirit and truth. Significantly, two other characteristics of devotion are underscored: to pray in secret (Matthew 6:5), and 'with weeping' (Ez. 10:1, KJV).

Thus *Gelassenheit*, or the behaviour connected to *Gelassenheit*, entails peaceful acceptance of God's will, even if it does not match the believer's requests. In other words, God always answers prayers, but not always as frequently or as exactly as expected. That is because, as the prophet Isaiah says (55:9, KJV): 'For as the heavens are higher than the earth, so are my ways higher than your ways, and my thoughts than your thoughts'. Living in the ethos of *Gelassenheit* means taking for granted that earthly problems and inappropriate responses are caused by human fault: 'Ye ask and receive not, because ye ask amiss, that ye may consume it upon your lusts' (James 4:3, KJV). As an Amish man, who signed his article just as 'grandfather', writes: 'We have the right to pray for those things which we need. But that is not the most important form of prayer. [...] So, when we teach our children how to pray, it is better if we teach them to pray for people than for things. [...] The purpose of prayer is not to make God do what we want. The purpose is to be sensitive to what God wants us to do' (Grandfather 1998: 29).

In the Amish worldview, devotion can play different roles. For instance, prayer can be utilized as a substitute for voting (Nolt 2004) – the Amish are discouraged from casting a ballot because they do not believe that any political administration could ever solve human problems, and they maintain that praying for the government (Anonymous 1994: 16) is the best way to engage in politics.

Although the Amish are not very inclined to talk about religious issues, the question of teaching religion and praying to children has become a matter of discussion (Grandfather 1998). The main question concerns who has the responsibility of transmitting religious notions to children: parents, older relatives, teachers at school, ministers at church, or the entire community? Even if different opinions are debated among the Amish, it is clear that the family has the major responsibility in teaching children how to pray.

Silent Prayer

Silent prayer occupies a prominent position in Amish religiosity. It goes without saying that praying wordlessly is a practice present in most Christian churches, both in institutionalized forms and as an expression of personal devotion. However, silent prayer is particularly important among the so-called Plain People, and especially in Amish congregations. My argument is that this is related to the ethos of *Gelassenheit*.

I observed such prayer at mealtimes. During my fieldwork I joined my 'Amish family' for supper each evening at five o'clock. Before the meal, the husband and father exhales a long and noisy breath, bows his head, and keeps silent for twenty to thirty seconds. All the members of the family, including the guests, imitate the same behaviour. During this time, everybody seated at the table is supposed to pray wordlessly. When the silent prayer is over, the head of the household makes another long and noisy breath, thus indicating that the thanksgiving to the Lord has been given, and the supper can begin. At the end of the very quick meal, as soon as everyone has finished eating, another ritual silent prayer takes place, following the same ritualized pattern as the opening one.

Anthropologist John A. Hostetler (1993: 161), who was raised in the Amish faith, wrote that: 'At mealtime at the table [a family member] repeats silently his memorized meditation. Children, upon reaching the age of puberty or earlier, are expected to say their own prayers. These prayers are memorized in German,[4] and they may consist of the Lord's Prayer or a prayer about the same length taken from a prayer book'. It seems to me doubtful that all Amish offer the same prayer every day, even though prayers suitable for mealtimes are taught to all Amish. Hostetler (1993: 162–3) reported two examples: Prayer before meal: 'O lord God, Heavenly father, bless us and these thy gifts, which we shall accept from thy tender goodness. Give us food and drink also for our souls unto life eternal, and make us partakers of thy heavenly table through Jesus Christ. Amen'. [Lord's Prayer is repeated], and Prayer after meal: 'O Lord, we give praise and thanks for thy sacred food and drink, for thy manifold great grace and goodness; Thou who livest and reignest, a true God till eternity. Amen'. [Lord's Prayer is repeated]. Yet, in the Amish view, it is not mandatory to follow these formulas because the thought which is 'inspired' by God should be free of any human influence.

Amish tradition highly values silence as a necessary instrument for preparing the soul to listen to God's word. A community publication reports the exhortation of the Anabaptist teacher Christopher Dock (c. 1698–1771) to consider both speech and silence as necessary, even though he recognized the primacy of silence: 'Speech has its time, and silence also has its time. But this rule is very hard for the children to adjust to; and it seems that we adults ourselves have not yet completely learned this lesson – that speech and silence have their proper times. We ought to regard our speaking and being silent' (Hostetler 1989: 145).

One of the most common accusations against the Amish, made especially by the Evangelicals, is that they would not pray aloud because they would not pray at all, and they would not know what to tell God. Some maintain that the Amish do not talk about God, or with God, because they do not have a clear

---

    [4]   Again, the word 'German', in this case, means neither the common modern German, nor the Pennsylvania Dutch, but the so-called Luther's German.

idea of God. It is true that Amish theology is basically existential and practised rather than systematic (Friedmann 1973), and this may also influence a form of prayer that does not rotate around deep theological speculation. Yet, when I asked an Amish informant about the Evangelical allegation, he answered with the usual ironic mood and disarming simplicity: 'Can the Evangelicals read into my mind?'

There are particular social benefits of silent prayer. A key value of Anabaptism is the rejection of clergy, seen as a link between earth and heaven. For such radical Reformers, every believer is a priest, and, consequently, nobody can be put in a higher position, closer to God. Allowing the breadwinner to present such prayer is a sort of 'cultural compromise', through which the Amish head of the family can emphasize his supremacy without claiming the responsibility of an intermediary between his own family and God.

There may seem to be a tension not only between personal silent prayer and the communitarian emphasis of the Amish, and between the inward waiting upon God and the effort to respect the outward forms, codified in the *Ordnung* (Hostetler 1993: 83–4). In many ways the Amish idea of Christianity is the quintessence of congregationalism. In general terms, the Amish believe that in order to be saved it is necessary to be baptized as an adult and to belong to a Christian church. But silent prayer must be situated in the communitarian context, being highly regulated by the *Ordnung*, rather than being interpreted as a sort of free expression of Faith. For the Amish, it goes without saying that God can read human thoughts just as easily as He can hear words uttered, as one can infer by reading Psalm 139:23 (NIV): 'Search me, O God, and know my heart; test me and know my anxious thoughts'; Jeremiah 12:3 (NIV): 'Yet you know me, O LORD; you see me and test my thoughts about you'; Matthew 12:25–6 (NIV): 'Jesus knew their thoughts ...'. Moreover Jesus said: 'But when you pray, go into your room, close the door and pray to your Father, who is unseen. Then your Father, who sees what is done in secret, will reward you' (Matthew 6:6, NIV). The most cited verse by the Amish that indicates the validity of unspoken prayers is: 'Pray without ceasing'. To pray unceasingly cannot signify that Christians have to pray out loud all the time. Rather, it means that they have to be in a constant state of God-consciousness, and therefore to address for every issue to the Father, as emphasized in II Corinthians 10:5 (NIV). For the Amish, a Christian can do, say, or think nothing that is hidden from God, who does not need to hear human voice to know people's thoughts. He has access to all prayers directed to Him, either spoken or silent. Since from a scriptural perspective there is nothing wrong with praying silently, as long as Christians are not doing it out of embarrassment, to pray silently fulfils the spirit of *Gelassenheit*. Praying aloud, to 'keep on babbling' or 'standing to be seen by men', would be against the Amish idea of Christianity, based on humility.

Thus addressing God privately allows everyone gathered for a service or meal to choose the words or thoughts that they believe are suitable in a specific situation. It involves listening to God, not just asking Him, which is evaluated as the right behaviour in front of God. And it is faithful to Jesus who considered verbosity and display a threat to purity of heart.

Prayer in Religious Rites

Predictably, prayer also plays an important role in the communal religious rites of the Amish church. During the Sunday service there are two main moments dedicated to prayer. First, silent, kneeling prayer occurs after the opening sermon and lasts for a few minutes. Then, following a scripture reading by the deacon and the main sermon, there is a second kneeling prayer, which is read by a minister from a traditional prayer book. To offer a spontaneous prayer during an Amish worship service, as is fairly common in many Christian denominations, would be bold. It would be against humility and submissiveness, and thus against the spirit of *Gelassenheit*.

In Amish tradition there are two days each year in which prayers have greatest importance: Good Friday and St Michael's day, October 11th. The reasons are both historical and theological. A major cause of the schism between the Swiss Brethren and the Amish in late seventeenth-century Alsace was the practice of celebrating communion twice a year, as the Anabaptists had done since their beginning. The progressive faction of Swiss Anabaptists preferred to take communion just once a year, while Jacob Ammann and his followers, who eventually were labelled the Amish, wished to keep the ancient habit. The Amish nowadays celebrate Holy Communion at Easter and the Sunday after Saint Michael's day (Michaelmas). Both days are occasions of fasting and praying in order to prepare body and soul for receiving the bread and the wine which symbolize the body and the blood of Christ.[5]

Fasting, as well as praying, occupies a central role in the Amish faith. In the words of the Amish man Elmo Stoll (1985: 9): 'We also need to spend time in prayer and fasting, asking God to reveal his will to us. Perhaps we might

---

[5]   Regarding the debate on the nature of the bread and the wine during the Holy Communion, Anabaptists endorse the position which rejects the idea that the two elements are the real body and blood of Christ (transubstantiation), but maintain that bread and wine just symbolise body and blood.

sum it up by saying that we do not believe in preparing our sermons, but we believe in preparing ourselves, so that God can provide the sermon'. *Gelassenheit* entails that men and women are just instruments in the hands of God. From a theological point of view this issue is particularly significant, because for many Protestants the proclamation of the Word of God and the sermon are the heart of the religious service. I would suggest that for the Amish, prayer is the main element in Sunday worship. Although sermons are very long[6] and deeply-felt by the ministers, who sometimes cry while preaching, they are in their essence the exposition of human thoughts addressed to other human beings. Prayers, by contrast, are either a form of devotion directly taught by Jesus Christ, as in the 'Our Father', or, at the very least, human words addressed to God.

Prayer is also present in every major occasion of Amish religious life. For instance, during the so-called lot, the customary practice of leadership selection, the members who are selected by the community as eligible candidates, after having accepted the nomination, kneel and pray to God. Similarly, during the plain service held for funerals, the last rite of the earthly life, the community offers prayers while ministers read hymns, scriptures and preach a sermon.

Fieldwork Notes: the Difficulty of Studying Private Prayer

This essay is based on anthropological research that has been conducted for several months over the course of the last seven years in a community of the Old Order Amish in Lancaster County, Pennsylvania. Gaining access to this community is exceptional, since the Amish aim to keep the contacts with outsiders to a minimum. Non-Amish people, whether neighbours, tourists, or social scientists, are perceived as a threat to the integrity of the church.

From a methodological point of view, I have conducted my fieldwork following the so-called Geertzian approach. According to anthropologist Clifford Geertz (1975), the ethnography is always a translation of a culture through concepts which are understandable by people belonging to another culture. However, if describing or giving an account of customs or practices, such as dress, language, or external habits, comes relatively easy, an analysis of inner, private matters, like prayer, is particularly complex. Indeed, in anthropological terms, prayer could be considered as belonging to the area of 'cultural intimacy' (Herzfeld 1997), to those aspects of a culture that are not usually shared with outsiders. Moreover, in the Amish case, there is a second level of intimacy: the

---

6   The first sermon lasts some thirty minutes, while the main one lasts nearly an hour.

'personal' one. Among the Amish, much more that in a (post)modern context in which the outward expression of emotions has become more and more usual, individual feelings or beliefs are kept secret, not just for foreigners, but for fellow members as well. According to this vision prayer is a sort of special and very private relationship between God and the believer, experienced in a community which leaves little room for individuality.

During my fieldwork, I realized how this 'cultural intimacy' can jeopardize the success of an anthropological analysis. Methodologically, the first step is to get information upon which to construct a scientific theory. Nevertheless, the common answer I received from the Amish about the reason for praying silently before and after the meals was highly cryptic: 'That's tradition'. Or, in other words, 'it is how it has always been'. This makes it harder to access personal 'deep motivations' for keeping alive a peculiar practice. Furthermore, the Amish emphasize humility before God, so speaking of God is seen as disreputable, inappropriate, almost shameful, because the human knowledge of God is never reducible to conceptual expression. For the Amish, quite paradoxically, discourse on God would be a reduction of His greatness.

Given such a framework, the main task of a worthwhile anthropological analysis is to overcome this hindrance, in order to understand the value of praying in Amish religiosity, and, in particular, the cultural relevance of silent prayer. I tried to achieve this goal through several methodological devices:

First, the ethnographic approach. By living with an Amish family, I shared the moments of prayer with the members of the community. In this way, I was able to perceive the ethos, I would even define it the 'aura', of those spiritual instances.

Second, I made an effort to take part in the above mentioned 'cultural intimacy' with my Amish friends and informants, in order to be able to understand the importance of the Amish silent communication with God, especially through indirect observation and questions. This methodological strategy allowed me to overcome the reticence of the Amish to talk openly about devotional issues.

Third, it has been essential for my research to construct a comparative analysis, by studying the forms and the meanings of the prayers in other Christian denominations which belong to the same religious tradition of the Amish, in particular, Brethren and Hutterites (Bowman 1995; Janzen and Stanton 2010). This comparative perspective has revealed many aspects which could be hidden if I had analysed only the Amish approach with regards to the prayer.

Finally, my personal friendship with some former Amish who have converted to another faith has helped contribute to increase my knowledge and comprehension of some of the more obscure traditional and theological reasons the Amish take into consideration in keeping alive the practice of praying silently.

Conclusion

Far from having their individuality crushed by harsh ordinances and external rituals, my suggestion in this chapter is that in the inner moments of silent prayer, the Amish tradition carves out room for a direct relationship with God, without imposing any standardized form, and, in this way, underscoring personal independence. The different forms of Amish prayers – silent, spoken, communitarian, private and ritualized, show how diverse prayer is within this community. However, as Kauffmann (1992) affirms, despite this diversity, 'the really important part is that our prayers be "in spirit and in truth"' (John 4:24). With these words, Kauffman underscores the inner goal of Amish spirituality, which aims to be based much more on *Gelassenheit*, rather than on *Ordnung* alone. The connection between *Gelassenheit*, the heart of the Amish ethos, of *Ordnung*, the patterning of Amish daily life, and of prayer, the most direct form of dialogue between a believer and God, is summarized by the Amish in the words of Jesus who prayed in the garden: 'Not as I will, but as thou wilt'. (Matthew 26:42, KJV), but such a stance also allows the individual considerable independence.

References

Anonymous (1994). 'A Matter of Prayer', *Family Life*, August/September: 14–16.

Ausbund (1996). Lancaster, PA: The Amish book committee.

Blank, Benuel (2009). *The Scriptures have the answer*, Sugarcreek, OH: Carlisle Printing.

Bowman, Carl (1995). *Brethren Society: The Cultural Transformation of a Peculiar People*, Baltimore, MD, and London: Johns Hopkins University Press.

Dock, Christopher (1770 c.). 'Speech and silence must have their time', in John A. Hostetler (ed.), *Amish Roots: A Treasury of History, Wisdom, and Lore*, Baltimore, MD, and London: Johns Hopkins University Press, 145–6.

Friedmann, Robert (1973). *The theology of Anabaptism*, Scottdale, PA: Herald Press.

Geertz, Clifford (1975). *The interpretation of cultures: selected essays*. London: Hutchinson.

Grandfather, (1998). 'Teaching Religion to the child', *Family Life*, February: 29–31.

Herzfeld, Michael (1997). *Cultural intimacy: social poetics in the nation-state.* New York, NY: Routledge.

Hostetler, John A. (1989) (ed.). *Amish Roots: A Treasury of History, Wisdom, and Lore*, Baltimore, MD, and London: Johns Hopkins University Press.

Hostetler, John A. (1993). *Amish society.* Baltimore, MD, and London: Johns Hopkins University Press.

J.P.R. (1996). 'The Hat – A religious Symbol?', *Family Life*, August/ September: 11–12.

Janzen, Rod and Max Stanton (2010). *The Hutterites in North America.* Baltimore, MD, and London: Johns Hopkins University Press.

Kauffman, Daniel (1992). *1001 Questions and Answers on the Christian Life.* Aylmer, ON, and Lagrange, IN: Pathway Publishers.

Kraybill, Donald B. (2001). *The Riddle of Amish Culture.* Baltimore, MD, and London: Johns Hopkins University Press.

Kraybill, Donald B. and Carl Desportes Bowman (2001). *On the Backroad to Heaven: Old Order Hutterites, Mennonites, Amish, and Brethren.* Baltimore, MD, and London: Johns Hopkins University Press.

Luthy, David (1981). 'A History of "Die Ernsthafte Christenpflicht"', *Family Life*, February: 19–23.

Nolt, Marcus (2004). 'Casting our votes', *Family Life*, November: 17–18.

Nolt, Steven M. (2003). *A History of the Amish.* Intercourse, PA: Good Books.

Olshan, Mark A. (1994). 'Conclusion: What good are the Amish?', in Donald B. Kraybill and Mark A. Olshan (eds), *The Amish struggle with modernity.* Baltimore, MD, and London: Johns Hopkins University Press, 231–42.

Oosterbaan, J.A. (1997). 'The reformation of the Reformation: fundamentals of Anabaptist theology', *The Mennonite Quarterly Review*, July: 171–95

Stoll, Elmo (1985). 'Physician, Heal Thyself', *Family Life*, December: 8–10.

Wight, Fred H. (1953). *Manners and Customs of Bible Lands.* Chicago, IL: Moody Press.

Chapter 8

Filipino Catholic Students and Prayer as Conversation with God

Jayeel Serrano Cornelio

In the Philippines where 80 per cent of the population professes to be Catholic (National Statistics Office 2008), prayer is a predictably highly-practised religious activity. According to the most recent national survey on religiosity, 73 per cent of Filipinos pray at least once a day, compared to 55.4 per cent in the US and 19 per cent in the UK (ISSP Research Group 2008).

Prayer is often inseparable from the many and various forms of piety in the country. Feasts as expressions of pious devotion to the Black Nazarene, the Santo Niño and Our Lady of Perpetual Help, for example, are typical (Bautista 2011; Cannell 1999). To describe their participation, devotees often refer to *panata*, the local term to express one's commitment to continually participate in religious rituals, including those that may not necessarily be sanctioned by the Catholic Church. Individuals getting crucified in some provinces during Lent, for example, describe their act as *panata* or, translated loosely, a sustained and repeated act of gratitude (Bräunlein 2012).[1] And every week, throngs of people gather in Manila for the El Shaddai prayer rally led by Brother Mike Velarde. The overnight vigil typically comprises Charismatic worship with emphasis on tithing and financial 'love offering' in which prayer requests are included. These requests reach El Shaddai's headquarters where they will be prayed for by staff (Wiegele 2005).[2]

Given its prominence in everyday religiosity, a social scientific approach to the study of prayer amongst Filipinos is warranted. In this way, I echo Giordan's (2012) observation that in various surveys in the West, prayer is often cited as the most practised religious activity, but remains understudied in the sociology

---

[1]   This, of course, is not unique to Filipino Catholicism. One may refer to the study of Oktavec (1995) on the Latin American followers of St Francis.

[2]   For more on Charismatic worship in the Philippines, see Kessler and Rüland (2008).

of religion. This is particularly true in the Philippines where the sociology of religion is still in its emergent stage.

In the examples above, the anthropological focus has been on the rituals or forms of piety more than on how the religious actors understand and articulate prayer. To address this gap, and as a contribution to this volume, this chapter will look at prayer as an everyday phenomenon among Catholics in the Philippines. Specifically, I will probe two areas: (1) the ways in which Filipino Catholic students understand the nature of praying and (2) how they perceive God responds to their prayers. If prayer is 'interpersonal communication *with God*', the latter dimension is equally important (Howard 2008: 300).[3] Researchers may have the tendency to only explore one area, namely, how prayer is carried out by individuals (Baker 2008; Collins-Mayo 2008). Giordan (2012: 83) is therefore right in asking 'what does it mean that [one's] prayer "has been answered"'?

Towards the end, I will argue that the way prayers are answered reveals who God is in the religious subjectivity of Filipino Catholic youth today. This is an attempt to respond to the questions raised by Bade and Cook (2008) concerning the relationship between the image of God and the kind of prayers individuals employ. That the divine is immanent, personal, and creatively experiential suggests an individualised God in the context of a Catholic identity. This is different from the moral therapeutic deism described by Smith and Denton (2005) and the religious instrumentalism often stereotypically assumed to be characteristic of Filipino Catholic youth (Macasaet 2009). This view of God suggests a spirituality that is reflected upon and authentic to the self, but always in relation to a Catholic identity. Thus this can be considered as a form of God who is *indwellingly individualised*.

The data which informs this chapter comes from interviews with sixty-two tertiary students involved in Catholic organisations in twelve colleges and universities in Metro Manila, the capital region of the Philippines. These are state, private non-sectarian and private Catholic universities, and the range indicates the various class positionalities of my respondents. To further diversify the sample, students have been selected according to gender, subject discipline and the type of religious organisation they are part of (charismatic, campus ministry-affiliated, liturgical, catechetical). The propositions offered here are not generalisable to all Filipino youth – especially because my informants are socially-included and considerably more religiously involved than the average

---

3   Such a definition necessitates a belief in a personal God, which Catholicism embodies. If the higher being is perceived as a form of power, for example, prayer might be construed in terms of meditation (Baker 2008). This connection between prayer and the image of God will be revisited towards the end of the chapter.

Catholic youth, a point I take from Vincett and Olson (2012). However, given the novelty of the sociology of prayer in the Philippines, their nuances are theoretically important and may inform future research in the area. Baker (2008), for example, has called on observers to pursue a qualitative study of the ways individuals pray. Furthermore, by drawing from the subjectivity of Catholic youth, this chapter may also be seen as a contribution to the emerging literature on religion and youth (Collins-Mayo and Dandelion 2010).

Prayer and Youth

In a way that reflects the thrust of the natural sciences, the study of prayer in the social sciences seems to be generally interested in how prayer is a coping mechanism for marginalised groups or individuals in distress (Nelson 2009). Praying or turning to prayer healing, for example, appears to be heightened when one is sick (Javaheri 2005). And according to the Baylor Religion Survey in the US, prayer is most frequent among women, African–American and lower income individuals and usually revolves around issues of financial security, health and confession of sins (Baker 2008). Reflecting the tone of many other studies, Baker (2008), therefore, argues that prayer is generally a form of coping mechanism among marginalised groups.

In a more recent study, though, Bade and Cook (2008) tease out the various functions that the religious act serves for its practitioners. They argue that the functions of prayer revolve around three dimensions: whether the issue being prayed for is approached or avoided, whether the prayer is concerned about the self or other people, and whether it is directed to the self only or to a higher being who can intervene in one's affairs. Ultimately, of course, the common denominator among these functions is that issues or crises exist for the individual who prays and they must be dealt with. In a way, they are various forms of coping. Another possible approach to understand the various functions of prayer is by looking at its different forms. For this, the study made by Poloma and Pendleton (1989) can be instructive. They argue that prayers can be meditative, ritualist (structured), petitionary, or colloquial (or conversational), each of which has effects on an individual's overall quality of life. The study, therefore, implies once again the coping function of prayer.[4]

---

[4]   There are, of course, other studies on prayer but they approach the phenomenon with different questions. The work of Loveland et al. (2005), for example, looks at how private prayer is correlated to participation in social service activities. They explain that private prayer encourages cognitive connection with other people and their needs. My work

In recent years, the study of prayer among young people seems to have been gaining ground and moving theory away from the typical theme of prayer as a coping mechanism. These studies are varied and substantive with regard to the questions they are asking – in terms of, for example, content, characteristics and overall connection to the youth's everyday life. One landmark project is the National Study of Youth and Religion in the US (Smith and Denton 2005) which has found that mainstream adolescents harbour a belief in a detached God who can be called on only when the need arises, and whose job is to administer happiness (moral therapeutic deism). Prayer to them, therefore, is first and foremost about making themselves feel good and is carried out according to necessity.

This finding of a rather detached attitude to prayer runs contrary to findings in other contexts where a post-materialist orientation is emergent. Among Dutch youth, for example, the content of their prayers has generally revolved around issues of personal happiness (Janssen et al. 1990). In another study, the young adult Italians Giordan (2012) has interviewed are more comfortable with conversational prayers with God in which the main theme involves finding meaning in life. Interestingly, the positive relationship between prayer and sense of meaning in life has been asserted by Francis and Robbins (2009) in their recent study of secondary school students in England and Wales. And based on typologies designed by Ladd and Spilka (2002), Zaha (2010) has discovered that among undergraduate students in Christian colleges and universities in the US, the most practised form of prayer is the one that examines the self. Other forms of prayer like intercessory and sacramental forms are not as prominent.

A possible explanation for this relationship between prayer and personal meaning is that prayer acknowledges a transcendent reality through which young people may discover themselves. And the fact that they are adolescents means that they are in the development stage that compels them to seek and ascertain for themselves their identity. Another possibility is the condition of subjectivisation in which authentic forms of spirituality can be discovered through personal explorations or reflections (Heelas and Woodhead 2005; Taylor 1992). Perhaps this is the reason why the members of Generation Y in England mostly conduct their prayers in the bedroom, even if many are largely unexposed to church practices.[5] This 'bedroom spirituality' recognises the

---

on evangelism on the Internet also looks at online prayer partnerships and groups as a form of virtualised spiritual experience (Cornelio 2009).

[5]   The prayers employed are also conversational in nature and fall under any of three categories: petitionary, confessional or thanksgiving. The typology suggests the lingering influence of Christianity as a default template for English youth (Collins-Mayo 2008).

privacy of their rooms where they can be honest to themselves alone, a point suggested by Collins-Mayo et al. (2010: 45) in their study of young people in England.

Even if the sociology of religion and youth is still emergent (Collins-Mayo and Dandelion 2010), it is encouraging to know that consideration is being given to the prayer life of young people. As shown by the literature above, strides have been made to look at prayer not merely as a coping mechanism but as significant strategies for discovering the self and one's meaning. To add to this developing picture, some additional areas are still of interest.

One important gap remains rather unfilled in the qualitative study of prayer among youth. As mentioned at the outset, if prayer is to be regarded as communication with God as is expected in the Christian tradition (Howard 2008), then observers need to ask how it is in fact answered. In the social sciences, the answer to this question, of course, does not lie in divine revelation but in the very subjectivity of people who pray. How do they know their prayers have been answered? Towards the end, I will also argue that this question entails another one: What do these ideas reveal about the image of God in the minds of young Filipino Catholics today? Finally, it must be reiterated that the attention given to Filipino youth in this chapter is an attempt to complement the emphasis on Western youth in the sociology of religion (Collins-Mayo and Dandelion 2010).

Prayer as Conversations: Talking to God

According to a landmark national survey on Filipino Catholic youth, praying is more practised than any other religious activities such as 'receiving the sacraments' or even 'doing good deeds to others' (Episcopal Commission on Youth 2003: 78). Such primacy of prayer over other religious activities in itself implies that a degree of religious individualisation is in operation among young Filipinos (Collins-Mayo et al. 2010). Prayer, after all, is an individual activity first and foremost. What will further confirm this possible trend is if there is a representative study on the very nature and content of the prayers young people make. In his work on the evolution of prayer, Mauss (2003), for example, argues that memorised prayers from rituals have been replaced by more individualistic thoughts and reflections. In the Philippines, there tend to be hints of such a trend but literature merely offers some reflections on the religious life of young people. The suggestion of the president of a technical college, for example, is that the participation of youth in worship activities seems to have been 'lost in a subjective, touchy-feely criterion of self-satisfaction' Macasaet (2009: 11).

Other observers tend to argue that the prayer life of young people tends to be instrumentalist since God is often perceived to be 'a gratifier of wants' (Ramos 2003: A9).

While I will argue that the conversational and spontaneous nature of praying is evident in the nuances of my young Catholic informants, I have some reservations about immediately claiming that they are 'touchy-feely' or 'instrumentalist'. This is because they understand and practise prayer in the context of an emotional relationship with God first and foremost (Ramos 2003: A9). The description of Kat (18 years old), a female student of information technology, seems most appropriate: 'For me, prayer is really about talking with God ... It's like writing an entry in your diary but you say it verbally to God ... So when I feel it, I tell Him my problems'.

Indeed, many of my informants have described prayer as conversations with God and even done in the most mundane settings like when one is riding the jeepney (a local form of transport) or walking home from school. Some take the chance to pray before eating and sleeping, for example. Although the college chapel or parish may be important, too, the diversity of spaces where prayer can be done is not simply a trivial matter because it suggests how young people are appropriating their religious life even in mundane geographies (Vincett and Collins-Mayo 2010). These possibilities also suggest the spontaneity of prayer, which is in fact heavily contrasted to the norms of piety typical among many Catholics in the country. Most of my informants do not follow memorised prayers, for example. This becomes very clear in my interview with She (20 years old), who is a scholar at a Catholic university and comes from a rural family: 'I always pray, but it doesn't have to be novenas and all that. Prayer for me must express what I want to tell God and it's mostly thanking Him'. Her statement indicates that not only are prayers meant to be spontaneous but also sincere. Interestingly, this view seems to have been shaped by an experience she had when she was still staying with nuns in a convent in Manila. 'One time I asked the sisters "Do you not sometimes think that you've had enough of these early morning prayers?" One actually admitted to me that sometimes their prayers were no longer heartfelt to her since everything is simply memorized'.

Do these statements suggest that traditional forms of prayer have been completely abandoned by my informants? Not necessarily. They still go to Mass and even organise traditional religious events like Taizé in their respective communities.[6] With their families, some of them still lead the rosary, too. One

---

6   This observation must be taken in context. Mass attendance among Catholic adults in the Philippines has declined over the years. Survey data show that weekly attendance has

of my informants also carries with him prayer cards for Our Lady of Guadalupe and saints like Josemaria Escriva. The main sociological insight, however, is that these rather traditional forms of piety do not necessarily reflect their personal nuances concerning prayer.

Interestingly, I have also encountered informants who believe in the importance of the mass, for example, and yet choose not to participate in it, arguing that 'God would understand my heart if I'm busy so I just pray instead'. Personal prayer, in other words, is deemed to be able to compensate for one's inability to participate in other religious activities. So apart from the spontaneity and sincerity of personal prayer, it is also in this way that the finding that prayer is more practised than 'receiving the sacraments' among young Filipinos makes sense (see above).

Treating prayer as a conversation with God must be understood as an experience in the context of an emotional relationship with God where personal sincerity is valued. When I asked Lea (18 years old), a journalism student, why she considers praying a 'conversation with God', she tells me 'because I feel that wherever I am, if I pray, the Lord will listen to me'. Indeed, the content of my informants' prayers often include petitions and thanksgiving for answered prayers but they cannot be automatically assumed as being instrumentalist in orientation. After all, they prefer to express whatever is 'in my heart', a description often conveyed by my informants, be it be about relational problems in the family, economic hardship, academic struggles, or conflicts among friends. So they are not at all following in the footsteps of the moral therapeutic deism of their American counterparts (Smith and Denton 2005).

One way of comprehending prayer as conversation is in terms of a combination of what Ladd and Spilka (2002) consider as 'examen' or prayers that 'emphasize honest self-evaluation' (477) and 'prayers of the heart' or those that express 'intimacy, love, and tenderness toward the divine' (478). Prayer as conversations with God is therefore both inward and upward in orientation. This combination may give us a glimpse of how young people are navigating the issues of their everyday life. Prayers allow them to abandon their conditions to a higher being but at the same time they are avenues for self-reflection as to what went wrong and what could have been done better in their lives. In this sense, therefore, prayer as conversations with God can be interpreted as 'a way of constructing reality, a way of making sense in a multi-interpretable world' (Janssen et al. 1990: 105). In the developing condition of the Philippines highly characterised by economic vulnerability, aspirations for globalisation, and

---

declined from 64 per cent in 1991 to 37 per cent in 2013 (Mangahas and Labucay 2013).

strong religiosity, a sense of authenticity within the self and towards the divine is a formidable anchor for the self (Janssen et al. 1990: 105).

Prayer as Conversations: Hearing from God

Framed by my informants as conversations with the divine, their personal prayers imply avenues for listening to the responses of God. How God answers, however, is an area not fully explored in the sociology of prayer. To be sure, one can look at the different effects of prayer on the person as divine answers, such as when Howard (2008) discusses heightened awareness to the things around and the overall effect on well-being, for example. Another approach might be to investigate the very structure itself of the narratives believers construct about their answered prayers (Lindgren 2005). Following an interpretivist approach, however, this chapter focuses on how my informants have heard from God. More specifically, what I probe are the different ways by which they deem God is talking to them: through *relationships*, *circumstances* and *technology*.

Through Relationships

Such a theme of prayer as conversations with God also came up when I was interviewing Ken at the rather noisy cafeteria of his private college located in the central business district. Living away from his parents who are in the province, the computer science major recounted to me several events in his life when he felt lonely, so God was the only one he could talk to. This compelled me to ask whether he thought God was answering his prayers:

> Yes ... whenever I am lonely, He makes ways to lighten up my mood. He has in fact given me friends here to keep me company. There was a time when I broke up with my girlfriend, I became alcoholic and insomniac – which they noticed. They convinced me to move on and accompanied me in the process. They never failed to invite me to movies and bond with them at the mall.

For Ken and many of my other informants, the importance of friends and relatives – relationships, essentially – are crucial in experiencing the response of God to prayer. A typical pattern in the construction of their narratives is the existence of crisis wherein certain significant individuals become central in its resolution. Apart from issues of loneliness in the university, another common problem especially among students of provincial and lower income backgrounds is whether they will have sustainable finances to support their education. Again, the presence of relatives intervening in their needs is a typical divine response. What is interesting among these stories is that the relationships they speak of are not necessarily found in religious settings like the parish or their respective Catholic organisations, which may be expected since they are part of small groups after all (Lindgren 2005). These may be friends from the university or extended kin who do not even have to be religiously inclined themselves. Nevertheless, they are perceived as manifestations of God talk. That God speaks through relationships is a significant contrast to the findings of Day (2009) concerning English youth, about whom she argues that the locus of their beliefs is not in God per se (God is arguably absent) but the relationships they deem important. To a great extent, such relationships govern their morality and sense of personal security – a strong case for 'believing in belonging' among English youth (264).

Through Circumstances

Another theme that recurs among my respondents is that God offers His response through the very circumstances they are going through. Oftentimes, these are ordeals and the typical explanation is that they are trials as God's way of testing and causing them to mature. Such testing appears to be about strengthening one's faith, a point raised by Marvin when he described the pain of losing his father to cancer. Teary-eyed, the 20 year old recounts, 'perhaps I haven't gotten over it yet, but I should focus on why God allowed it to happen – to build the faith of my family and mine'. Indeed, today, Marvin is involved in the campus ministry of his state university. Interestingly, this positive appraisal of trials as God talk came up, too, in my interview with EJ, a female English major at a prominent Catholic university. Her narrative deserves considerable space:

> When I finished high school, I had to stop studying because my brother was also in college at that time. For me it was like blackout since there was no way I could be supported to go to college. At that time my mother would tell me that everything is going to be under control, God will be there. So every Wednesday I would go to this church (Our Lady of Guadalupe) just to talk to God in silence. 'Why is this happening? Did I do anything wrong?' When I prayed that I remembered what I learned before that trials do come to test one's strength and faith ... But at that time I was already doubting God and how He can really be a father. And when I cried, I thought to myself, 'No, don't be like that. Don't give up. God is always there. He just gave you a challenge and you must continue'. So I would tell God, 'God, I'm here and I'm ready for all the challenges you will give me ... I know you

want a better life for me'. That's how God and I talk, face to face, while staring at his image.

To be sure, the individuals who helped in resolving their tribulations are taken by my informants as God's divine response to them, like the ones mentioned in the previous section. But as recounted by my informants above, the very circumstances themselves are also taken as positive developments in their lives. Also, the events do not have to be sheer afflictions. This, in particular, became clear to me in my conversation with Vincent, a geological engineering major and president of his student organisation. Talking about his own answered prayers, Vincent muses 'yes, like the safety of my family even if we seldom see each other ... And that they are happy'. To an outsider, this brief statement may be easily perceived as a polite token gesture. But this is not the case for Vincent who hails from a far province in the south of Manila and is therefore away from his family.

So whether the event is an ordeal or a cause for celebration, they are deemed positive as demonstrating God's overall goodness. This element of gratitude is one reason why their prayers cannot be simply read as a coping mechanism (Nelson 2009). Furthermore, their prayers and the way they view reality reflect a personal spirituality that allows them to find God in all things, whether good or bad. As Cassie (20), a female nursing student at a medical college puts it: 'I always think that God is everything everywhere. For example, when I am on the jeepney and I pray, I will look in front and will see a picture of Jesus. To me, it's a sign that God is already answering me'. Interestingly, such readiness to read transcendence into my informants' moments – significant or mundane – is absent from the nuances of teenage boys Engebretson (2004) has interviewed in Australia. Instead, these teenagers' sense of hope and peace resided in 'a strong connection to family and friends' and in activities that made them reflect such as 'listening to music' and 'being in nature' (273).

Through Technology

Perhaps true to the character of finding God in all things, the other intriguing revelation from my interviews is that my informants also see God as answering their prayers through popular forms of media technology such as mobile phones, radio and even the Internet. Concerning the Internet, my informants have talked about how God talks to them through messages they see on forwarded emails, graphic arts and even social networking sites. In this section, however, I will focus on mobile phones and radio since the nuances I have gathered deserve attention. Elsewhere, I have published on how spiritual activities are virtualised or replicated in cyberspace (Cornelio 2009).

In a country declared to be the 'world's text messaging capital' (Anonymous 2010) where young people are touted to be part of a 'text generation' (Batan 2005: 80), it might not be surprising that God answers through text messages. When I asked Niza (18 years old) to describe to me how she sees God, the engineering student from a state university tells me: 'I consider God my friend. I tell Him if I need something, and sometimes I even quarrel with Him. Then He responds by nagging me through the Gospel and through text messages'. Niza then explains to me what she means by such nagging: 'It's like God seeks me. My classmates text me godly messages. I then feel that my pride becomes a hindrance to drawing closer to Him'. Niza's account suggests that apart from conventional sources of divine revelation (like the Gospel at Mass), she and many of her peers are open to hearing from Him in alternative avenues, which in this case are text messages from her friends. Based on the study of Roman (2006: 5) among undergraduate students at a Manila university, an example of a creative and religiously inspired forwarded text message is as follows:

> Without 'JESUS CHRIST', days are
> 'moanday' 'tearsday'
> 'wasteday' 'thirstday'
> 'fightday' 'shatterday'
> & 'sinday'
> so allow Him to be
> w/'U' everyday. !
> GOD BLESS U

It was also a text message that Faye (19 years old), a nursing student, saw as God-inspired. Although she has read Rick Warren's very popular *Purpose-driven Life*, it was her mother's text message on the last day at a camp that confirmed what to her was its most profound message: 'You are not an accident'. As the founding president of her medical college's Charismatic group, Faye has gone through a series of discouragements, notwithstanding her mother's on-going cancer. It was indeed a timely message that made her say: 'This, I think, is my purpose'.

Another intriguing story comes from Jed (20 years old), a computer science major, who recounts to me how God has spoken to him at a café near his college known for its courses in information technology. When he tells me that God helps him, I probe by asking how he knows that it is indeed from God:

Jed: I typically ask for a sign. There's a story to it. Last year I joined
a campus pageant here. I was extremely busy and no longer knew what to do. I
prayed, 'God, give me a sign, tell me what to do – I have my studies and exams
and my family is struggling financially'. And when I turned on my mp3 player, the
song was 'Take It One Step at a Time'.

Me: Alright

Jed: Then I realized that through that song, yeah, why was I hurrying
myself when I could take things one at a time? After listening to that song, I went
down the café and there was sign above the staircase: Please watch your step. As I
prayed, I felt like God was telling me to take it one step at a time but as I took each
step, I had to be sure it was the right one.

Jed confirms to me that the song is not even a religious one but it has not
stopped him from hesitating to receive it as God's sign. Such religious character
of technology use among my informants enriches the observation of Batan
(2005) concerning the use of mobile technology among Filipino adolescents.
Describing how he uses cellphones for courtship, one of Batan's informants
muses: 'A text message creates a bridge to every heart' (84). For my informants,
such bridging certainly includes signs from God.

In his seminal chapter on the emergence of 'charismatic technology' or that
feature of technology that inspires optimism about its positive contributions to
the quality of life, Lim (2009: 4) asks how the relationship between religion
and technology must be analysed. There are two ways to approach this issue. On
one hand, a technological society has the tendency to fully subject individuals,
relationships and everyday life to instrumental rationality (Taylor 1992). But
the appropriation of technology as God's voice box, as it were, can be deemed as
countering this tendency since individuals are finding it as extensions of personal
and religious relationships. This notion of personal authenticity is revisited at
the end of the chapter.

Another approach might come from Turner (2009) who argues that the
advancement in media technologies will facilitate popular religion's further
democratisation. To a great extent, a form of democratisation is indeed what is
emerging from my informants' nuances in the sense that conventional sources of
religious wisdom such as priests and religious counsellors are not as prominent
although they can also be present. The Bible, which is sometimes quoted, is also
not very prominent. It is not that these conventional sources are pitted against

the ones they currently rely on. If anything, the appropriation of technology as divine signs points to their immediate accessibility, which they may not be enjoying from their respective local parishes. I have noted elsewhere that my informants have a sense of detachment from their own parishes and religious leaders (Cornelio 2011). Put differently, the divinity of technology reveals at the very least the frailty of formal and institutional religious socialisation.

The Image of God as Indwellingly Individualised

In a recent study, Bade and Cook (2008) have recommended that future research should look into the relationship between how people pray and the notions they have about God. Observing Dutch youth, Janssen and colleagues (1990) have asserted that a view of God as a person tends to shape prayers in terms of dialogues whereas a view of God as force or indefinable power influences prayers in terms of meditation. In this section, I argue that instead of merely looking at the forms and functions of prayer, the very ways by which prayers are answered reveals a more direct access to their understanding of who God is. Doing this would help observers avoid a more dismissive posture that prayers, for example, are merely forms of coping mechanism or generally instrumentalist in character (see discussion above). Drawing from Riis and Woodhead's (2010) recent work on religious emotion, my informants must be compelled by a particular view of God if their prayers are embedded in an emotional relationship with Him.

Since God speaks through relationships, circumstances and technology, I posit that God is deemed to be immanent, personal and creatively experiential. His immanence lies in His perceived willingness to intervene in daily affairs. He is personal because in many ways God is seen as friend and as father, ideas that reflect relationality. Indeed, the national survey on Catholic youth (Episcopal Commission on Youth 2003: 77) shows that the top three personal concepts of God are as 'parent', 'provider' and 'friend'. Finally, God may be described as creatively experiential. This is a God who is willing to appropriate technology to answer prayers, for example.

Collectively, these ideas suggest that even if prayer assumes some distance between God and the person and even if it is in the context of the Mass or some other forms of traditional piety, prayer as religious practice for my informants points to a God who has arrived in the here and now. In response, it is the self that experiences how God answers and reveals Himself. Indeed, while He is still the God above who tests, tries and rewards, He is more than that. He is a God who is caring, sincere and intimate. To simply argue that the young people today are instrumentalist or coping may be missing all this richness of their contemporary faith.

Such nuances bring to light what may be considered an individualised notion of God. This needs to be carefully qualified. In the sociology of religion, individualisation is often described in terms of how traditional religion gives way to alternative forms of spirituality that the self purposively seeks. Invoking Luckmann (1967), religion becomes 'invisible' or privatised. A cognate term might be detraditionalisation, which connotes that the sources of religious authority, beliefs and practices are taking shape outside established religious institutions (Woodhead and Heelas 2000). Another possible term is subjectivisation or the cultural turn to the self prevalent in the West which accounts for the decline of traditional religions and the rise of spiritualities of life in the form of eastern practices, horoscope, meditation and even homeopathic medication (Heelas and Woodhead 2005).

In the case of my informants, there is no clear intent on their part to leave Catholicism. Their nuances concerning answered prayers and the image of God they entail are all framed within their Catholic identity. My informants, it needs to be recalled, are all active members and officers of Catholic organisations on campus and they are convinced that their everyday religious practices are part of being Catholic (Cornelio 2010). In other words, their prayers and the way they perceive answered prayers are all to them ways of experiencing the Catholic faith even if they may not be the conventional or institutionally sanctioned. Following this train of thought, the image of God generated by the way they understand how God talks to them, is also part of their Catholic experience. It is therefore in the light of this indwelt framing that God is individualised or personalised. More specifically, God as the immanent, personal and creatively experiential divine for the Filipino Catholic youth I have interviewed is *indwellingly individualised*.[7]

To elaborate, these students, I argue, are arguably discovering a more authentic faith in the context of their personal experiences but without converting out of the religion. Employing Wuthnow's (1998) terms, they are not necessarily 'seeking' outside Catholicism. They are still 'dwelling' in their Catholic identity. But within that dwelling, they are discovering new ways to experience their religion in personal and authentic ways. The highly experiential and accessible nature of how God answers their prayers through relationships, circumstances and technology – areas where they have a mastery of as young

---

[7]   Coining this term has been influenced by Baggett (2009: 67) who describes as 'indwelt seekers' his Catholic informants in the US who internalise their religion more meaningfully by engaging its doctrines in the light of rationality and increasing cultural diversity.

people – allow these Filipino Catholic youth to achieve a sense of personal authenticity concerning their religion. Indeed, if God is immanent, personal and creatively experiential, that only means that He resides in the present and can speak into their lives effectively and not only through institutional or sacramental forms. He responds not just to provide for their needs but also to inspire them with assurance and hope for the day. These are matters that resonate with my informants' sense of self as Filipino Catholic youth living in the challenging conditions of a developing society that is globally connected. In a way, these themes resonate with the expressive and post-materialistic forms of prayer Giordan (2012) discusses in the context of Europe. Therefore, to consider their prayer life as sheer instrumentalism or a coping mechanism betrays such personal authenticity. To view it as a form of moral therapeutic deism (Smith and Denton 2005) is also inappropriate as it may suggest that they are taking prayer and religion lightly.

Conclusion

At a lecture I delivered at the Ateneo de Manila University, one of my students pointed out that the ways in which prayer is understood and practised by my informants are certainly typical. But she suggested that more than being problematic, these should be perceived as deepening Catholic spirituality. I leave it to the ministers of the faith to comment on the validity of such a statement, a point I take from Day's reflections (2009). Indeed, the report of the Episcopal Commission on Youth (2003: 74) laments that 'the Filipino Catholic youth have a personalist knowledge and experience of an inadequately Christian God'. From my point of view as a sociologist, however, the nuances presented above remain important in understanding how young people are practising their faith at the everyday level (McGuire 2008).

In a way that enriches the emerging sociology of prayer, the sociology of religion and youth, and the study of religion in the Philippines, the contribution of this chapter to this volume lies in three respects. First, the fundamental interest has been in understanding what prayer means to the Filipino Catholic students I have interviewed. As discussed at the outset, prayer to them is a conversation with God in the context of an emotional relationship with Him. Second, a major interest has been in the nuances Filipino Catholic students have about answered prayers or how God is perceived to respond to prayers. I have presented above that my informants see divine response through the relationships they are part of, the circumstances they are going through, and technology of which they have mastery. When I delivered this paper at the ISSR conference in France, I described these themes collectively as suggesting that 'God does not speak in mysterious ways'. And indeed, as far as my respondents are concerned, He does not. This is where the third contribution of the chapter comes in.

By looking at how they perceive divine response, my informants' nuances are able to unravel who God is in their religious subjectivity. I have argued in the latter part that the image of God being revealed is that of an immanent, personal and creatively experiential divine being. These are attributes implying some degree of religious individualisation especially because they have nothing to do with traditional and doctrinal notions of the Catholic God as being enveloped in mystery as a trinity, for example, or as a God of justice and righteousness. Nevertheless, the attributes of being immanent, personal and creatively experiential are not in contradiction to the God that Catholicism embraces. It is for this reason that such religious individualisation must be taken in the context of a Catholic identity. In other words, the God discernible from my informants' nuances concerning divine response is one who is indwellingly individualised.

Drawing from these insights, I am convinced that the sociology of prayer must not only be concerned with describing prayer per se. It must give attention to first, the relationship of prayer with other aspects of everyday religion. In the case of this chapter, I have looked at the image of God in the subjectivity of my informants. Other possibilities include the relationship of prayer to morality, religious authority, decision-making and beliefs concerning fate, the afterlife and even one's freewill. Two, the sociology of prayer must also consider the wider trends concerning religious change. This chapter has looked at religious individualisation, for example, although other trends such as sacralisation, universalisation, and even secularisation may prove worthwhile as well (see Woodhead and Heelas 2000). This angle becomes even more pressing when considering the religious condition of young people as a glimpse of the future of religion. Finally, even in its emergent stage, the sociology of prayer must start considering the experience of non-Western societies where religiosity is significantly stronger as they can open up novel ways of thinking about religious change.

References

Anonymous (2010). 'The Philippines is Still the World's Text Messaging Capital', *The Daily Blend*.

Bade, Mary and Cook, Stephen (2008). 'Functions of Christian Prayer in the Coping Process', *Journal for the Scientific Study of Religion*, 47/1: 123–33.

Baggett, J.P. (2009). *Sense of the Faithful: How American Catholics Live Their Faith*. Oxford: Oxford University Press.

Baker, Joseph (2008). 'An Investigation of the Sociological Patterns of Prayer Frequency and Content', *Sociology of Religion*, 69/2: 169–85.

Batan, C. (2005). 'Texting as Style: Preliminary Observations on Cellular Phone Use Among Filipino College Students', in H. Helve and G. Holm (eds), *Contemporary Youth Research: Local Expressions and Global Connections*. Aldershot: Ashgate, 77–88.

Bautista, J. (2011). *Figuring Catholicism: An Ethnography of the Santo Niño De Cebu*. Quezon City: Ateneo de Manila University Press.

Bräunlein, Peter (2012). '"We are 100% Catholic:" Philippine Passion rituals and some obstacles in the study of non-European Christianity', *Journal of Religion in Europe*, 5: 384–413.

Cannell, F. (1999). *Power and Intimacy in the Christian Philippines*. New York: Cambridge University Press.

Collins-Mayo, S. (2008). 'Young People's Spirituality and the Meaning of Prayer', in A. Day (ed.), *Religion and the Individual*. Aldershot: Ashgate, 33–46.

Collins-Mayo, S. and Dandelion, P. (eds) (2010). *Religion and Youth*. Farnham, Surrey, England; Burlington, VT: Ashgate.

Collins-Mayo, S. et al. (2010). *The Faith of Generation Y*. London: Church House Publishing.

Cornelio, J.S. (2009). 'The New Face of Global Evangelism: Virtualizing Spiritual Experience', in F.K.G. Lim (ed.), *Mediating Piety: Technology and Religion in Contemporary Asia*. Leiden and Boston: Brill, 183–207.

Cornelio, Jayeel Serrano (2010). 'Being Catholic as Reflexive Spirituality: The Case of Religiously Involved Filipino Students', *Asia Research Institute Working Paper Series*.

Cornelio, Jayeel Serrano (2011). 'Foregrounding the Study of Generations in Education Research: The Case of Filipino Students and the Isolated Generation', *Reformare. Journal of Education Research*, 1/1: 9–35.

Day, Abby (2009). 'Believing in Belonging: An Ethnography of Young People's Constructions of Belief', *Culture and Religion: An Interdisciplinary Journal*, 10/3: 263–78.

Engebretson, Kath (2004). 'Teenage Boys, Spirituality and Religion', *International Journal of Children's Spirituality*, 9/3: 263–78.

Episcopal Commission on Youth (2003). *The National Filipino Catholic Youth Survey 2002*. Manila: Catholic Bishops' Conference of the Philippines.

Francis, Leslie and Robbins, Mandy (2009). 'Prayer, Purpose in Life, and Attitudes Toward Substances: A Study Among 13- to 15-Year-Olds in England and Wales', *Counselling and spirituality*, 28/2: 83–104.

Giordan, G. (2012). 'Toward a Sociology of Prayer', in G. Giordan and J.W.H. Swatos Jr (eds), *Religion, Spirituality, and Everyday Life*. London: Springer, 77–88.

Heelas, P. and Woodhead, L. (2005). *The Spiritual Revolution: Why Religion is Giving Way to Spirituality*. Oxford: Blackwell.

Howard, E. (2008). *The Brazos Introduction to Christian Spirituality*. Grand Rapids: Brazos Press.

ISSP Research Group (2008). 'International Social Survey Programme 2008: Religion III (ISSP 2008). GESIS Cologne, Germany Za4950 Data File Vers. 2.1.0, Doi: 10.4232/1.10773'., 2010.

Janssen, Jacques, De Haart, Joep and Dan Draak, Christine (1990). 'A Content Analysis of the Praying Practices of Dutch Youth', *Journal for the Scientific Study of Religion*, 29/1: 99–107.

Javaheri, Fatemeh (2005). 'Prayer Healing: An Experiential Description of Iranian Prayer Healing', *Journal of Religion and Health*, 45/2: 23–43.

Kessler, C. and Rüland, J. (2008). *Give Jesus a Hand! Charismatic Christians: Populist Religion and Politics in the Philippines*. Quezon City: Ateneo de Manila University Press.

Ladd, Kevin and Spilka, Bernard (2002). 'Inward, Outward, and Upward: Cognitive Aspects of Prayer', *Journal for the Scientific Study of Religion*, 41/3: 475–84.

Lim, F.K.G. (2009). 'Charismatic Technology', in F.K.G. Lim (ed.), *Mediating Piety: Technology and Religion in Contemporary Asia*. Leiden and Boston: Brill, 1–28.

Lindgren, Tomas (2005). 'The Narrative Construction of Muslim Prayer Experiences', *International Journal for the Psychology of Religion*, 15/2: 159–74.

Loveland, Matthew et al. (2005). 'Private Prayer and Civic Involvement', *Journal for the Scientific Study of Religion*, 44/1: 1–14.

Luckmann, T. (1967). *The Invisible Religion: The Problem of Religion in Modern Society*. New York: Macmillan.

Macasaet, M. (2009). 'The Spiritual Journey of Young Filipinos', in G. Leung (ed.), *The Y Factor: 2009 Yearbook on the Filipino Youth*. Makati: Salesian Missions, 10–15.

Mangahas, Mahar and Labucay, Iremae (2013). '9% of Catholics Sometimes Think of Leaving the Church', http://www.sws.org.ph/pr20130407.htm.

Mauss, M. (2003). *On Prayer*. Oxford and New York: Bergahn Books.

McGuire, M.B. (2008). *Lived Religion: Faith and Practice in Everyday Life*. Oxford: Oxford University Press.

National Statistics Office (2008). 'Philippines in Figures 2008', http://www.census.gov.ph/data/publications/PIF2008.pdf.

Nelson, J. (2009). *Psychology, Religion, and Spirituality*. New York: Springer.

Oktavec, E. (1995). *Answered Prayers: Miracles and Milagros Along the Border*. Tucson, AZ: University of Arizona Press.

Poloma, Margaret and Pendleton, Brian (1989). 'Exploring Types of Prayer and Quality of Life: A Research Note', *Review of Religious Research*, 31/1: 46–53.

Ramos, Melanie (2003). 'Youth and Religion', *Philippine Daily Inquirer*, Opinion: A9.

Riis, O. and Woodhead, L. (2010). *A Sociology of Religious Emotion*. Oxford: Oxford University Press.

Roman, Anthony (2006). 'Texting God: Sms and Religion in the Philippines', Paper presented at the 5th International Conference on Media, Religion and Culture, Stockholm. http://www.freinademetzcenter.org/pdf/Texting%20God%20SMS%20and%20Religion%20in%20the%20Philippines.pdf .

Smith, C. and Denton, M.L. (2005). *Soul Searching: The Religious and Spiritual Lives of American Teenagers*. Oxford: Oxford University Press.

Taylor, C. (1992). *The Ethics of Authenticity*. Cambridge, MA: Harvard University Press.

Turner, B.S. (2009). 'Technologies, Religion and Social Mediation', in Francis Lim (ed.), *Mediating Piety: Technology and Religion in Contemporary Asia*. Leiden and Boston: Brill, 29–46.

Vincett, G. and Collins-Mayo, S. (2010). '(Dis)Engagements With Christianity Amongst Young People in England and Scotland', in Giuseppe Giordan (ed.), *Annual Review of the Sociology of Religion: Youth and Religion*. Leiden and Boston: Brill, 219–49.

Vincett, G. and Olson, E. (2012). 'The Religiosity of Young People Growing Up in Poverty', in L. Woodhead and R. Catto (eds), *Religion and Change in Modern Britain*. London and New York: Routledge, 196–202.

Wiegele, K. (2005). *Investing in Miracles: El Shaddai and the Transformation of Popular Catholicism in the Philippines*. Honolulu: University of Hawaii Press.

Woodhead, L. and Heelas, P. (2000). *Religion in Modern Times: An Interpretive Anthology*. Malden, MA: Blackwell Publishers.

Wuthnow, R. (1998). *After Heaven: Spirituality in America Since the 1950s*. Berkeley: University of California Press.

Zaha, J. (2010). *Prayer, God-image, and moralistic therapeutic deism.* PsyD thesis, George Fox University.

Chapter 9

The Embodiment of Prayer in Charismatic Christianity

Michael Wilkinson and Peter Althouse

Introduction

In the early 1990s a revival broke out in Toronto, Canada, and quickly became known as the 'Toronto Blessing'. People from around the world came to experience renewal with many claims of healing, forgiveness, deliverance and miracles. One activity was playfully referred to as 'carpet time' where people would appear to spontaneously fall to the floor and 'rest' in the Spirit for great lengths of time. The practice, over time, was transformed into a more regularized activity known as soaking prayer. Soaking prayer is an adaptation of previous types of prayer that brings together resting, waiting, healing, forgiveness, contemplation and experiences of divine love into a new form of charismatic prayer. Catch the Fire (CTF), formerly Toronto Airport Christian Fellowship, has developed Soaking in His Presence Weekends, Soaking Prayer Schools and a network of thousands of participants of soaking prayer throughout the world. Based upon extensive fieldwork and interviews, we present some of our findings on soaking prayer and offer a discussion based upon theoretical work on embodiment.

Charismatics and the Body

Charismatics are not afraid to talk about the body and they certainly celebrate it more than their classical Pentecostal cousins, shaped by holiness notions of the body that sought to control it. The body for charismatics, however, is not a site for a battle between the spirit and the flesh where the flesh is something to regulate or even to fear. The charismatic body is understood to be holistic where spirit and flesh come to dwell together. It is where God meets men and women, unified by the work of the Spirit. The body experiences God as an energizing, loving force where the flesh is restored, renewed and healed. The body communes with God through dreams and visions. Bodies communicate with each other and God through prophetic speech. It is a communion, a unity of the divine and the human. This convergence of spirit and body makes classical Pentecostals nervous and evangelical Protestants have long criticized the charismatic body as indulgent.

The body has become an important area of research in the social sciences especially in the fields of gender and sexuality. However, the location of the body in society and religion cannot be reduced to these issues, as important as they are in the discipline. Sociology of religion and the body needs to particularize the way in which charismatic Christians embody religion. Interpreting the charismatic body in some ways is not unlike interpreting the writings of charismatics and their theologies. However, the 'text' we read and interpret in this case is the body. An embodied theology tells us something about charismatics. First, it signals for the observer something about religious experience and the charismatic view of the body. Charismatics appear to enjoy their faith and their bodies express this joy through dance, singing, laughing, twirling, resting, falling down and ecstatic utterances. The admonition to discipline or mortify the body is not part of the discussion though there is an emphasis on sanctification or holy living in a general sense. Christian discipline is not absent from charismatic theology. It is just not at the centre of their practice.

Bryan Turner (1996) has identified important shifts for understanding the body and embodiment in contemporary society. Sociological discussions of the body have primarily focused on the nature of bodies especially their form and function. Issues surrounding gender, sexuality and health, especially in the area of medicine, were often the focus of sociologists. Turner rejects this type of sociological work on the body, which tends to reify the body. Embodiment, on the other hand, focuses on notions of the body, how bodies are constructed in social space, the social discourse surrounding bodies, and how bodies are represented or the phenomenology of bodily experience. For our purposes, embodiment focuses on how charismatic Christianity is expressed through bodies and as a vehicle for signifying the presence of the Spirit and what charismatics describe as the Father's love. In turn, embodiment also allows researchers to view what charismatics do with their bodies observing these encounters between Spirit and body.

The major issues in the sociology of the body have revolved around two different approaches including constructionism and foundationalism (Turner 1996). Sociological approaches to the body shaped by foundationalism, writes Turner, tend to focus on the body as a set of social practices in everyday life including how the body is regulated and the physiological potentiality of bodies, especially in the structural work of Giddens and Bourdieu (see Turner 1996: 24–31). The weakness of this approach is the tendency to reduce the discussion of bodies to materialist explanations, which can be avoided by paying attention to the interaction of bodies. As Turner (1996: 26) states: 'Because sociology is ultimately a social science of interaction which pays especial attention to the question of the meaning of actions, the sociology of the body must be grounded in some notion of embodiment in the context of social interaction and reciprocity'.

Another approach to the study of the body comes from studies of signs and symbols where the body is viewed as a system of signs. For example, the work of anthropologist Mary Douglas (1966; 1970) examined the importance of the body in ritual, culture and religious expression. For Douglas, the body is a system of symbols, a metaphor for society, shaped by notions of pollution, risk and taboo where the body requires control. Some feminist studies are also shaped by this approach where the body is a site for the struggle over power and sexuality. Critique of the body focuses on the differences between male and female bodies with attention given to how gender is constructed as a symbol and sign of inequality. Turner's approach is to incorporate these other approaches from signs and symbols and structuralism, which allows one to examine in our case how bodies are constructed around notions of the charismatic body as well as the way in which bodies interact and are culturally structured. In other words, we can take a phenomenological viewpoint that examines the meaning of embodiment among charismatics, especially over time.

Anthropological studies of the Catholic charismatic renewal and healing by Csordas (2002) are informed by a perspective of methodological embodiment. Csordas makes the argument that bodies are like texts that can be read semiotically. Embodiment, however, is a methodological orientation that sees bodies as existentially grounded in culture. The body is a biological, material entity, but embodiment is an indeterminate methodological field defined by sensory perception, presence and engagement in the cultural world, rather than a bodily response to the cognitive mind. Embodiment, argues Csordas, is the starting point for analysing human cultural activity. Indeterminacy is rooted in the ambiguity of human existence as perceiving beings-in-the-world.

Csordas brings together two strands of interrogation with regard to a theory of embodiment: the anthropology of the body and embodied phenomenology. Previous work in the anthropology of the body, including the work of Douglas, Foucault, Victor Turner and Bourdieu saw the body as the locus of social practice. The phenomenology of the body, however, views embodiment as an existential condition grounded in culture and the self, and starts from the perspective of the lived body or being-in-the-world. For Csordas, both the anthropology of the body and the phenomenology of the lived body are complementary as long as the modernist mind–body dualism is resisted.

Influenced by Merleau-Ponty, Csordas argues that bodily sensory perception is preobjective and embedded in culture so that 'somatic modes of attention' allows the observer to identify different cultural practices. Somatic modes of attention mean both an attention to and attention with one's own body and other bodies within an intersubjective milieu of culture. This is a social process in that it is concerned with the cultural elaboration of sensory perception rather than the body in isolation. The sensory elements in charismatic phenomena are examples of a cultural elaboration of embodiment.

The relationship between body and Spirit has specific theological implications when observing Pentecostal-Charismatic Christianity. For the early Pentecostals from the Methodist-holiness background ascetic notions of the body were dominant. The body in many ways was perceived as dangerous where much war was battled over the flesh. The body had to be controlled and regulated. The body was thought to be the 'Temple of the Holy Ghost' and therefore needed to be pure or clean for the Spirit to indwell. The Spirit would not indwell impure flesh. The body was often the vehicle of unruly, ungovernable and irrational passions that required self-control. Emotions and fleshly desires were to be under the control of the Spirit. Sanctification and perfection shaped notions of the classical Pentecostal body. Pentecostals, through the work of self-control, modesty, moderation and the Spirit, subjugated their bodies to the control of the Spirit, which governed everything from speech, food and drink that entered the body.

The charismatic movement, beginning in the 1960s within the mainline Protestant churches and Roman Catholic Church, signalled a shift in the understanding of the body. Classical Pentecostals were not sure what to do with these new charismatics who often consumed alcohol and smoked cigars. In the 1980s when evangelicals embraced a charismatic view of embodiment they also redefined the relationship between body and Spirit. These changes, however, were not simply theological. They also reflected cultural shifts often identified as the postmodern turn with attention given to consumption, self and identity. Bodies, however, were not objects of mortification. Rather, bodies were expressions of freedom, individuality, creativity and the joy of the Spirit-infused life.

David Lyon (2000) captured this shift in the nature of the body and charismatic Christianity. In his analysis of religion and postmodernity, Lyon focused on the relationship between consumption and the body where the body is no longer objectified. Rather, the individual 'shops' for religious experience which in turn shapes the self and identity. Poloma (2003) referred to these globetrotting spiritual pilgrims as 'main street mystics' where a reversal of body control is characteristic of charismatics who search for experience from one holy site to another. Religion may be fragmented but it is also a cultural resource for its re-imagination (see Hervieu-Léger 2000). Religion is embodied and experienced as emotive, playful, theatrical, intimate, therapeutic and sensual where bodies emit all kinds of sounds, including groaning, crying, moaning, laughing and weeping.

Methodologically, our findings are based upon our observations, interviews with participants and participation. We had opportunity to observe soaking prayer in small home groups, seminars, large renewal events and church based centres. We conducted interviews with 126 participants. On occasion we participated in soaking prayer practices although we cannot claim to experience the many things we describe like visions, dreams, healings and bodily experiences like weight, smell or heat. The one experience both researchers had was a feeling of rest, relaxation, or peace, which was therapeutic. However, on many occasions we were uncomfortable with the prayer meetings (especially the groaning, laughing, snoring etc.) and spent much time debriefing after our observations. The discomfort we think was due to our position as outsiders of this particular church tradition and not regular practitioners of soaking prayer, which raises questions about whether or not regular practice and participation may eventually lead to the shared experience often talked about by soaking prayer practitioners. We also discussed the difficulties researchers have speaking about the impact of research on our own bodies and the appropriate venues with which to discuss these issues (see Droogers and van Harskamp 2013; Yong 2012).

Soaking Prayer

In our observations of soaking prayer we have noted that while there is some variety, how people practice soaking prayer has much similarity. Soaking prayer is practised in churches, conferences, seminars and homes. Soaking prayer is practised in small intimate groups, among family members or on one's own. A common structure is observable in that people will gather together for a time of prayer. As people gather together they socialize and talk about the concerns of the day, or needs they might have. Gathering together for prayer is a time to develop deep emotional relationships among those who pray. At a predetermined time the group starts the time of soaking. The lights are turned down; sometimes candles are lit if they are available. Pillows and blankets appear and people find a place to lie down in order to soak, usually on the floor, a number of chairs strewn together or on couches if available. Music and lyrics are an important component to the practice of soaking prayer. Most participants play soaking CDs as they pray or, if they are involved in a worship event or soaking school, have worship musicians playing in the background.

As the music plays, people will soak without speaking. Soaking prayer is a form of meditative or contemplative prayer that cultivates hearing from God rather than intercessory prayer when people pray for their needs or the needs of others. The music usually progresses through a series of slow, melodic sounds that help participants to centre the heart and calm the body. The use of music is distinct from earlier forms of contemplative prayer in that prayer was conducted in silence. We have heard of some people (usually musicians) who soak in silence, but more often music is used to help centre the self. One participant, whose parents were music ministers in the church, described it as follows: 'I found that our culture is so busy that I think soaking is really relevant in our particular culture because I think people have a hard time settling down and relaxing and emptying. I guess it's not really emptying but it's centring. I think people have a hard time with that. And I think at first I really relied on the music a lot. Like certain kinds of music that would help me to focus. Now most often I soak in silence' (P13). Those who produce soaking music often describe it as a prophetic practice where the musicians speak prophetically while singing and playing. Soaking prayer will take about an hour or longer, after which the group will come together again to share what they have experienced with each other. We have heard examples where one person in the group will share a prophetic word for another person in the group and will speak to a social situation. At other times people may simply share what God has said or shown them.

While people soak together their bodies are involved in the process in subtle ways. For the most part, people soaking together will lay still or roll to one side in order to relieve the pressure of staying in one position too long. We observed a husband and wife in their middle years holding each other intimately while they soaked. On another occasion we observed a mother, father and child soaking together. Intimacy is an important experience of love that permeates soaking prayer and its social consequences. One man explained: 'It all comes down to intimacy. Intimacy with God breaks down all the barriers that we think are in our lives that keep us from living this way' (P51). However, sometimes sobbing could be heard as people claimed to experience a profound love of the Father or were healed of past hurts, disruptions in relationships and emotional pain.

At other times, participants would laugh softly, which sometimes would ripple through the room. At one soaking meeting near Ottawa, Ontario, we observed a woman moving her hands in a way that mimicked the movement of air or breath.

Soaking prayer allows people to engage the sacred and cultivate the charismatic gifts. Unlike other religions that assign sacred space to a permanent location, soaking prayer occurs in space that has multiple uses. The practice of prayer makes the space sacred, which can occupy any space such as hotel conference rooms or private homes. However, churches also provide sacred space for the practice of soaking prayer, either in the main sanctuary or in an adjacent room. The sacred objects are the pillows and blankets, which support the idea that soaking is a time for resting in the Father's love and presence. We have observed that some people will fall asleep and this is acceptable. According to CTF teaching, God can speak to a person while asleep. If a person falls asleep while soaking then it probably indicates that the person needs to rest. Unlike earlier forms of Pentecostalism, which mortified the body, soaking prayer includes the body as a site for the sacred. We have identified a number of bodily experiences that indicate the spiritual significance of soaking for charismatics such as resting, breathing, groaning, weight or pressure, odours, dreams and visions, heat, tingling, tears and shaking.

Rest refers to the physical act of lying down and making oneself comfortable with a pillow and blanket. Soaking music facilitates the goal of resting as does dimming the lights and lighting candles. Some people find that resting leads to sleeping and on more than one occasion we heard people snoring. Resting is sometimes linked with the idea of Sabbath, a Judaeo–Christian practice based upon the Genesis creation account where God rested after creating, or the command of Moses to keep the Sabbath holy. As one participant said: 'And I think soaking is more like the Sabbath that you take every single day. I mean in the Old Testament, you get six days of work and one day of rest. But we don't [do] that now. On Sunday people are so busy in their work. People go to church and then after church they do all these things. But then I feel like what God wants us to do is have a time of rest every single day' (P48). Here you get the sense that resting is not just limited to a day of the week but is an important spiritual practice that is incorporated into the daily life of charismatics. Rest becomes the first step of preparation for listening and receiving.

Along with rest is the practice of breathing with its rhythm of inhalation and exhalation, the in and out process of physical air moving through the body. Breathing is often associated with de-stressing and relaxation. In our observations and interviews this is what we most often heard as people described their bodies slowing down and their breathing becoming more regulated. This was our own experience too as we participated in the practice of soaking, noticing how our breathing changed within minutes and the muscles in our bodies started to relax. As the breathing deepened, the body relaxed, the mind calmed down and the heart slowed, as far as we could perceive. Exhalation would deepen and come from the diaphragm. Either in prayer, in worship, or in conversation there would be an exhalation of contentment and noticeable relaxation in their bodies.

One young woman relayed a vision she experienced while soaking in prayer that was related to her breathing. As she was praying she was being drawn deeper into the Father's love but began to get panicky and couldn't breathe. She said: 'And then I realized how deep I was. And I couldn't breathe. I couldn't breathe'. But then her perception began to change and she felt more comforted: 'When I was lying on my back on the sofa and I was just so paralyzed. And I felt my chest was breathing in and out. And I know that He [God] was giving me the breath' (P59). Another person commented: 'And so, I tend to just breathe in prayer, like I automatically pray' (P100).

Cleo McNelly Kearns (2005) developed the work of Luce Irigaray on the relationship between breathing, spiritual discipline, and the body, offering insight for understanding soaking prayer. Specifically, Kearns investigates the role of breathing and speaking in the spiritual practices of Yoga and the Western philosophical religions and argues that respiration and diverse kinds of breathing resists the emphasis on the mind in the West by giving attention to the body and its senses. Furthermore, spirituality or religion that focuses solely on speech without breathing and silence disrespects lived life. According to Kearns, breathing has an important impact on speech and prayer in the following ways: '(1) that speech should be organically related to but may in fact be divorced from or counterproductive of breath and silence; (2) that a more flexible way of breathing – and hence speaking and praying – may be cultivated, even to the point of spiritual transformation; and (3) that breath itself and the kinds of religious discipline related to it are situated in the body and may hence be, at least in some of its manifestations, gendered' (2005: 104–5). Kearns's observations hint at a theoretical framework for embodied prayer in which breath, rest, silence and pause form the rhythms of speech.

The rhythms of speech can be constructed so that breathing and silence are supported by, or divorced from, embodied experience. When speech becomes forced, organic breathing becomes gasping and grabbing for the next breath or an anxious pause at the end of breath's exhalation. Improper breathing in speech can constrain the torso, create laxness and loosen body posture so that the body's core is weakened. The relationship between prayer and breathing can affect health: positively in that proper breathing can support mental clarity and enhance communication and negatively in that improper breathing can detract from good speaking techniques. Prayer that cultivates proper breathing patterns supports the breathing patterns needed in speech. Once again drawing on Irigaray, Kearns (2005: 105) writes:

> The material and somatic support for spirit both East and West – has not only health effects but effects on clarity of mind, on pertinence of thought, and on communication as well. It produces speech that is, as we say, 'dry' or 'vapid', but also dogmatic, alienated, and dull, lacking elemental qualities of authority, force, flow, inspiration, and spaciousness or organic relationships of context. At the other end of the breathing spectrum are those who underarticulate, or swallow their words. Stammering, muttering, and poor articulation are gross manifestations of the counterproductive relationship between speech and breath, but those are manifestations at the level of content and effect as well. Talking here becomes a substitute for or an impediment to flexible and responsive speech, a way of galvanizing and forcing a constricted bodily practice that becomes narrowed by anxiety and chronic tension and forcing it into at least a semblance of oxygenation and life support.

Groaning or moaning (also a kind of breathing) is often heard among people who soak and with comparable sounds to making love, childbirth, a longing or a desire. Some people are physically positioned on the floor, which supports the comparisons with childbirth or lovemaking. No one appears to be uncomfortable with the sounds and some will say out loud phrases like 'yes Lord' or 'more Lord' along with other sounds of 'ooh' and 'ah'. Bodies will remain still or shake or tremble or spasm. Some people will laugh or you may even hear a gentle crying. It is not always the entire group groaning or moaning but usually one or two people while others may be resting, sleeping, or simply remaining still and quiet. The groaning is often associated with Romans 8 where Paul writes about the Spirit interceding on behalf of those in need with groans. One participant said in a way that is suggestive of gestation and birth: 'I remember I went into a season of eight months of really a groaning in me for just more, and more, and then suddenly bam I got hit with a fresh anointing, and revival started breaking out. So I'm in a place of hunger, desperation, and borderline depression just wanting more of God' (P97).

Weight or pressure is another experience regularly described by people who soak. It is often talked about as a heavy weight felt on the body, especially in the chest. Some have spoken of the presence of God as an entombing experience where they were unable to move. People will lie on the floor for several hours and say they were unable to get up because of the great weight upon them. Some have explained it as God laying hands on the person. 'Laying on of hands' between people is thought to be an act of transferring the anointing or power of God from someone who is especially empowered by God to another person. In soaking prayer it is God who, metaphorically speaking, directly lays hands on the person praying and bypassing any other person. One participant said: 'The Bible talks about God's glory as a "weight of glory". I feel it's perfectly fine for God to show up in that way when somebody lays his hands on you. He [God] is putting weight on you. And when the All Mighty God, the Father God – He's probably so huge – when He lays His hands on you, you're going to feel a little bit of weight. And His hand is probably bigger than your whole body. You know, when we lay hands on people, we feel a weight and we feel a touch and then we feel love' (P48).

Smell or olfaction, the physical experience of sensing the perfume of flowers, fruit or some other enjoyable odour is another experience. It is not that common but in some of our interviews people spoke of sensing a specific odour of some kind during prayer. In many cases it was usually something enjoyable or if it was an unpleasant smell it was interpreted with some tension often signalling a call to spiritual warfare prayer where they were to battle in the heavenly realms some demonic attack. Smelling perfume or flowers was the more common experience while engaging in soaking prayer. In this case, the smell was identified as the presence of the Lord: 'I've smelled different smells. In fact, I've had the experience where I woke up in the night and I smelt the presence of the Lord. It was strong enough to wake me up. So, I went, wow, you're here, Lord. I turned over and suddenly I could smell it again' (P63).

Dreams and visions are one other kind of experience that illustrates how charismatic Christianity is embodied. The key text for dreams and visions among charismatics is based in Acts 2 and thought to be the confirmation of the prophecy given in Joel 2:28: 'Your young men shall see visions, and your old men shall dream dreams' (Acts 2:17). Dreams and visions are not understood metaphorically in the renewal as, for instance, hopes and plans for the future, but as embodied experiences that involve mental impressions or pictures. Dreams are the normal process of experiencing night dreams, but according to charismatics dreams are occasionally special moments of divine communication. Visions are similar to dreams, but occur during waking hours as spontaneous mental impressions or images. As one participant said: 'It's just one of those mysterious things that happens. You can't really explain it. I try to come up with words to explain the visions, but "they is what they is". It's an encounter with somebody invisible, but it's not really invisible anymore because you're in that realm where He is' (P10). Often visions are described as visual and colourful. As one person said: '... and in my vision, it was just all these colours and shapes and like what you'd picture in some '70s psychedelic movie or whatever' (P57).

Droogers (1994) views the experiences of dreams and visions, healing and prophecy in Pentecostalism as resistance to the mind–body dualism prominent in modernism. Charismatics, argues Droogers, oppose any kind of polarity such as the priority of reason over emotion, the profane over the sacred or the mind over body. Instead charismatics seek a rehabilitation of the individual, the body, the sacred and the emotions that is more holistic and integrated. Experiencing dreams and visions then allows for wholeness as the emotions are validated and prized alongside reason.

Dreams and visions have taken on a more therapeutic interpretation in the twentieth century, which in some ways is appropriated by charismatics. John A. Sanford (1978), an Episcopal priest with ties to the mainline charismatic movement, who later became a Jungian therapist, interpreted dreams as both spiritual and psychological. Dreams are rooted in natural life but reflect the divine through the *imago dei*. For Sanford, God is the inner source and energy of life and dreams link humans indirectly to this source of life. Sanford (1978: 183) states: 'The experience of God, psychologically speaking, is the experience of the depth, the height, and the unity of our own psyche. The search for God is the search for the depth and height of our own being, for the complete Christ like being who is waiting within us to be consciously realized and expressed in our human relationships'. In other words, through dreams and visions people are indirectly touched by the divine energy within, which is the divine source of life.

The feeling of heat, tingling or electricity in the body is another experience talked about among charismatics, often associated with healing. One of the soaking coordinators in the United States explained: 'It just feels like electricity like you just put your finger into a plug and you encounter God's raw power, you just feel like raw electricity because there's no way my body could shake like that in the natural, and like I said, I've tried' (P1). Another person described the sensation as follows: 'Sometimes there's shaking, but there's this electricity or heat that is just powerful. And I've had two healings. I think I may have mentioned this to you. Personally, I've had two healings during soaking' (P56). In some cases the sensations of heat, tingling or electricity for charismatics signifies the presence of God.

Another common experience is spontaneous laughter that can be heard among charismatics. Sometimes it begins with just one person and then it spreads from one person to another like a wave across the group. Laughter is associated with happiness, joy and having fun. One person said: 'And I'm just out on the floor laughing hysterically and I don't really know why I was laughing. I was just laughing hysterically' (P40). A man in Florida who teaches physics and considers himself very analytical began to laugh following a time of prayer. He said: 'I just started laughing, like flat out, all out laughing. And I couldn't stop. I tried to stop, and I laughed harder to the point that the next day my stomach hurt. I laughed so loud and it was uncontrollable. Then [I think] I need to stop laughing and I was just laughing louder' (P61).

Love is the central experience among charismatics that captures all of the other experiences described above. The embodiment of love is the defining quality where charismatics talk about it as a baptism of love, a love revolution, or a river of love. One interviewee said: 'I had a vision one time at home where I actually felt like I experienced the Father's love for the first time. I actually experienced Him as my Father, that He truly loved me as a daughter. And that was amazing. That just gave me a new perspective of God' (P17). The sense that one is loved by a higher power, a greater love, by the heavenly Father, is empowering, enriching and enlivening for charismatics. It fills them with a sense of wholeness, peace, acceptance, and shapes their identity. It is also described as a love that is not just experienced by the individual but often people talk about feeling a greater love for other people (see Sorokin 2002). Over and over we heard similar comments like this one: 'I don't know anybody that has received deeply of the Father's love that hasn't in some remarkable way or some very obviously new and different way found a way to love those people around them' (P53).

Experiencing the Father's love and reciprocating that love is important in the practice of soaking prayer. As one soaking prayer coordinator said: 'sometimes just being with my wife and we might not be even saying something but we're in each other's presence ... I guess we find that the company you keep has an effect on the way you are as a person, and hopefully, as we keep company with the Lord, as we try to get into His presence, that we'll become more like Him' (P123). At the same time, soaking prayer is a way to cultivate the spiritual discipline of hearing God and discerning what God is saying through the ears and eyes of faith. Hearing, however, is more than the physical act of hearing with the ears, but a way of knowing God and being guided by the Spirit.

Hearing God's voice and experiencing mental images or pictures are common occurrences for people who practice soaking prayer; and they are related to surrender, intimacy and presence. One west coast participant commented: 'When you're just on the ground, surrendered to Him and you just feel His presence, and you [are] in this place of a deeper peace than you've ever felt before ... and you just hear those words I love you, I accept you, I choose you' (P51). A Christian counsellor in Florida explained that hearing God's voice was part of an emotional healing process: 'This was a step, a part of my own healing journey of learning to relax and to hear God speak. That He would speak in such a manner, that it would be very personal, and I found that initially He would simply say the same thing over and over, "I love you" and He would say it until I got it' (P22).

Some people who soak speak of hearing God's voice as an impression of the heart or still small voice. Others, however, speak of hearing an audible voice (see Luhrmann 2012). One woman in Florida was quite open about hearing God in an audible voice in her early Christian life, but that as her relationship with God progressed she no longer needed the audible. She commented: 'But for the first year-and-a-half of walking with the Lord, I literally heard him audibly' (P10). Probing what she meant by this statement she responded: 'I would hear him speaking audibly all the time. I mean, just nonstop, you know, in my car, as I was praying, I would just hear him audibly'. As she continued her story she revealed how at a later part in her spiritual journey God revealed to her that she would now hear only by faith:

> And one day, driving down the road, going to work, He [God] said, 'Now, I want to tell you this', and He was very sweet. He said, 'This will be the last time you hear my voice like this because now I want you to start to listen to my voice by faith, walking by faith is what you're going to learn next'. And I really didn't like this. I loved hearing Him audibly but I was really thankful that He prepared me and let me know that it didn't mean that I'd done anything wrong. It didn't mean that I was missing Him. He warned me. He didn't just like, 'Okay, I'm cutting it off, let you figure it out for yourself'. It was very sweet the way He did that.

The story is one that suggests there is progress in the Christian journey in which the believer becomes more intimate or more deeply enveloped in the Father's love. The life of progress in prayer is a story that kept coming up in our interviews and is related to the mystical tradition in Christianity (see Poloma 2003).

However, hearing God's voice is not just for one's own personal development though this was an important element of prayer, but hearing from God was also so that the person could act as a conduit to speak love into the lives of others. As one participant said: 'This also translates into the prophetic – how to hear God's voice because hearing God's voice, it's inward in that it's outward. Prophetic is where it's kind of outward' (P46). One of the leaders of the renewal commented: 'So for us, the people that are the deepest – the ones who encounter God the deepest are the ones that have the most profound impact on loving people but also on delivering people. They hear – they're so accustomed to the voice of the

Lord ...' (P121). When asked about the impact of soaking prayer, a woman from Washington explained: 'Well intimacy, hearing God's voice and through that being able to hear God's voice for others. Being able to prophesy over others. Being able to hear what God is saying for someone else maybe is one of the impacts. I think that prophesy was a gift I had that I never knew and it really didn't start to emerge until after that experience that I talked about in the Bible study and through soaking prayer has sort of sharpened it' (P13).

Soaking prayer then is an embodied spiritual practice in which the charismatic Christian experiences love by gazing upwardly to the source of unlimited love. The reception of love is experienced bodily as sensations, deepened breathing, groans, laughing, sounds, smell or the feeling of weight or lightness. Speaking in tongues, prophecy, dreams, visions and hearing God are also embodiments of love that spur the charismatic to share this love with others. Charismatics are fond of swaying, dancing, jumping around and freely expressing themselves in worship. Claims of bodily and/or emotional healing are the most dramatic examples of the embodiment of love, where love is experienced as wholeness. Charismatics celebrate the body as a site for sacred encounter that resists the rationalization of belief. In their spiritual practices of soaking prayer charismatics reflect postmodern culture in a way that resists the mind–body dualism that relegates the body to a secondary role, or social hierarchies that force the body into mundane modes of stressful work. Embodied prayer celebrates the body as a ritual site for the sacred.

References

Catch the Fire Ministries (2009). Student manual: soaking prayer center training school.

Csordas, Thomas J. (2002). *Body/ meaning/ healing*. New York: Palgrave.

Douglas, Mary (1966). *Purity and danger: An analysis of the concepts of pollution and taboo*. New York: Routledge.

_____ (1973). *Natural symbols: Explorations in cosmology*. New York: Pantheon Books.

Droogers, André (1994). 'The normalization of religious experience: Healing, prophecy, dreams and visions', in K. Poewe (ed.), *Charismatic Christianity as a global culture*. Columbia, SC: University of South Carolina Press, 33–49.

Droogers, André and Anton van Harskamp (eds) (2013). *Methods for the study of religious change*. London: Equinox.

Hervieu-Léger, Danièle (2000). *Religion as a Chain of Memory*. New Brunswick, NJ: Rutgers University Press.

Kearns, Cleo McNally (2005). 'Irigaray's *Between East and West* Breath: pranayama, and the phenomenology of prayer', in Bruce Ellis Benson and Norman Wirzba (eds), *The phenomenology of prayer*, New York: Fordham University Press, 103–18.

Luhrmann, Tanya (2012). *When God talks back: understanding the American evangelical relationship with God*. New York: Alfred A. Knopf.

Lyon, David (2000). *Jesus in Disneyland: Religion in postmodern times*. Cambridge, UK: Polity Press.

Poloma, Margaret M. (2003). *Main street mystics: The Toronto Blessing and reviving Pentecostalism*. Walnut Creek, CA: Alta Mira.

Sanford, John A. (1978). *Dreams and healing*. Mahwah, NJ: Paulist Press.

Sorokin, Pitirim A. (2002 [1954]). *The ways and power of love*. Philadelphia: Templeton.

Turner, Bryan S. (1996). *The body & society*. London, UK: Sage.

Yong, Amos (2012). 'Observation-Participation-Subjunctivation: Methodological Play and Meaning-Making in the Study of Religion and Theology'. *Religious Studies and Theology* 31(1) 17–40.

Chapter 10

Prayer Requests in an English Cathedral, and a New Analytic Framework for Intercessory Prayer

Tania ap Siôn

Introduction

A small but growing body of international research has begun to explore the rich resource of intercessory prayers posted on the prayer boards in churches, cathedrals and hospital chapels for illuminating the religious and spiritual quests of ordinary men, women and young people whose sense of the transcendence has been enriched by these buildings. However, the integration of findings from these international studies has been frustrated by the absence of a recognised analytic framework through which the data have been analysed or by the means of which rigorous replication studies could be presented. It is within this context and in response to these issues that the ap Siôn Analytic Framework for Intercessory Prayer (apSAFIP) was developed and tested.

The aims of the present chapter are twofold. The first aim is to describe and to justify the approach taken by the apSAFIP, rooted within theoretical frameworks proposed by empirical theology, ordinary theology and the psychology of religion, and to review the findings of those initial studies through which the approach was developed. The second aim is to apply the approach to a discrete sample of 1,658 prayer requests taken from over 10,000 prayer requests systematically harvested from Lichfield Cathedral over an 18-month period. This data source is important for three main reasons: it is the largest collection of intercessory prayers so far available for analysis; the systematic collection throughout a calendar year will permit attention to seasonal variation and location within the wider context of local, national and international events; and Lichfield Cathedral provides a conducive environment for individuals to reflect on their prayers and to write them undisturbed.

As the apSAFIP has been developed within the discipline of empirical theology, and is informed by the constructs of both ordinary theology and the psychology of religion, these will first be examined before reviewing previous empirical studies of intercessory prayer. The new empirical study of Lichfield prayer requests will then be introduced and the apSAFIP applied in the analysis. On the basis of the results emerging from the Lichfield prayer requests, a number of conclusions will be drawn.

Ordinary Theology

The construct of 'ordinary theology' was pioneered by Astley (2002) in his seminal book *Ordinary Theology: Looking, Listening and Learning in Theology*, and further clarified when applied to the rural ministry context (Astley 2003).

Ordinary theology is defined as 'the theological beliefs and processes of believing that find expression in the God-talk of those believers who have received no scholarly theological education' (Astley 2002: 1). This ordinary God-talk or ordinary theology is a deeply personal 'lived' theology and may be hesitant or inarticulate because it has not been subjected to the same objective, analytical rigours required for academic theology. Ordinary theology is also concerned with understanding how the processes of believing work, and that requires an appreciation of individual learning contexts and an understanding of how people learn (Astley 2002: 17ff). Astley argues that learning takes place in 'experiential learning contexts' which are located outside the person (for example, the religious community) and inside the person (for example, individual life experiences), and that these two contexts for learning exist in a dialogical relationship. Therefore, in a real sense, individuals have their own theology, informed by their reflections on their individual experiences, and this theology is in a continual state of change and adaptation as individuals reflect on and incorporate new information arising from individual experiential learning contexts. Astley, therefore, asks whether the Church and the Academy may benefit from listening carefully to the voices belonging to those who are theologically unqualified (ordinary) people.

Building on the theoretical model of ordinary theology provided by Astley, a number of empirical studies have sought to access aspects of ordinary theology in practical, church-related contexts. For example, the qualitative studies of Christie (2007: 2012) examined ordinary Christology, Christie and Astley (2009) examined ordinary soteriology, and Littler and Francis (2005) examined ordinary ideas of the holy. A significant strand of empirical research relevant to ordinary theology is the growing number of studies analysing the intercessory prayer requests left by ordinary people in a variety of church-related contexts (a recent list of these is provided by ap Siôn, 2012). The study of ordinary people's prayers offers a distinctive insight into ordinary theologies because personal prayer is often argued to lie at the heart of Christian practice, and knowing how ordinary people pray, why ordinary people pray, and what ordinary people pray can provide important insights into their perceptions of the nature of the relationships existing between themselves, the world and God.

Psychology of Religion

It is clear from the definition of ordinary theology and the empirical research tradition growing around it that this area can be informed by (as well as inform) the study of prayer in the psychology of religion. Empirical studies related to psychology and prayer were reviewed by ap Siôn and Francis (2009) in the *International Handbook of Education for Spirituality, Care and Wellbeing*, where they were placed within three distinct themes, namely: the subjective effects of prayer, investigating the correlates of prayer among those who engage in the activity; the objective effects of prayer, investigating the outcomes of prayer on those who do not know they are being prayed for (with a focus on controlled medical experiments); and the content of prayer, providing a means of studying the religion and spirituality of ordinary people. Of these three areas, questions relating to the content of personal prayer have generally been given less attention by researchers, although there has been growing interest in exploring the relationships between prayer content (or what people believe about prayer) and psychological effects.

Such interest in the relationship between prayer content and associated psychological effects is illustrated by the research tradition concerned with personal prayer and coping in health-related contexts. Although most research in this area concentrates on who uses personal prayer as a coping strategy and the perceived effectiveness of personal prayer (for example, Brown and Nicasso 1987; Ai, Bolling and Peterson 2000; Hank and Schaan 2008), a number of studies have begun to identify the specific components of personal prayer and their subjective effects. One example of this type of study includes work conducted by Krause, Chatters, Meltzer and Morgan (2000), and Krause (2004) measuring correlations between prayer expectancy (expected outcomes of prayer requests), self-esteem and race. Another example is the *Prayer Functions Scale*, which was developed by Bade and Cook (1997) and applied by Harris, Schoneman and

Carrera (2005) and Bade and Cook (2008), with a focus on how prayer is used by individuals in coping contexts.

The Study of Ordinary Intercessory Prayer

There has been a growing research tradition concerned with the content analysis of ordinary people's intercessory prayer requests left in a number of church-related contexts, including churches or shrines (ap Siôn 2007, 2008, 2009, 2010, 2011; Brown and Burton 2007; Burton 2009, 2010; Lee 2009; Schmied 2002), a cathedral (ap Siôn in press a), hospital chapels (Grossoehme 1996; Hancocks and Lardner 2007; Cadge and Daglian 2008; Grossoehme, VanDyke et al. 2010; Grossoehme, Jeffrey Jacobson et al. 2011; ap Siôn in press b), and a Church of England website (ap Siôn and Edwards 2012). There has also been one study of prayers collected on the street by Church of England bishops (ap Siôn and Edwards 2013). And see Collins, in this volume.

Although these studies have produced some useful results, which have contributed to an understanding of what people pray, many of them were single studies that were not replicated, and as a result, the wider applicability of their findings have not been tested. In addition, there has generally been little attempt to construct a robust analytical framework designed to make such replications possible. It was for this reason that ap Siôn (2007) first developed an analytical framework for intercessory prayer requests, and applied the framework to a variety of church-related intercessory prayer contexts. The ap Siôn Analytic Framework for Intercessory Prayer (apSAFIP) was employed in its original form in five studies of prayer requests (2007, 2009, 2010, 2012; ap Siôn and Edwards 2013) and in modified forms in four studies of prayer requests, where the apSAFIP was adapted to focus on particular aspects of intercessory prayer, styled as 'health and well being' (2008, 2013) and 'activity of God' (2011 in press a, in press b).

In terms of the studies employing the original form of the apSAFIP, it was shown that the instrument worked consistently well in a variety of different prayer request contexts, including those related to church prayer boards, online prayer provision, and prayers collected on the street (the latter two studies were part of the Church of England's 'Say One for Me' 2010 and 2011 Lent initiatives). It was also shown that intriguing differences emerged which were related to prayer request context (ap Siôn and Edwards 2012 and 2013). For example, when the online prayers (ap Siôn and Edwards 2012) were compared with the traditional prayer cards from previous studies (ap Siôn 2007, 2009), the following similarities and differences were observed. First, both the online requests and the prayer card requests from church prayer boards focused on 'illness' more than any other category (26 per cent for online prayers; 21 per cent and 29 per cent for prayer cards); however, when compared with the two previous prayer board studies, the online prayers had far greater focus on 'relationships' (24 per cent compared with 5 per cent and 7 per cent), 'work' (18 per cent compared with 3 per cent and 3 per cent) and 'growth' (18 per cent compared with 5 per cent and 5 per cent), and far less focus on 'death' (4 per cent compared with 16 per cent and 20 per cent) and 'open intention' (1 per cent compared with 24 per cent and 18 per cent). Secondly, both the online requests and the prayer board requests focused mainly on prayers for other people known to the prayer author; however, when compared with the two prayer board studies, the online prayers had fewer prayers for people known to the prayer author (57 per cent compared with 63 per cent and 75 per cent), more prayers for the prayer authors themselves (34 per cent compared with 4 per cent and 5 per cent), and fewer prayers for world or global issues (9 per cent compared with 27 per cent and 16 per cent) and fewer prayers for animals known to the prayer author (0 per cent compared with 5 per cent and 4 per cent). Thirdly, differences were found in the use of primary control (where the desired outcome for prayer was stated) and secondary control (where no desired outcome for prayer was stated) when the online study is compared with the two prayer board studies. The majority of the online prayers favoured primary control rather than secondary control (PC 83 per cent and SC 17 per cent), while primary control and secondary control were more evenly balanced in the two prayer board studies (SC 57 per cent and PC 43 per cent; PC 55 per cent and SC 45 per cent).

In terms of prayers collected on the streets by bishops participating in the 2011 'Say One for Me' Lent initiative (ap Siôn and Edwards 2013), the concerns reflected in the requests followed a very similar pattern to those recorded in the two earlier prayer board studies (ap Siôn 2007, 2009) rather than the 'Say One for Me' online prayers (ap Siôn and Edwards 2012). In a similar way, the predominant focus of the prayer authors on the street was on their families and friends (84 per cent). However, the prayers collected on the street exhibited one distinctive feature that set them apart from both the prayer board requests and the online prayer requests. The majority of prayers collected on the street did not make an explicit attempt to direct the prayer outcome; their concern was simply presented, using varying amounts of detail. In total, 74 per cent of the prayer requests fell into this 'secondary control category', compared with 57 per cent and 45 per cent of the earlier church-based prayer requests and 17 per cent of the 'Say One for Me' website prayer requests.

Method

Sample

Lichfield Cathedral is situated in one of the largest dioceses in the Church of England in the northwest Midlands. The Shrine of St Chad (d. 672) is located in the Cathedral and at the shrine people are invited to say a prayer, to light a candle and to fill in a prayer card. The prayer cards begin with the words, 'Please pray for' and provide four lines for the writing of the prayer request. The prayers left at the shrine are used in the Cathedral services each week. A total of 1,624 prayer cards were collected from the shrine over a two-month period from July to September 2010.

Analysis

Of the 1,624 prayer cards, 1,570 were examples of supplicatory prayer, with thanksgiving and supplication present in ten cases and adoration and supplication present in one case. The other prayer cards included 24 other language cards, 9 illegible cards, 19 thanksgiving-only cards, one adoration-only card, and one confession-only card. The analysis for this study is based on the 1,570 supplicatory prayer cards within which there were 1,658 individual prayer requests.

A content analysis of the 1,658 supplicatory prayer requests employed the ap Siôn Analytical Framework for Intercessory Prayer (apSAFIP). According to this framework, three elements intrinsic to all examples of prayer of this type are identified: prayer intention, prayer reference and prayer objective. *Prayer intention* seeks to establish the concerns of the individual prayer authors, which are categorised within eleven areas: health and illness, death, growth (affective), work, relationships, disaster and conflict, sport, travel, housing, open intention and general. *Prayer reference* seeks to establish for whom the prayer is being offered, and identifies four foci: the prayer authors themselves; other people personally known to the prayer author (friends and family); animals known to the prayer author (pets); and the world or global context. *Prayer objective* seeks to distinguish between the effects of prayer anticipated by the prayer authors, described as primary control and secondary control. Prayer authors employing primary control are explicit about the desired outcome of the prayer request, while prayer authors employing secondary control do not suggest a desired outcome. The primary control component of prayer *objective* was further delineated between prayer authors who requested material changes to the physical world and those who requested affective changes. The former is labelled primary control one (PC1) and the latter is labelled primary control two (PC2). Secondary control is referred to as SC.

Results

Table 10.1 (see page 189) presents the quantitative results relating to the analysis of the 1,658 prayer requests and the three constructs of the analytical framework: prayer intention, prayer reference and prayer objective. In relation to *prayer intention*, 464 (28 per cent) requests were concerned with health and illness, 452 (27 per cent) death, 307 (19 per cent) open intention, 144 (9 per cent) general, 81 (5 per cent) growth, 74 (4 per cent) relationships, 70 (4 per cent) conflict and disaster, 53 (3 per cent) work, 6 (0.4 per cent) housing, 6 (0.4 per cent) travel and 1 (0.06 per cent) sport.

In relation to *prayer reference* 1,426 (86 per cent) were requests for other people who were known to the prayer author (friends and family), 132 (8 per cent) for global concerns, 79 (5 per cent) for the prayer authors themselves and 21 (1 per cent) for animals known to the prayer author (pets).

In relation to *prayer objective*, primary control was employed in 839 (51 per cent) of requests and secondary control was employed in 819 (49 per cent) of requests. Of the 839 primary control requests, 803 (96 per cent) were categorised as PC2 (which requested affective prayer outcomes) and 36 (4 per cent) were categorised as PC1 (which explicitly requested God to intervene in a material sense). Of the 36 PC1 requests, 32 (88 per cent) were situated in the health and illness category.

The following exemplification of the content of these requests explores the eleven *prayer intention* categories: health and illness, death, open intention, general, growth, relationships, disaster and conflict, work, housing, travel and sport.

Health and Illness

Of the 464 prayer requests related to health and illness, 437 (94 per cent) were for other people (family and friends), followed by 16 requests for prayer authors themselves, 10 requests for global contexts, and one request for animals (pets). Of these, 268 (58 per cent) employed primary control 2, 164 (35 per cent) employed secondary control, and 32 (7 per cent) employed primary control 1.

The majority of the prayers were concerned with family and friends who had physical illnesses, which (when specified) included terminal conditions, cancer, MS and strokes among other health problems. Some prayers simply referred to family and friends as being unwell, hospitalised, or undergoing an operation. A substantial minority of requests were concerned with mental illnesses such as depression, alcohol and drug addiction, and dementia:

> Mum. In NAME Hospital having tests. NAME and NAME [SC]
> NAME from PLACE. Please help her to recover well from her illness soon. Thankyou. [PC2]
> NAME. Self worth and confidence with depression. [PC2]
> NAME (most especially battling with alcoholism) and his wife and children. Amen. [SC]
> NAME. My wife who has senile dementia and in care. Husband [SC]

For both physical and mental illness, there were cases of multiple prayers being offered by prayer authors for the same person, over the two-month period covered in this sample of prayer cards.

One group of prayers was concerned with promoting the continued health of family and friends, and this was often combined with requests for a long life and requests for affective gifts such as happiness, peace and success. Another group of prayers was concerned with healthy pregnancies and successful births of babies:

> All my family and friends to live a healthy and happy life. [PC2]
> All my friends and family and bless them with continued health, happiness and success as well as good insight and that they remain on the path of good. [PC2]
> NAME, NAME and family for health and peace. [PC2]
> NAME – safe delivery of a healthy baby [PC2]

There were relatively few examples of prayer requests using primary control 1 and where these occurred there was a clear request for divine intervention in the healing of the sick person or people concerned. In many of these requests the term 'healing' appeared to be employed in a distinctively religious way, and in one example a parallel was drawn with a healing miracle in Luke's gospel. In another example, experience of answered prayer was followed by a further request for healing. A few requests asked for the conception of a child after difficulties had been experienced in the past:

Thank you Lord for giving us this day and being with us coming around the cathedral. I love you with all my heart. NAME – and husband – He has had a tumour but now has a blood clot on the brain. Please heal him Lord. Amen. [PC1]
NAME – our prayers have helped my son come through horendous injury – my thanks and request for further healing. [PC1]
DATE NAME PLACE Suffering from kidney carcinoma. May she touch the hem of His garment. INITIALS. [PC1]
NAME whos not feeling well and make him get better thank you amen. [PC1]
DATE. I am NAME from [India] my second son and d-in-law NAME and NAME must be blessed with a son. 5 years have passed. Pray for them – Lord must bless. NAME. [PC1]

However, most of the prayer requests were less specific in stating the desired outcome of prayer or sought more affective help for the ill person and their families, such as strength, love or faith:

NAME As she faces radiotherapy and chemotherapy in her brave battle – send her your love Dear Lord. [PC2]

Prayers for health and illness set in a global context were concerned with sick people in general and the people who look after them (sometimes as part of a prayer for a sick family member or friend), the discovery of a cure for a specific disease, and the hope that God would heal 'here' (which was perhaps a reference to the prayer requests left in the Cathedral):

A cure to be found for cancer [PC2]
Bring comfort to the sick and to their carers. [PC2]
Pray for NAME and all who are ill or struggling with life. [SC]

Prayers for the authors themselves followed a broadly similar pattern to prayers for family and friends, with requests for physical and mental illnesses, the maintenance of current good health, and issues relating to starting a family:

<u>Me</u> NAME / Bad ache / bowel [SC]
NAME. I love her so much I just wish I could stop drinkin xxxx [PC2]
Keep me safe from and in good health. [PC2]

success of my IVF treatment [PC2]

Death

Of the 452 prayer requests related to death, 432 (96 per cent) were for other people (family and friends), followed by 10 requests for animals (pets), 8 requests for global contexts and 2 requests for prayer authors themselves. Of these, 259 (57 per cent) employed secondary control and 193 (43 per cent) employed primary control 2. It is probable that a number of the prayers in the large 'open intention' category were also prayers for people who had died, but insufficient detail was present to allocate these requests with confidence in the 'death' intention category.

The majority of prayers were concerned with family who had died, most often parents, grandparents, children (including babies) and partners. These ranged from very recent deaths (in the same week or within the year) to a few years previous or more. A large group of these prayers were presented as memorials and were offered around the time someone had died, on their birthday, on a wedding anniversary, or simply 'in memory of' or 'to remember' the deceased:

> NAME born sleeping DATE. My shining star love you always Grandma xxx [SC]
> Baby NAME, Happy 13th Birthday on DATE. We will always love you and
> remember you. God bless you son. [PC2]
> My wife. NAME that died on this day DATE. Your loving husband NAME. [SC]
> NAME I will love and miss you always our 52nd anniversary DATE. Wife NAME
> Grandaughter NAME [SC]

Many of these prayers were used as opportunities to express the prayer authors' emotions in relation to the deceased and in many cases to communicate directly with them. There were concerns that the deceased were happy, at peace, at rest and safe. Where it was possible to identify with confidence prayers left by children and young people, it was apparent that many were using the prayer facility in a broadly similar way to adults in these respects:

> NAME "We all miss him so much". Love from [5 NAMES] and All the
> family. [SC]
> Lasting peace for my sister (RIP). [PC2]
> NAME. Keep him safe in your arms. I miss you Grandad. Love NAME 11 and
> NAME age 7 [PC2]

Nan, I'm writing to say how much I miss you. Hope your ok! Love you always xxx [SC]

Explicitly religious language was used in a minority of the prayer requests. 'Heaven' was referred to in around 25 prayers, and a few prayers referred to an afterlife with Jesus or God in heaven, or made use of liturgical expressions such as 'may she rest in peace and rise in glory'. These illustrate some of the religious beliefs about the afterlife along with beliefs that it is possible to communicate with the dead (through addressing prayers directly to them), the dead are somehow also present to the living, and loved ones are re-united with their families at death:

> My Grandad who is in heaven and make sure his life is good PLEASE [PC2]
> Lord, How I do miss my mum and dad, keep them safe until we meet again. NAME xxx [PC2]
> NAME, killed in a car crash DATE: for her husband [NAME], sons and daughter. May she rest in peace and rise in glory. [PC2]
> Our two grandsons who are with Jesus. Love nanny and granddad xx [SC]
> My dad, hope he is always there, well I know he is, love you dad xx [PC2]

Another group of prayers were concerned with people known to the prayer authors who had lost someone close to them. Some of these prayers simply requested that a prayer be said for them, while others also expressed empathy with their situation and the hope or the request for the necessary resources to cope with their loss. There were some examples of prayers requested for others within the same grieving family:

> Please pray for NAME who lost her boyfriend NAME. She misses him every day and he is with Jesus now. Keep him safe. Thank you. [PC2]
> NAME and NAME and their loss of their beautiful daughter aged only 5 years. Bless all their family and help them through this time. [PC2]
> My Dad NAME give him strength to cope with the recent death of my beloved Mom. We all miss her so much. May our whole family get through this difficult time whilst coping with our own illnesses and problems. NAME [PC2]

Pets that have died were the subjects of some prayer requests, and it is probable that many of these were written by children. In some respects, these prayer requests have certain features in common with those left for people who have died; for example, the way prayer is used to communicate with their pets, to express the author's emotions towards them, and to hope that all is well in the afterlife:

> NAME my rabbit who died a few weeks ago. Thank you. NAME Aged 5 [SC]
> NAME. NAME is my old pet rabbit and my pet pepsi, I miss them dearly tell them I said hi x. [PC2]
> NAME, my beautiful dog you mean the world to me I hope you are happy in heven. [PC2]

Slightly fewer prayer requests were placed within a broader global context. Where this occurred, personal bereavement was often connected with empathy for others who had also lost someone, or may have been a response to the written prayer requests of others:

> For my family and the people who lost someone very close to them I am sorry for your loss. NAME age 14. [SC]
> All those who mourn. In memory of my Dad, NAME, DATES. Sadly missed by all your family and friends. NAME and NAME. [SC]
> =All who mourn including me. [SC]

Open Intention

Of the 307 prayer requests related to open intention, 270 (88 per cent) were for other people (family and friends), followed by 21 requests for global contexts, 10 requests for animals (pets) and 6 requests for prayer authors themselves. None of these prayer requests included a specific intention but explicitly identified individuals or groups who were the subjects of prayer. For family and friends, a list of names was not uncommon, and in some cases some additional information was provided relating to location, age, personal qualities and the prayer author's emotions towards them. All of these were always examples of secondary control requests:

> 7 NAMES [people]. Rocky our beloved pets – please pray for our family and pets. [SC]
> All my family here on earth and in heaven. NAME. [SC]
> NAME – a lonely lady. [SC]
> NAME 98 years, much loved! Thank you. [SC]
> All of us. [SC]
> The human race. INITIALS. [SC]

The world. [SC]

All dead (or live) pets. [SC]

General

Of the 144 prayer requests related to the general category, 125 (87 per cent) were for other people (family and friends), followed by 10 requests for prayer authors themselves, and 9 requests for global contexts. Apart from one example (which did not fit into the other categories and was a primary control 1 request), all of these were examples of primary control 2 requests because of their focus on petitioning for affective qualities or gifts:

My Mother NAME for god to protect her and give her strength and peace in her life. NAME. [PC2]

My anty NAME and please look after her. Xxxxxxxxxxxxxx. [PC2]

Lord give me courage. [PC2]

NAME. For luck. [PC2]

God bless mum and dad and mum and gran and granddads. Love and kisses NAME and NAME xx [PC2]

My phone it got scratched + it is new please make it not scratched. thx. [PC1]

Peace in Ireland [PC1]

Growth

Of the 81 prayer requests related to growth, 48 (59 per cent) were for other people (family and friends), followed by 21 requests (26 per cent) for global contexts and 12 requests (15 per cent) for prayer authors themselves. Of these, 72 (89 per cent) were primary control 2 requests and 9 (11 per cent) were secondary control requests. These prayer requests were often concerned with religious or spiritual growth, or conversion for members of the family or friends. Other requests asked for guidance and direction in general or in specific circumstances. A few requests asked that God be revealed in more global terms:

Please guide my daughter safely on DATE [PC2]

A man: that he would find his calling and purpose as did St Chad. [PC2]

A husband for NAME who loves Jesus and wants to serve him. [SC]

Salvation for (NAME and NAME) my two sons and Kelly my daughter in law – they need Jesus Christ in their lives – and for my grandson NAME for God to protect and bring him to Himself. Thank you NAME God bless you! [PC2]

> All humankind. Bring peace to earth and end all wars. [PC1]
> God's Kingdom [SC]

Relationships

Of the 74 prayer requests related to relationships, 56 (76 per cent) were for other people (family and friends), followed by 17 requests for prayer authors themselves, and one request for a global context. Of these, 49 (66 per cent) were primary control 2 requests and 25 (34 per cent) were secondary control requests. These prayer requests were often concerned with problems experienced within relationships or were requests for happiness in relationships. Those requests falling into the secondary control category simply stated the prayer context without reference to the desired outcome for the prayer:

> Healing the relationship between NAME (mother) and NAME (daughter). [PC2]
> My dear friend NAME who's father has been from her and from her family.
> Xxx [SC]
> My mum, NAME. Forgive and forget x [PC2]
> NAME and NAME – a happy marriage. [PC2]
> Our relationship and happiness. [PC2]

Disaster and Conflict

Of the 70 prayer requests related to disaster and conflict, 59 (84 per cent) were for a global context, followed by 11 requests for other people (family and friends). Almost all of these requests were either examples of secondary control (57 per cent) or primary control 2 (39 per cent), with only three examples of primary control 1 (4 per cent). The focus of these requests was either related to prominent wars or natural disasters, and occasionally a relative or friend was involved and specifically referred to. A number of prayers asked for peace in the world:

> All troops injured now at NAME hospital. They fought for our freedom. [SC]
> god bless all the people who died fighting battels of yours and mine family. Armen
> NAME 9 [PC2]
> Pakistan please help people. [PC1]
> An end to war and conflict in the world. [PC1]

Work

Of the 53 prayer requests related to work, 37 (70 per cent) were for other people (family and friends), followed by 13 requests for prayer authors themselves, and 3 requests for global contexts. Of these, 41 (77 per cent) employed primary control 2 and 12 (23 per cent) employed secondary control.

The majority of prayers in this category were for friends and family, and included requests relating to examinations at school and university, as well as employment concerns. Prayers relating to employment included finding a job and job interviews, redundancy concerns, success and happiness at work, starting new jobs and businesses, and retirement:

> For our children to receive good Grades and a safe transition to University NAME. [PC2]
> please pray NAME does not lose his job thank you [PC2]
> NAME to have financial success at work [PC2]
> NAME and NAME. They have just started a business and are feeling apprehensive. [SC]

The requests for the prayer authors themselves echoed some of these themes with particular reference to school and university examination results and job concerns; however, additional areas were also identified such as a request for a work permit and multiple prayers for a forthcoming court case (the final prayer of which reported the successful vindication of the prayer author). Where these prayers were primary control 2 requests, the desired outcomes sought were guidance, justice and strength:

> Help me to know what to choose in my forthcoming decision at work. [PC2]
> My career prospects [SC]
> All those (including myself) who are awaiting A level results next week. Pray that we all reap what we have sown. [PC2]
> NAME pray for me for my case on DATE [July 2010] at TIME. Mercy [PC2]
> For the [?] coming application for a work permit. Please pray for me. NAME [SC]

For the few requests placed within a global context, one asked for the re-opening of a local community centre, and another for financial support for a charity with which the prayer author was involved:

The [community centre] has closed and a community is now sad and lost. Pray it
can re-open soon.
Please help Talkback UK that we may find the money to keep us going. People
with learning disabilities and their family carers should have a voice. Talkback helps
them. Thank you.

Housing

Of the 6 prayer requests related to housing, 4 were for other people (family and
friends) and 2 requests were for the prayer authors themselves. These were all
primary control 2 requests. The prayers reflected the concerns of buying and
selling and property, as well as being able to retain their homes:

> NAME to have a financial breakthrough and not lose her accommodation. [PC2]
> A family new to the district to find a suitable home to purchase within budget
> Thank You [PC2]
> Me that I find a buyer for my flat so that I can move back to my roots in a quieter
> part of the country now I'm retired. [PC2]

Travel

Of the 6 prayer requests related to travel, 5 were for other people (family and
friends) and one was for a prayer author. These prayers related to specific journeys
undertaken by family and friends or the prayer author, or were concerned with
family members who lived abroad.

> That my friend has a good journey home. Love you. [PC2]
> Our trip to New Zealand that we are safe and nothing bad happens. [PC2]

Sport

There was only one request related to sport, which fell into the other people
(family and friends) category and was concerned with winning the lottery:

> I wish my Nan would win the Euromillion and buy a really big [?] [PC2]

Conclusion

The aim of this chapter has been to describe, to contextualise, and to review the use of the apSAFIP, and to apply the analytic framework to the new context of an English cathedral. Three main conclusions are drawn as a result of this process.

Firstly, the apSAFIP worked well in the new intercessory prayer context of an English cathedral. The variety of prayer requests offered at St Chad's shrine in Lichfield Cathedral over a two-month period in the summer of 2010 were accommodated well within the framework, supporting the application and extension of apSAFIP to the cathedral context. The successful application of the apSAFIP to the cathedral context has allowed the results of the present study to be compared with the results of previous studies employing the same analytic framework in other intercessory prayer contexts. This supports the argument that devising a broad framework for analysing intercessory prayer and repeatedly applying that framework to a variety of contexts make a significant contribution to understanding the phenomenon of intercessory prayer content that goes beyond that which may be provided by single empirical studies.

Secondly, when the results of this study are compared with previous studies employing the apSAFIP (ap Siôn 2007, 2009, 2012; ap Siôn and Edwards 2013) a number of similarities and differences are found. In terms of prayer intention (for what people pray), the results of this study follow a similar hierarchical pattern to that found in both the church prayer board requests and the prayers from the street with requests relating to health and illness, open intention and death appearing with much greater frequency than the other prayer intentions. However, a distinctive feature of the prayer intention results for the current study is the emphasis placed on prayers for the dead with 27 per cent falling into this category compared to the 14 per cent, 16 per cent and 20 per cent for the other studies. This may well reflect an important function of cathedral intercessory prayer facilities for those who access them and who use them as 'memorials', as ways of remembering and connecting with family and friends who have died. The responses from the current study also continue to show a very different profile from those found with online requests, which (apart from illness) have a much greater focus on growth, relationships and work. In terms of prayer reference (for whom people pray), the results of this study follow a similar hierarchical pattern to that found in the prayers collected on the streets, where in both cases over 80 per cent of prayers were classified as for 'friends and family', which is higher than the prayer board requests and substantially higher than the online requests (57 per cent). In terms of prayer objective (expressed outcome of prayers), the results of this study follow a similar hierarchical pattern to that found in the church prayer board studies, with a fairly even balance found between primary control requests (51 per cent) and secondary control requests (49 per cent). This is in stark contrast to the online prayer requests where there was much greater emphasis on primary control (83 per cent) and the prayers collected on the street where there was much greater emphasis on secondary control (74 per cent). However, for the prayer request studies that differentiated between different types of primary control (ap Siôn and Edwards 2012 and 2013), no more than 5 per cent of these requests explicitly asked for God to intervene miraculously in the physical world. These results support the trends found in the studies so far, which have indicated that Anglican church-related intercessory prayer facilities provide for (or evoke) particular responses on the part of those who use them.

Thirdly, it is recommended that more replications of studies using the apSAFIP are conducted with the aim of further mapping the content of intercessory prayer and its characteristics. The current study has focused on one sample of prayer requests left at a well-known shrine in an English cathedral over the busy holiday period of mid-July to mid-September. Analysing intercessory prayers left at other times of the year may provide some different results linked to seasonal variations and how the prayer facility is being used and by whom. There is also a need to apply the apSAFIP to other pertinent denominational contexts. To date, the apSAFIP has been applied to Anglican contexts only, and it is likely that other denominational contexts may provide different results and emphases.

References

Ai, A.L., Bolling, S.F. and Peterson, C. (2000). 'The Use of Prayer by Coronary Artery Bypass Patients', *The International Journal for the Psychology of Religion*, 10: 205–20.

ap Siôn, T. (2007). 'Listening to Prayers: An Analysis of Prayers Left in a Country Church in Rural England', *Archiv für Religionspsychologie*, 29: 199–226.

_____ (2008). 'Distinguishing between Intention, Reference, and Objective in an Analysis of Prayer Requests for Health and Well-being: Eavesdropping from the Rural Vestry', *Mental Health, Religion and Culture*, 11: 53–65.

_____ (2009). 'Ordinary Prayer and the Rural Church: An Empirical Study of Prayer Cards', *Rural Theology*, 7: 17–31.

_____ (2010). 'Implicit Religion and Ordinary Prayer', *Implicit Religion*, 13: 275–94.

_____ (2011). 'Interpreting God's Activity in the Public Square: Accessing the Ordinary Theology of Personal Prayer', in Leslie J. Francis and Hans-Georg Ziebertz (eds), *The Public Significance of Religion*, Leiden: Brill, pp. 315–42.

_____ (in press a). 'Ordinary Prayer and the Activity of God: Reading the Prayer Board in a Welsh Cathedral', in J. Astley (ed.), *Studies in Ordinary Theology*, Farnham: Ashgate.

ap Siôn, T. and Edwards, O. (2012). 'Praying "Online": The Ordinary Theology of Prayer Intentions Posted on the Internet', *Journal of Beliefs and Values*, 33: 95–109.

_____ (2013). 'Say One for Me: The Implicit Religion of Prayers from the Street', *Mental Health, Religion and Culture*, 16.8: 922–35.

ap Siôn, T. and Francis, L.J. (2009). 'Psychological Perspectives on Prayer' in M. de Souza, L.J. Francis, J. O'Higgins-Norman and D. Scott (eds), *International Handbook of Education for Spirituality, Care and Wellbeing: Part One*, Netherlands: Springer, 247–67.

ap Siôn, T. and Nash, P. (2013). 'Coping through Prayer: An Empirical Study in Implicit Religion concerning Prayers for Children in Hospital', *Mental Health, Religion and Culture*, 16.9: 936–52.

Astley, J. (2002). *Ordinary Theology: Looking, Listening and Learning in Theology*, Aldershot: Ashgate.

Astley, J. (2003). 'Ordinary theology for Rural Theology and Rural Ministry', *Rural Theology*, 1: 3–12.

Bade, M.B. and Cook, S.W. (1997, August). 'Functions and Perceived Effectiveness of Prayer in the Coping Process', Poster session presented at the annual meeting of the American Psychological Association, Chicago, IL.

Bade, M.K. and Cook, S.W. (2008). 'Functions of Christian Prayer in the Coping Process', *Journal for the Scientific Study of Religion*, 47: 123–33.

Brown, A. and Burton, L. (2007). 'Learning from Prayer Requests in a Rural Church: An Exercise in Ordinary Theology', *Rural Theology*, 5: 45–52.

Brown, G.K. and Nicassio, P.M. (1987). 'Development of a Questionnaire for the Assessment of Active and Passive Coping Strategies in Chronic Pain Patients', *Pain*, 31: 53–64.

Burton, L. (2009). 'The Dear Departed: Prayers for the Dead on a Prayer Tree in a Rural English Parish Church', *Rural Theology*, 7: 17–34.

_____ (2010). 'Prayers on a Prayer Tree: Ordinary Theology from a Tourist Village', *Rural Theology*, 8: 62–77.

Cadge, W. and Daglian, M. (2008). 'Blessings, Strength, and Guidance: Prayer Frames in a Hospital Prayer Book', *Poetics*, 36: 358–73.

Christie, A. (2007). 'Who Do You Say I Am? Answers from the Pews', *Journal of Adult Theological Education*, 4: 181–94.

_____ (2012). *Who Do You Say I Am? Answers from the Pews*, Farnham: Ashgate.

Christie, A. and Astley, J. (2009). 'Ordinary Soteriology: A Qualitative Study', in L.J. Francis, M. Robbins and J. Astley (eds), *Empirical Theology in Texts and Tables: Qualitative, Quantitative and Comparative Perspectives*, Leiden: Brill, pp. 177–96.

Grossoehme, D.H. (1996). 'Prayer Reveals Belief: Images of God from Hospital Prayers', *Journal of Pastoral Care*, 50: 33–9.

Grossoehme, D.H., Jeffrey Jacobson, C., Cotton, S., Ragsdale J.R., VanDyke, R. and Seid, M. (2011). 'Written Prayers and Religious Coping in a Paediatric Hospital Setting', *Mental Health, Religion and Culture*, 14: 423–32.

Grossoehme, D.H., VanDyke, R., Jeffrey Jacobson, C., Cotton, S., Ragsdale, J.R. and Seid, M. (2010). 'Written Prayers in a Pediatric Hospital: Linguistic Analysis', *Psychology of Religion and Spirituality*, 2: 227–33.

Hancocks, G. and Lardner, M. (2007). 'I Say a Little Prayer for You: What Do hospital Prayers Reveal about People's Perceptions of God?' *Journal of Health Care Chaplaincy*, 8: 29–42.

Hank, K. and Schaan, B. (2008). 'Cross-national Variations in the Correlation between Frequency of Prayer and Health among Older Europeans', *Research on Aging*, 30: 36–54.

Harris, J.I., Schoneman, S.W. and Carrera, S.R. (2005). 'Preferred Prayer Styles and Anxiety Control', *Journal of Religion and Health*, 44: 403–12.

Krause, N. (2004). 'Assessing the Relationships among Prayer Expectancies, Race, and Self-esteem in Late Life', *Journal for the Scientific Study of Religion*, 43: 395–408.

Krause, N., Chatters, L.M., Meltzer, T. and Morgan, D.L. (2000). 'Using Focus Groups to Explore the Nature of Prayer in Late Life', *Journal of Aging Studies*, 14: 191–212.

Lee, D.B. (2009). 'Maria of the Oak: Society and the Problem of Divine Intervention', *Sociology of Religion*, 70: 213–31.

Littler, K. and Francis, L.J. (2005). 'Ideas of the holy: the ordinary theology of visitors to rural churches', *Rural Theology*, 3: 39–54.

Schmied, Gerhard (2002). 'God Images in Prayer Intention Books', *Implicit Religion*, 5: 121.

Table 10.1   Content of intercessory and supplicatory prayer by intention, reference and objective

intention	Other People			Global			Self			Animals			Total			TOTAL
	pc1	pc2	sc	pc1	pc2	sc	pc1	pc2	sc	pc1	pc2	sc	pc1	pc2	sc	
health/illness	29	252	156	1	5	4	1	11	4	1	0	0	32	268	164	**464**
death	0	181	251	0	3	5	0	1	1	0	8	2	0	193	259	**452**
open intention	0	0	270	0	0	21	0	0	6	0	0	10	0	0	307	**307**
general	0	125	0	0	9	0	1	9	0	0	0	0	1	143	0	**144**
growth	0	42	6	0	18	3	0	12	0	0	0	0	0	72	9	**81**
relationships	0	33	23	0	0	1	0	16	1	0	0	0	0	49	25	**74**
disaster/conflict	0	5	6	3	22	34	0	0	0	0	0	0	3	27	40	**70**
work	0	28	9	0	3	0	0	10	3	0	0	0	0	41	12	**53**
housing	0	4	0	0	0	0	0	2	0	0	0	0	0	6	0	**6**
travel	0	2	3	0	0	0	0	1	0	0	0	0	0	3	3	**6**
sport	0	1	0	0	0	0	0	0	0	0	0	0	0	1	0	**1**
total	29	673	724	4	60	68	2	62	15	1	8	12	36	803	819	**1658**
TOTAL	**1426**			**132**			**79**			**21**			**1658**			**1658**

Chapter 11

An Analysis of Hospital Chapel Prayer Requests

Peter Collins

Yet it is not only for exterior reasons that prayer should command our attention, but above all because of its very great intrinsic importance. From several aspects it is in fact one of the central phenomena of religious life (Mauss 2003: 21).

Introduction

This chapter is based on research carried out in nine NHS (National Health Service) acute hospitals situated in the north east of England (Collins et al. 2007). The project was funded by NHS Estates and focused on the material culture of chaplaincies, on chaplaincies as places. Ethical approval for the study was provided both by the NHS and Durham University.

At first sight, the acute hospital appears to be a particularly good example of a secular, rational universe. However, in the UK at least, every NHS acute hospital has a team of chaplains comprising religious professionals and volunteers, whose base generally comprises a suite of rooms grouped around what is in most cases called 'the chapel'. While there is a growing academic and professional literature on various aspects of hospital chaplaincy (Holst 1984; Dykstra 1990; Ruff 1996; Orchard (ed.) 2000; Street and Battle 2003; Department of Health 2003, 2009; Mowat and Swinton 2005; Norwood 2006; Mowat 2008; Swift 2009) there is a common function of the service which has so far remained almost entirely unresearched, the prayer request (PR), those ephemeral texts left by visitors in the chapel.

In addressing this gap, this chapter is meant to be both a contribution to the study of prayer, itself shamefully neglected by sociologists and anthropologists, and to the material culture of religion. I will present our classification and preliminary analysis of over 3,000 PRs collected from the chapels of two hospitals

within the South Tees Acute Hospitals Trust between 1995 and 2006.[1] I intend
also to indicate how these transient jottings might shed light on the condition of
'religion' and 'spirituality' in the UK in the early twenty-first century.

Context: Hospital Chaplaincy

Since the creation of the British National Health Service (NHS) in 1948, acute
hospitals have been expected to attend to the religious and spiritual needs of
their patients. The 1948 legislation included a section that called on all hospitals
to establish a chaplaincy service, an aim that has since been met (Swift 2009: 42).
The roots of chaplaincy in hospitals are Christian and managed in most cases by
an Anglican priest. A more obviously ecumenical approach has been adopted
during the last few decades, but only since the 1990s has hospital chaplaincy
attempted to cater for a far broader, multi-faith constituency. While chaplaincy
facilities are available in all acute hospitals, they can vary considerably in terms
of size, location, staffing and organisation. The chapel itself (which may in some
hospitals be called a 'prayer room' or 'multi-faith space') might be high church
elaborate (for instance at the Royal Victoria Hospital, Newcastle) or plainly
functional (at the Newcastle General Hospital). They may be integral to the
design of the building (at the City Hospital Sunderland) or constructed as a
separate entity (the Memorial Hospital, Darlington). In this regard the nine
hospitals we investigated were typically diverse. In this chapter, however, we will
focus almost entirely on the chaplaincy at JCUH, the James Cook University
Hospital, a large hospital situated in the suburbs of Middlesbrough.

The chaplaincy facility of JCUH is located along an internal corridor just
to the left of one of the two main entrances and is clearly signposted. The space
allocated to the chaplaincy in this instance comprises a chapel, two offices, a
seminar room and a Muslim prayer room with separate washing facilities. The
chapel itself (see Figure 1 below), carved out of existing space, was improved
in 2000 but conforms to the general design of other hospital rooms. However,
there are various artefacts that give the game away, as it were. The furniture is
arranged rather like a typical church, two banks of chairs divided by a narrow
aisle, facing what would generally be taken to be 'the front', marked by a lectern,

---

[1]   Middlesbrough General Hospital (MGH), situated in the town centre, was
demolished in 2002 and several of its departments were transferred to the second hospital,
The James Cook University Hospital (JCUH), a large hospital situated in the suburbs of
Middlesbrough. The earlier PRs (about 1000 of them) were collected from MGH, while the
rest were collected from JCUH. All PRs were stored at the JCUH.

table/altar, (electric) piano and hymn board. In addition, there is a movable cross that is often located on the table/altar. There is an aumbry for the Reservation of the Holy Sacrament, and items used during the Christian liturgy (chalice, patten, wine, wafers, etc.) are stored in a locked cupboard. Further clues clearly define the space as Christian, the display of flowers, the lectern cloth decorated with overtly Christian symbols and the words alpha and omega, signifying Jesus Christ. At the back of the room is a bookcase containing pamphlets relating to both health and illness and the religious life. There is a tabernacle directly opposite the entrance. Unusually (due to health and safety regulations), there is also a stand on which visitors can light a votive candle. The windows in the left wall are false, represent the sea, and were designed specifically to key in with the hospital's 'theme', Captain James Cook, explorer and local hero. The hospital chaplain explained during interview that the glasswork is intentionally ambiguous, thereby attempting not to alienate either those 'of faith or of no faith at all'. I will return to this issue below. Although situated on a major corridor adjacent to a main entrance, the chapel is generally quiet, though the voices of passers-by can be heard. The ceiling is clad with sound reducing tiles and visitors need to pass through two heavy doors in gaining access to the chapel (for a more detailed description of chaplaincy facilities at JCUH see Collins et al. 2007).

Figure 11.1   Chapel at The James Cook University Hospital. Photograph by the author

Prayer Requests

It is usual for hospital chaplains in the UK to provide materials in their chapel required to write PRs. In 2006 the lead chaplain at JCUH gave the author a set of PRs written between 1995 and 2005 that he hoped would contribute to our research on hospital chaplaincy. Lined sheets of A4 paper were the norm up until 2002. These sheets specified the date, ward, bed (seldom completed) and name (of the person to be prayed for). Each sheet is headed 'Please pray for those listed below'. In later years, other formats were made available, including A4 pads of lined paper, and smaller sheets of various sizes. The intention was to enable people to write longer pieces if they felt the need, and these less structured formats certainly facilitated greater variability in PRs (just visible on the wooden stand situated on the altar just below the cross in Figure 1). The collection also contains a variety of other formats, including bought cards and notepaper both decorated and undecorated. PRs have not so far been left in the Muslim prayer room adjacent to the chapel, but chaplains told us that they have been found in various locations around the hospital.

At the end of each day a member of the chaplaincy team would read the prayer requests left in the chapel and respond appropriately. A4 pads would be returned to the altar while individual and separate sheets of paper and similar ephemera would be removed and stored in a cupboard in the chaplaincy offices. There may be similar and perhaps more complete collections of prayer requests stored in hospitals around the country but as far as I know they have not been analysed. This is a more or less unique data set, the only other comparable material described in the academic literature is presented in Gilliat-Ray (2005), based on research undertaken at the chapel in the Millennium Dome (London), and in Cadge and Daglian (2008), who offer an interpretation of PRs left at the Johns Hopkins Memorial Hospital. The JCUH PRs provide an invaluable resource not only because of the light they shine on the meaning of the chapel and chaplaincy for users which could not easily be gleaned in any other way, but because they also provide a squint window, as it were, onto British vernacular religion at the turn of the millennium.

An Overview of JCUH Prayer Requests

The importance of this data set, comprising 3,243 PRs in all, lies in the fact that their writing was not prompted by a researcher. Whatever the motive of the person writing a PR, it was not a result of being asked by an academic! In an important sense, this is a study of ephemera, of texts that are apparently of little consequence in that each piece is a found object, a material inscription not intended for publication. As ephemera, the PR belongs in a class which includes, letters to the milkman, inscriptions on tombstones, and coins in wells – which we shall return to below. They are also documents, those artefacts largely ignored by social scientists that are, nonetheless, interpretable; that say something about the society in which we live (Riles 2006).

We use the term 'PR' as a shorthand here noting that this term refers to the form of the text rather than its content, PRs vary in several ways. All English hospital chapels visited by the author (about 60) make available a book, store of cards or lined paper on which visitors can write a PR or some other note or message. The earlier PR sheets are lined, constraining the writer, and most entries (2,521) are just a sentence or two in length, often just a name, 'My friend (name)', 'My dad (name)', 'To my dearest mam (name) who I miss so much', 'To Baby (name) – get well soon', '(name) undergoing treatment for cancer', 'Please pray for (name) to find suitable employment and get well soon'. In such cases, the request for prayer is most likely directed at the chaplains. A few are very long and fill an A4 page or more. The lined paper format does tend to encourage people to copy the content/structure of previous requests, a practice also noted by Gilliat-Ray (2005), and Cadge and Daglian (2008). The set does, however, include examples of many other formats, including cards of one sort or another, including one with a prayer or psalm printed on one side, and also loose sheets of paper of various kinds – these facilitate a wide variety of responses.

Of the 3,243 PRs collected, 1,640 are clearly repeats – suggesting that for some people the need to inscribe their hopes and fears is a recurrent need. In such cases the place of PRs in narratives of people's lives is particularly evident. The great majority are, like those analysed by Cadge at the Johns Hopkins Memorial Hospital (Cadge and Daglian 2008), either prayers of thanks or petition, or both of these. While pre-printed PR sheets described above naturally determine the form of submission and generate petitionary PRs, less prescriptive formats tend, unsurprisingly, to facilitate more varied PRs. However, many PRs presented on cards tend also to fall into one or both of these types:

> Dearest Lord
> Please give
> our darling (name)
> peace and
> rest while he is in
> for treatment.

Loving wife,
son, grandson,
mother and
family.

In this case the writer was evidently a woman, and while the gender of the writer is often impossible to determine, 366 are identifiable by name (or title) as female and 125 as men, the remainder either being jointly composed by members of both sexes or unattributable by gender. There are, then, probably more submitted by women than men – indicating a greater willingness of women to engage in public displays of religiosity. Direct observation in the chapel certainly supports this assumption. There is considerable evidence, also, to support the claim that women (in the UK) pray more regularly than men (Tearfund 2007). This tendency is noted by a number of contemporary writers describing religious faith and practice in the US (Baker 2008) and UK (Davie 1994).

We looked at the relation between the writer and the subject of the PR. A large proportion were written on behalf of family members, including 181 definitely written by individuals on behalf of a parent or parents. The fact that we suspect the number to be far higher confirms the common sense assumption that prayers are most likely to refer to close kin (and close friends). However, at least 66 PRs were written on behalf of the writer themselves, 'Please Lord help me though this difficult time. Lord Hear my prayers. From (name)'. There were in fact many more which refer to the writer but which also refer to others or to more general and sometimes abstract subjects. While these particular requests seem to conflict with one of the key 'rules of prayer' (that prayer should not be selfish) they appear to represent a last resort on the part of desperate people, those who are 'at their wits end'. They may also point to the growing individualism said to characterise modernity (Giddens 1991). It is possible that indirect requests were deemed more appropriate in petitioning God than direct commands, particularly those that might be considered 'selfish' (see also Brown 2001). In cases where a person begins by petitioning God regarding their own health, they often balance this apparent selfishness by going on to include others:

Thank you to the Holy Family, all Angels, and Saints for prayers answered. Please let me be free of cancer to be well and healthy. God bless and protect us all always. Bless the surgeons, doctors nurses and everyone in this hospital for their kindness to all who enter here. God bless the families of all patients. Please give them strength and faith in you Dear God.

We found a significant number of PRs were written by groups on behalf of a single subject – as if greater numbers lent greater force to the PR. Indeed an important role of the chapels is that of collective worship and group PRs can be seen as an example of this. The JCUH chapel is used for religious and non-religious meetings of one sort and another. A thanksgiving service, officially a humanist ceremony, was held to commemorate the life of a doctor who had worked at the hospital. The messages that people wrote following that gathering range from those which are explicitly religious to those which are entirely secular. It is clear in this case that the space is constructed on the basis of the individual's beliefs or world-view.

Given the location of the chapel (in an acute hospital), it is unsurprising that a large proportion of PRs (779) are explicitly related to sickness and health. Furthermore, a further 324 of those not specifically related to health concern the death in hospital of a loved one and thus directly related to health. In this regard, it is interesting that Gilliat-Ray's analysis of Millennium Dome requests also turned up a relatively large number of PRs relating to health (Gilliat-Ray 2005). Given that they may articulate a person's greatest immediate fears and anxieties, it is clear that prayers function, in large part, as a coping mechanism (see also Cadge and Daglian 2008). Here is the possibility of a talking cure which is simpler to perform and considerably less expensive than psychotherapy.

Whom do the PRs address? In 388 cases, it is clearly the hospital chaplain alone, and in a further 77 cases, the chaplain along with one or more others. There were 221 PRs explicitly directed to 'God' and 114 to 'Lord' and a further 27 addressed to an explicitly religious agent (such as 'the Pope', 'Our Lady of Lourdes', 'Almighty Father'). These cases multiply if one includes examples where the addressed is multiple for example 'the Lord and staff'. Indeed, in relation to the latter, a significant number of prayers are addressed entirely to some secular agency, the most common being 'hospital staff', 'A huge thanks to all those in A&E for saving my son's life'. The extent to which such notes are 'prayers' is a moot point – the writer wants to inscribe their thanks which might seem more permanent (and more public?) than a spoken utterance which is fleeting and somehow less substantial. Certainly, the writer believes that it is important to inscribe their gratitude to this social other, and the chapel is one place where they find an opportunity to do this.

Other PRs simply say 'thank you' for the chapel and/or chaplaincy, providing evidence (apart from the observations of chaplains themselves) that the chapel provides a useful space for those who need to stop and perhaps rest a while. In 1,728 cases, the PR articulates the love felt by one person for another without any overtly religious expression, though of course, here, we enter the realms of 'the spiritual'. Occasionally, the writer generalises from a single individual to a category of people, 'everyone in heaven' or 'all those who are sitting exams'.

Religiosity is indexed by use of certain terms, including 'Amen' (91 times), also 'faith', 'miracle', 'heaven', 'soul', 'mercy' and 'sins'. However, some PRs included the term 'kisses' with a turn towards the informal and perhaps increasingly secular. The language and tone of these PRs suggests that writers assume a deity (usually 'God') who is both 'there' and 'willing to listen'. For example, 'Hi God, its (sic) me again. Today I've been wondering what its like up there. I hope everyone is happy. Speak to you again soon'. This is, then, an anthropomorphic God – a God that one can approach without fear, one that is reasonable and from whom one might expect a response.

There is a measure of religious diversity in the PRs. A few are addressed to Allah, another requesting a Baha'i prayer, another concerning a gypsy fortune teller. It should be said, however, that these represent a tiny proportion of PRs which, where manifestly religious, are mainly Christian in perspective. This suggests that the Chapel is not perceived to be an obviously multi-faith space. Muslims will gravitate in any case to the prayer room in which there has been no provision for writing PRs.

PRs often contain qualifiers such as 'If it is God's will ...', which serves to indicate the omnipotence of God. The remainder of the PRs refer to specific though broad categories of people, 'all those who have suffered', 'the bereaved', 'members of the armed forces', 'sinners', the victims of natural disasters and so forth. There is an overwhelming tendency, then, for the PRs to be other-oriented and this in itself may be described as a spiritual if not religiously inspired orientation. 1,283 of the PRs are overtly religious in content. Just 13 entries are submitted by individuals who claim to be agnostics who are, as one put it, 'turning to God in a desperate time of need'. There are only three categorically non-religiously oriented PRs – substantiating Bruce's claim that atheists are rare in Britain (Bruce 1995). While the entries in the Millennium Dome discussed by Gilliat-Ray (2005: 296) 'were strikingly free from the typical language and terminology of prayer', this is not true of JCUH PRs. While there is considerable variety with regards structure, the majority are couched in prayer-like language. Furthermore, the relatively large number of people making requests to the Chaplain, to God, The Lord, Jesus, Mary Mother of God, and so forth. However, attempting to relate prayer and religiosity in any simple way is a mistake. As one person wrote, 'I'm not a very religious person but I pray every night'.

The purpose of PRs is very diverse. A key theme is 'love' (509 PRs) generally expressed towards an individual; related to these are those which relate to someone 'missed' (163) or 'valued' (114). Other, fewer, expressions of love are directed towards God and Jesus. Submissions frequently included pleas for 'help' (351), 'strength' (258), 'healing' (202), to 'look after/watch over' (167), 'peace' (155), 'to be kept safe' (129), 'hope' (51), 'comfort' (28) and 'support' (27).

Eighty-nine requests involved the idea (if not the term) 'remembrance'. In these (and some others) allusions are made to 'heaven', 'those up above' 'watching over us' or 'with God'. As well as the use of PRs for this purpose, hospital chapels will in most cases maintain a book of remembrance – and often two (one for adults and one for children). JCUH still, despite increasingly restrictive health and safety regulations, offers visitors the opportunity to light votive candles. Commemoration is a key function of chapel use, then. Such functions are possible because the space might be seen as liminal – as a space between hospital space and the space of everyday life. Turner (1969) indicates the extraordinariness of liminal space (and time) which he believes is perceived to stand in opposition to ordinary (or profane) space. The chapel provides the space and the time to inscribe what is on one's mind probably at a time of increased emotionality. It is possible, but would be hard to prove, that inscribing these thoughts and feelings help the person make them easier (both in the emotional and cognitive sense) to understand and cope with. One writer put it as follows, '... I know you are taking her so she can carry on helping people forever. In your goodness you have seen fit to prevent any more pain ... now give me strength to cope'.

This set of PRs suggests that the chaplain's remit to cater for those of all faiths and none is met – at least to an extent. The diversity of PRs in terms of structure and content suggest that visitors relate to the chapel, the hospital, to God and others, in a variety of ways. Although there is, typically, a tension between the sacred and secular orders in the hospital, the benign environment of the hospital chapel seems to encourage the tension to be played out in a number of intriguing ways.

Further Reflections on this Taxonomy

Having stepped onto the lowest rung of analysis through the classification of the PRs, what follows is a number of tentative, even speculative – and admittedly terse – reflections intended to develop this analysis in a variety of directions. My aim, here, is to establish what might seem fairly obvious comparison, alongside others which may be rather more surprising, with the objective of generating further discussion on this almost entirely neglected mode of discourse.

Prayer and Prayer Requests

The literature on prayer is dominated by theologians and clerics, who attempt in their writing to lead people to 'true prayer'. However, the phenomenon has been largely ignored by social scientists, and empirical studies are rare (Giordan 2012). Marcel Mauss, both anthropologist and sociologist, published an unfinished, though important, account of prayer in 1909. Mauss wanted, above all, to present prayer as a fundamentally social phenomenon (2003: 32–6), as one might expect of the nephew of Émile Durkheim and leading member of the *L'Année Sociologique* school. According to Mauss:

> A prayer is not just the effusion of a soul, a cry which expresses a feeling. It is a fragment of a religion. In it one can hear the echo of numberless phrases; it is a tiny piece of literature, it is the product of the accumulated efforts of men and women over generations. What we are saying is that prayer is beyond doubt a social phenomenon because the social character of religion is now sufficiently well established ... Even when prayer is individual and free, even when the worshippers choose freely the time and mode of expression, what they say always uses hallowed language and deals with hallowed things, that is, ones endorsed by social tradition (ibid.: 33).

It is illuminating to revisit Mauss's account of prayer in this study of prayer requests both in order to identify differences and similarities. In the first place Mauss, adopting the evolutionary perspective common at the time, underlines the importance of prayer in our understanding of religion; he writes: 'The evolution of prayer is in part the evolution of religion itself, the progress made by prayer is similar to that made by religion' (2003: 23–6).

Mauss (ibid.: 57) defines prayer as 'a religious rite which is oral and bears directly on the sacred'. Although it might seem obvious that, if nothing else, prayer 'bears directly on the sacred', this is not true of all PRs, even if we stretch the meaning of 'the sacred' beyond what is reasonable. For Mauss prayer is speech (ibid.: 23), and 'does not exist apart from some form of ritual' (ibid.: 33). On both counts, Mauss seems to be excluding prayer requests from his definition of prayer. Given his evolutionist perspective, and his Durkheimian tendency to begin by identifying 'elementary forms' his focus on spoken prayer is unsurprising. However, the first characteristic of the PR is its textual nature, it is a written document, and we would widen Mauss's definition to include this characteristic of some prayers. Mauss analysed many accounts of prayer as demonstrated in 'primitive religion'. Again, his focus led him to emphasise the close, even necessary relationship between prayer and ritual. This necessary relationship is not always apparent in PRs, though it may not be entirely absent. However his evolutionism led him to predict that: 'Beliefs for their part become intellectualised and, growing less and less material and detailed, are being reduced to an even smaller number of dogmas, rich and varied in meaning. While becoming more spiritual, religion has tended to become increasingly individualistic' (2003: 23–4). And lest we make the mistake of assuming that his perspective was a narrow and dry view of prayer, the following passage indicates clearly that, for Mauss, prayer is multifaceted and dynamic:

> Infinitely supple, it has taken the most varied forms, by turns adoring and coercive, humble and threatening, dry and full of imagery, immutable and variable, mechanical and mental. It has filled the most varied roles, here it is a brusque demand, there an order, elsewhere a contract, an act of faith, a confession, a supplication, an act of praise, a hosanna (2003: 21).

The OED defines prayer as: 'A solemn request to God, a god, or other object of worship; a supplication or thanksgiving addressed to God or a god'. Certainly, 'talking to God' is generally taken as the key definition characteristic of prayer (Phillips 1965). Given this generally accepted definition, there might be a tendency to assume that since the writer is responding to an invitation to submit a *prayer* request that all prayer requests are therefore necessarily prayers. Indeed, a large proportion of the PRs are easily recognisable as taking the form of prayer. For instance many represent some attempt to achieve ontological security, a large number are directed at God, or some deity.

But 'talking to God' is no simple matter, particularly if a person has no clear idea of what 'God' is. For this reason I do not think that it is helpful simply to exclude all those items in the set that seem to fall outside the dictionary definition of prayer. Prayer requests are not, or at least are not necessarily, prayers as usually conceived, and can be considered a form *sui generis*. There are examples here of what appear to be concrete poems, doodles, nonsense; there is a letter in an envelope, addressed to 'God', that has been torn into a hundred pieces, a series of cartoons, drawings of those being prayed for, of Father Christmas, The Virgin Mary, Jesus, and characters from the Bible and from mythology; there are Christmas cards, letters of several pages, and essays on various subjects. The prayer request is a material object and may be a token of many different things. As the taxonomy indicates, while a PR may be an inscribed prayer, it may also be a statement of intent, an admission of guilt, a drawing or cartoon, or a smutty comment or remark. The point is that all these various forms are presented as, in one sense or another, acceptable as prayer requests. Perhaps the most important shared characteristic is their very framing.

Framing

This study is, then, a study of ephemera, of texts that are apparently of little consequence in that each piece is a found object, a material inscription not intended for publication. Thus, it belongs in a class which includes letters to the milkman and inscriptions on tombstones. However, while the PR has little else in common with a note in a milk bottle, it is similar to the tombstone inscription in one very significant aspect, its framing (Goffman 1974; Cadge and Daglian 2008). Whatever the content of the chaplaincy PRs – and whatever their structure – they are framed as 'religious' and/or 'spiritual' documents by virtue of their physical context. I described the way in which the material culture of the chapel ensures that it will be presented and will be read as an overtly Christian space. Visitors are invited to write a 'prayer request'. The majority of those who do endeavour, with greater or lesser success, are producing, in material form, what we might agree is a form of prayer. The variety of forms is almost certainly a result of the ambient social and individual ambivalence with regard to 'religion', as well as the sheer individuality of authors, each of whom has a unique biographical trajectory. And let us remember that Mauss, despite his overwhelming emphasis on the social nature of prayer also wrote:

> But when we say prayer is a social phenomenon, we do not mean that it is in no way an individual phenomenon. That would be a misunderstanding of our thesis. We do not think that society, religion and prayer are extraordinary things, that is, are conceivable without the individuals who live within them. But we do believe that, while it takes place in the mind of the individual, prayer is above all a social reality outside the individual and in the sphere of ritual and religious convention (2003: 37).

Ambiguous Religion

Despite the framing of PRs as religious/spiritual texts, their identity is made less certain as the meaning of the terms 'religion' and 'spirituality' have grown increasingly contentious both among academics and within the public sphere since the mid-twentieth century. What has been called 'the secularization thesis' is now a lengthy discourse involving many academics, not only sociologists. There is insufficient space here to discuss this debate in any depth but I have included a range of references in the bibliography representing the work on scholars central to that debate (Berger 1971, 1999; Bruce 1992, 1995, 2002; Casanova 1994; Davie 1994; Martin 1969, 1978, 2005; Taylor 2007; Wilson 1966, 1998). The argument has raged over the 'decline' of religion in modern society – an observation already prevalent among the 'founding fathers' of sociology, notably Marx, Durkheim and Weber. Unsurprisingly, the key problematic concerns the definition of 'decline'. While it is relatively easy to prove that attendance at worship by Anglicans in the UK has declined in recent decades, it is rather more difficult to prove that religious belief has similarly reduced (Davie 1990, 1994).

During the past twenty years, attention has shifted from the concept of 'religion' (which is often taken to mean traditional, institutionalised religious practice), towards 'spirituality' (which is more individualised, less obviously visible and therefore less amenable to empirical research). Indeed some have spoken of a 'spiritual revolution' (Heelas and Woodhead 2005). Even among hospital chaplains there is a strong sense that chapel users are more likely to identify themselves as spiritual rather than religious. In practice, this has meant that the goal of hospital chaplaincy to 'provide for those of all faiths and none' has become a considerable challenge. The nine chapels comprising our study meet this challenge in various ways, though in each case, the space remains primarily Christian. While prayer rooms are increasingly provided for Muslim staff, patients and visitors, other faiths have little choice but to make do with a space that is overtly Christian.

In contemporary British society, religious belief is extraordinarily varied. Belief might still be a composite formed through processes of socialisation and discipline within a faith group, but is more likely to represent the fragmented narrative of an individual's unique biographical trajectory, a cut-and-paste process which is dynamic, which struggles to comprehend what there might be beyond the quotidian. Chaplains recognise this overwhelming plurality and understand that chapel space might well alienate those of other faiths, but in particular those who claim no religious affiliation, or more likely, nominal affiliation (Day 2011). Several scholars have drawn our attention to the complexity of the belief/nonbelief spectrum, including Storm (2009) who spoke of 'fuzzy fidelity'.[2] Towler (1984) analysed the voluminous correspondence between John Robinson, the Bishop of Woolwich and author of *Honest to God* (1963), and members of the public who wrote to him in response to that book. Many of these letters included accounts of their authors' beliefs. Setting aside the nominally

---

[2]   After Zinnbauer et al. (1997).

Christian tenor of the letters, Towler focuses on the practical outcome of an individual's beliefs, on what he calls 'conventional belief'. He identifies five types of 'religiousness' in the letters: exemplarism, conversionism, theism, gnosticism and traditionalism. Suffice it to say, here, that each represents a quite different understanding of Christianity. He notes, most significantly in this context, that individuals hold beliefs regarding the spirit, the transcendent realm, and the nature of humanity that are quite different from and even contradictory to religious and metaphysical systems. Towler's analysis suggests that even among those who identify themselves as 'Christian', there exists an extraordinary dynamism in the variety or types of religiosity. There are tensions here, as well as ambiguities and contradictions. The following are a few examples:

> Altho I don't really believe in god, I think that jesus was a good person who can
> help others. So please can you make (name) better soon.
> Still miss you millions (name). Lots of love, (name).
> Dear God in heaven save my dad and I will be with you for evermore.

Given the immense complexity of belief/nonbelief it is hardly surprising that hospital chaplains are faced with a considerable challenge. Two strategies are most regularly employed to mitigate against this negative outcome. First, the paraphernalia of Christian liturgy is generally made portable – stored away out of sight except when needed. In several chapels, however, a large cross (and in one case crucifix) remains visible when permanently fixed to the wall and other items (including the aumbry) are difficult to hide. A second strategy is to include items, especially artworks, which are considered 'uplifting', 'inspiring' and so forth, but which are not overtly religious. Most common are representations of the natural environment, including photographs, paintings, tapestries and abstract art. In some cases, artists have been commissioned to produce works which simultaneously capture the 'religious' the 'spiritual' and that which is neither, a colourful sunset which might be cruciform for instance, or a seascape that might remind one of a verse from Genesis, or another of the potential of the self, and another of the beauty of the natural world. The range of PRs, even greater I suspect than John Robinson's letters, both reflect this apparent ambivalence and ambiguity, and at the same time contribute to it.

Prayer and Healing

In recent years there has emerged a growing literature on the relationship between religion/spirituality and health. There is a rapidly growing literature – both popular and academic – on the relationship between spirituality and health (see for example, Cobb, Puchalski and Rumbold 2012; Meier, O'Connor and Van Katwyk 2005; Robinson, Kendrick and Brown 2003). Hundreds of studies have examined this relationship in an attempt to discover whether or not religious beliefs and experiences can have a positive effect on health, the majority of which focus on the person offering the prayer, and 'especially on the measurable benefits to the person' (Wuthnow 2008: 333). Many focus in particular on prayer as a coping mechanism (Giordan 2012). The role that prayer requests (PRs) play in hospital chapels suggests that there is an abiding folk belief that prayer can work for the benefit of the sick.

While the outcome of prayer is naturally an important issue, and some of these PRs do speak of outcomes (though hardly measurable outcomes), they have much to say in addition. Given that the PRs were offered in a hospital chapel one might be forgiven for assuming that they would typically petition for the recovery of a loved one – and many do. Wuthnow (ibid.: 335) claims that: 'Prayer is not so much about the sheer belief that gods exist or function in certain ways; it is more about relationships between those who pray and those to whom prayers are offered'. While it is true that many of these PRs can be simply understood as petitionary, even incantatory or spell-like (Phillips 1965: 112–30), many speak of the significance of well-being rather than sickness:

> Jesus. We don't expect dad to be the way he was before but we pray that he will soon be happy and more content soon.
>
> Can you please pray that (name) will be more like their old cheerful self when they leave this hospital. And help him see that he has so much going for him.

and of healing not illness but relationships:

> Dear God I am so sorry for being mean to my mam please make her well again.
>
> Oh Lord, they say that every cloud has a silver lining and so this terrible illness is bringing me and my little sister closer together after such a long time. Please let her operation work out OK.

Wishing and Praying

If we are willing to accept that the submission of PRs constitutes a constellation of possible actions, then the search for comparisons, for those actions which have a 'family resemblance' (Wittgenstein 1953) outside of what we would understand as 'prayer', is both straightforward and interesting. PRs would seem to be related to those actions which seek to effect a particular future. I have space here for just one example. There is a relatively large literature, especially within folklore studies, relating to wishing, and particularly with reference to wishing wells. Rattue (1995), in his historical overview of holy wells, describes what he calls the 'hydrolotatrus instinct', which he shows to be common not only in Roman and Celtic Britain but across the ancient world, 'the spring or well is the repository of spiritual power' (21). Coins and other objects have for centuries been tossed down wells and into fountains by those wishing to determine the course of future events.

In the Roman and Greek worlds, such places were religious sites, inhabited by the gods and their minions. Nowadays, we observe that the hydrolotatrus instinct continues to prompt people to drop coins not only into genuine wells and fountains, but into their obviously fake counterparts at tourist sites, which suggests that we are dealing less with religious/spiritual beliefs and more with superstition, fate and luck. In a recent article Hu and Law (2007) describe the development of a piece of community-ware which involves 'the concept of a network-mediated system for making wishes and sending them remotely to people whom we care about' (2007: 80). They believe that such a system would be helpful to those facing personal crises, that this 'system will have positive emotion effects on both the wish-senders and the wish receivers' (2007: 80). The chaplaincy staff we interviewed believed that this was a key component of PRs, except of course, the 'wish receivers' may not be aware of the wish-givers' action.

While the PRs are more likely to demonstrate 'hopes' rather than 'wishes' the two intentions are closely related, even overlapping in their meaning. When people wish, we must assume that they hope the wish is granted. Hu and Law (2007: 80) establish that wishes are either 'me-oriented':

A little prayer for my operation this afternoon. J.

or 'them-oriented':

For all who work here, caring for the sick, for all the sad, lonely and depressed. (Name)

Most of the PRs are other-directed, although there are plenty of exceptions. There are PRs, however, which elide this simple dichotomy in various ways, for instance in those cases where a 'wish' is explicitly 'them' oriented but implicitly meant to benefit 'us' (as patient or friend or family member):

Dear Lord, give the consultants wisdom and a listening heart – in Jesus name – Amen.

Conclusion

The PR is a form of document *sui generis* and diverse in both form and function. Like oral prayers, PRs are communicative acts. As Bender (2008: 477–9) suggests, prayer is generally an attempt made by a person to communicate with God (or some other supernatural entity). However, while the writers of PRs apparently intend to communicate, their target may be some supernatural agent, a person (living or dead), a group or institution, some inanimate object, or sometimes their self. Partly for this reason, the PR may be more or less 'religious', more or less 'spiritual'. What is perhaps most significant about the PRs is their existence, their very production, rather than their content, structure or function. The PRs, together, suggest that making material (and public) one's deepest emotions is a necessary, meaningful and social act.

If prayer provides the criteria for deciding what is religious what do PRs speak of? They speak eloquently of the continued need among many people not to rely exclusively on the scientific and the rational during times of personal crisis. Few, if any, writers deny the value of clinical practice, but the majority appear to believe that such work can be supplemented by appeal to that which exists on the other side of science and technology. The PRs point also to the significance of hope in times of despair; hope that may or may not be inspired by religious belief. Most significantly the PRs provide yet more evidence that belief is very often complex, diffuse and ambiguous; belief may or may not be hitched to religious faith and practice. The emotions and ideas that comprise a person's beliefs are rarely systematic and may embrace profound tensions and contradictions.

The set of PRs represents a large and probably unique data set. While there are undoubtedly patterns in terms of structure and content, I would not want to underestimate the extraordinary variety of submissions. It is important to remember, also, that only a tiny fraction of chapel users write PRs and only a miniscule proportion of hospital users ever enter the chapel. It remains true however, that these writings conclusively prove that the chapel is an important resource for many people, people who are suffering, who are most likely worried, stressed, anxious and afraid.

In this study, we began (but do not end) with the PRs themselves – they reach us unadorned by subjects' glosses, explanations, comments or revelations.

Cadge and Daglian (2008) refer, on several occasions, to the absence of data that might elucidate the motivation and intention of writers, and their perception of the outcome of their PR. All we have to go on, apart from the PRs, the context, and ad hoc comments from chaplaincy staff, are the PRs themselves. Somehow, however, these small, largely unregarded documents speak volumes – about hospitals and the bio-medical approach to health and illness, about the tension between the secular and the sacred on the one hand and between the spiritual and the religious on the other; they speak of suffering and compassion, of belief and its absence. Despite their brevity, together they illuminate not only hospital life in Britain today, but also the ambiguity which characterises the nature of belief.

Acknowledgments

I would like to thank Natalie Coe, who tabulated the data and produced an initial taxonomy, and NHS Estates and Facilities who kindly funded the research on which this paper draws (Pathfinders Grant P(05) 04).

References

Baker, Joseph O. (2008). 'An Investigation of the Sociological Patterns of Prayer Frequency and Content', *Sociology of Religion* 69/2, 169–85.
Bender, Courtney (2008). 'How Does God Answer Back?' *Poetics* 36, 476–92.
Berger, Peter (1999). '*The Desecularization of the World:* A Global Overview'. In *idem* (ed.), *The Desecularization of the World. Resurgent Religion and World Politics*. Grand Rapids, MI: Eerdmans, 1–18.
_____ (1971). *A Rumour of Angels, Modern Society and the Rediscovery of the Supernatural*. Harmondsworth: Penguin Books.
Brown, Callum (2001). *The Death of Christian Britain. Understanding Secularisation 1800–2000*. London: Routledge.
Bruce, Steve (ed.) (1992). *Religion and Modernization, Sociologists and Historians Debate the Secularization Thesis*. Oxford: Clarendon.
_____ (1995). *Religion in Modern Britain*. Oxford: Oxford University Press.
_____ (2002). *God is Dead. Secularization in the West*. Oxford: Blackwell.
Cadge, Wendy and M. Daglian (2008). 'Blessings, Strength, and Guidance, Prayer Frames in a Hospital Prayer Book', *Poetics* 36, 358–73.

Cobb, Mark, Christina M. Puchalski and Bruce Rumbold (2012). *Oxford Textbook of Spirituality in Healthcare*. Oxford: Oxford University Press.

Casanova, Jose (1994). *Public Religions in the Modern World*. Chicago, IL: University of Chicago Press.

Collins, Peter, Simon Coleman, Jane Macnaughton and Tessa Pollard (2007). *NHS Hospital 'Chaplaincies' in a Multi-faith Society. The Spatial dimension of Religion and Spirituality in Hospital*. NHS Estates.

Davie, Grace (1990). 'Believing Without Belonging, is this the Future of Religion in Britain?' *Social Compass*, 37, 456–69.

_____ (1994). *Religion in Britain since 1945. Believing Without Belonging*. Oxford: Blackwell.

Day, Abby (2011). *Believing in Belonging, Belief and Social Identity in the Modern World*. Oxford and New York: Oxford University Press.

Department of Health (2003). NHS Chaplaincy, *Meeting the Religious and Spiritual Needs of Patients and Staff. Guidance for managers and those involved in the provision of chaplaincy-spiritual care*. London: HMSO.

Department of Health (2009). *Religion or belief? A Practical Guide for the NHS*. London: HMSO.

Dykstra, R. Craig (1990). 'Intimate strangers, the role of the hospital chaplain in situations of sudden traumatic loss', *Journal of Pastoral Care*, 44(2), 139–52.

Fuller, Robert C. (2001). *Spiritual, but Not Religious, Understanding Unchurched America*. Oxford: Oxford University Press.

Giddens, Anthony (1991). *Modernity and Self-Identity, Self and Society in the Late Modern Age*. Cambridge: Polity.

Gilliat-Ray, Sophie (2005). 'Sacralising Space in Public Institutions, A Case Study of the Prayer Space at the Millennium Dome', *Journal of Contemporary Religion*, 20, 357–72.

Giordan, Giuseppe (2012). 'Toward a Sociology of Prayer', in Giordan, Giuseppe and William H. Swatos Jr (eds), *Religion, Spirituality And Everyday Practice*, Dordrecht: Springer, 77–88.

Goffman, Erving (1974). *Frame Analysis, An Essay on the Organization of Experience*. New York: Harper and Row.

Heelas, Paul and Linda Woodhead (2005). *The Spiritual Revolution, Why Religion is Giving Way to Spirituality*. Oxford: Blackwell.

Holst, Lawrence E. (1984). 'The Hospital Chaplain. A Ministry of Paradox in a Place of Paradox', *Care Giver*, 1(2), 7–13.

Hu, Catherine and Simon M.S. Law (2007). 'PixelWish, Collective Wish-Making and Social Cohesion', *Online Communities And Social Computing* 4564/2007, 80–85.

Martin, David (1969). *The Religious and the Secular*. London: Routledge and Kegan Paul.

_____ (1978). *A General Theory of Secularisation*. Oxford: Blackwell.

_____ (2005). *On Secularization, Towards a Revised General Theory*. Aldershot: Ashgate.

Mauss, Marcel (2003). *On Prayer*. Edited by William S.F. Pickering, Oxford: Berghahn.

Meier, Augustine, Thomas O'Connor and Peter Van Katwyk (eds) (2005). *Spirituality and Health, Multi-Disciplinary Explorations*. Waterloo, Ontario: Wilfrid Laurier University Press.

Mowat, Harriet and Swinton, John (2005). *What do Chaplains do? The Role of Chaplains in Meeting the Spiritual Needs of Patients*. Report CSHD/MR001. University of Aberdeen.

Mowat, Harriet (2008). *The Potential For Efficacy Of Healthcare Chaplaincy And Spiritual Care Provision In The NHS. A Scoping Review of Recent Research*. Aberdeen: Mowat Research Limited.

Norwood, Frances (2006). 'The Ambivalent Chaplain, Negotiating Structural and Ideological Difference on the Margins of Modern-day Hospital Medicine', *Medical Anthropology* 25(1), 1–29.

Orchard, Helen (2000). *Hospital Chaplaincy Modern, Dependable?* Sheffield: Lincoln Theological Institute for the Study of Religion and Society.

_____ (ed.) (2001). *Spirituality in Health Care Contexts*. London: JKP.

Phillips, Dewi Z. (1965). *The Concept of Prayer*. London: Routledge and Kegan Paul.

Rattue, James (1995). *The Living Stream, Holy Wells in Historical Context*. Woodbridge: Boydell Press.

Riles, Annelise (ed.) (2006). *Document, Artifacts of Modern Knowledge*. Ann Arbor, MI: University of Michigan Press.

Robinson, Simon, Kevin Kendrick and Alan Brown (2003). *Spirituality and the Practice of Healthcare*. Basingstoke: Palgrave Macmillan.

Ruff, Rob A. (1996). '"Leaving Footprints", the Practice and Benefits of Hospital Chaplains Documenting Pastoral Care Activity in Patients' Medical Records', *Journal of Pastoral Care* 50(4), 383–91.

Storm, Ingrid (2009). 'Halfway to heaven: Four types of fuzzy fidelity in Europe', *Journal for the Scientific Study of Religion*, 48, 702–18.

Street, Alexandra and Battle, Tim (2003). *National Survey of Chaplaincy, Spiritual Healthcare Issues*. South Yorkshire NHS Workforce Development Confederation.

Swift, Christopher (2009). *Hospital Chaplaincy in the Twenty-first Century.* Farnham: Ashgate.

Taylor, Charles (2007). *A Secular Age.* Cambridge, MA: Harvard University Press.

Tearfund (2007). *Prayer in the UK.* Teddington: Tearfund.

Towler, Robert (1984). *The Need for Certainty, A Sociological Study of Conventional Religion.* London: Routledge and Kegan Paul.

Turner, Victor W. (1969). *The Ritual Process. Structure and Anti-Structure.* London: Routledge and Kegan Paul.

Wilson, Bryan (1966). *Religion in Secular Society.* London: C.A. Watts.

———— (1998). 'The Secularisation Thesis, criticisms and rebuttals', in R. Learmans, B. Wilson and J. Billiet (eds) *Secularisation and Social Integration.* Papers in Honor of Karel Dobbelaere. Leuven: Leuven University Press, 45–65.

Wittgenstein, Ludwig (1953). *Philosophical Investigations.* Oxford: Blackwell.

Wuthnow, Robert (2008). Prayer, cognition, and culture, *Poetics* 36: 333–7.

Zinnbauer, Brian J. et al. (1997). 'Religion and spirituality, Unfuzzying the fuzzy', *Journal for the Scientific Study of Religion*, 36, 549–64.

Conclusion

Prayer as Changing the Subject

Linda Woodhead

Describing her experience of sitting in court looking at the person accused of harming her, a victim of crime explains how she was emotionally 'boiling over' to the point where:

> I thought, no, I'm not stooping to your level. I'm better than this. I looked at him and thought, he's not worthy of these emotions, he's draining me. I said, right, you're going to have to do it, and I was battling with myself, then I sat there and did it – I said a prayer for him.[1]

Reading and editing the fascinating studies of prayer presented in this book and its companion volume *Prayer in Religion and Spirituality* (Giordan and Woodhead 2013) has prompted many new thoughts about the nature of prayer, particularly prayer in its contemporary manifestations. For me, it has led to the idea of prayer as 'changing the subject' – prayer as switching the conversation in one's head, taking a new subject-position or viewpoint (including God's), moving to a new emotional register, altering focus, or dissociating from one state and entering another 'higher' one – just as in the example quoted above.

In this conclusion I will discuss this idea after consolidating some of the general insights from the chapters which precede, and explaining how they enlarge our understanding of prayer. My aim is to draw out the implications of the studies we have gathered in this volume for how we define, study and approach prayer in contemporary societies.

What is 'prayer'?

To start with a fundamental issue: how can we make sense of the sheer variety which lies hidden under the deceptively simple label of 'prayer'? As Marcel

---

[1]   Tulisa Contostavlos, *The Guardian Weekend*, 02.08.14, p. 20.

Mauss, quoted many times in this volume, points out, prayer is 'by turns adoring and coercive, humble and threatening, dry and full of imagery, immutable and variable, mechanical and mental ... here it is a brusque demand, there an order, elsewhere a contract, an act of faith, a confession, a supplication, an act of praise, a hosanna' (Mauss 2003: 21). The research collected in this book illustrates even more variety: prayer which is bound up with bodily practices (from lying on the floor to chanting), social and individual prayer, prayer which is politically-charged, coercive, subversive, meditative, wordless, addressed to all sorts of beings both human and divine – or not focused upon any deity at all. And although this book looks chiefly at prayer in Muslim, Christian, and post-Christian societies, what about Hindu *puja*, Jewish *davening*, or Buddhist meditation? Do all these count as 'prayer'?

An established way of defining prayer is as the attempt to communicate with God, whether collectively or individually. Judged in the light of the findings presented here, this may seem too narrow, for it excludes some of the activities exposed in this book, either because they are not best described as 'communication', or because they don't have to do with God or theism. Here we find 'prayer' used to describe activities as diverse as expressing love for God, chatting with a deceased person, emptying one's mind of all thoughts, and sending a message to doctors and nurses who care for a loved one. Of course it is possible to stick with the established definition and exclude these from consideration as prayer, and there would be gains – such as clarity and comparability – in doing so. But there would also be loss.

Before making a decision about how to define prayer, it would therefore be sensible to consider, first, the main varieties of 'prayer' discussed in the book, and second, the commonalities which also emerge.

Variations in Prayer Participation, Frequency and Content

The fact that the percentage of people who pray varies considerably across nations is well known. For example, according to a recent national survey on religiosity, 73 per cent of Filipinos pray at least once a day, compared to 55.4 per cent in the US and 19 per cent in the UK (ISSP Research Group 2008, cited by Cornelio in this volume). In the previous volume, Garelli and Ricucci assemble statistics on regular prayer in Europe, which vary from 84 per cent for Poland and 40 per cent for Germany (Giordan and Woodhead 2012: 66).

Nationally-representative surveys I carried out in Great Britain with YouGov in 2013 also find significant variations between different segments of the population within a single country, as well as between different religious groups and affiliations: 21 per cent of the population aged 18 and over said they had prayed in private in the last month, a percentage which rises to 72 per cent amongst Muslims and falls to 3 per cent amongst those who report 'no religion'. Gender is also an important variable: whilst only 16 per cent of men say they pray monthly, 26 per cent of women say the same (Woodhead 2014). These findings are confirmed by other population surveys for the UK, which find that around 30 per cent to 20 per cent of the population pray regularly, and that higher frequency of prayer is correlated with greater age, being female and attending church (Collins-Mayo 2008: 34).

What is less well known, yet revealed by several studies in this book, is that what people pray for – the contents of prayer – also differ considerably. Typologies of prayer, several of which are proposed and discussed here, help us to see this more clearly. Because they generally work with implicit definitions of prayer as petition and communication with an addressee, they make it possible to separate and compare components of prayer. These may include form, theme/content, referent-prayed-about (e.g. grandad), prayer objective (e.g. healing) and addressee (e.g. God, grandma). This can help us to make interesting comparisons between different studies, even though the varied nature of these studies – in terms of method, research site, type of prayer, nature of the sample and so on – mean that the comparison is useful merely as an indication of something of the breadth and variety of 'prayer' in contemporary Christian or post-Christian societies.

In his study of committed young Catholics in Australia using a survey preceded by interviews, Michael Mason in this book uncovers the following list of prayer contents, arranged in descending order of frequency:

> Ask God for guidance in making decisions
> Thank God for blessings
> Pray for individual people you know
> Ask God to forgive your sins
> Express your love for God
> Pray for the world – e.g. for peace, justice, relief of poverty
> Ask God for material things you need

Jayeel Cornelio's study of young active Catholic Filipinos also finds that asking God for help in decision-making is an important concern. Sylvia Collins-Mayo's (2008) study of young people in Britain who have had contact with Christian youth workers, but are not as deeply committed to church Christianity as

Mason's and Cornelio's subjects, finds that petitionary prayer is their most common form of prayer, followed by 'confession' as 'the telling of self', followed by thanksgiving and gratitude.

By contrast, Tania ap Siôn's study of prayer requests left by visitors in an English cathedral discovers rather different content and a very different order of priorities. In descending order of frequency, requests were concerned with:

Health and illness
Death
Open intention (e.g. 'pray for the human race')
General (mainly for family and friends but no specific request)
Growth
Relationships
Conflict and disaster
Work

Peter Collins' study of prayer requests left in the chapel of an acute NHS hospital in England finds something different again. Not surprisingly, the largest proportion are concerned with health and illness, and the next largest with death and bereavement. Most do not address God at all. The most frequent theme by far is an expression of love towards an individual. Related to this are those prayers which refer to someone 'missed' or 'valued', but make no mention of a divine being. Others, though fewer, are directed towards God and Jesus. Submissions frequently include non-directed pleas for 'help', 'strength', 'healing', to 'look after/watch over', 'peace', 'to be kept safe', 'hope', 'comfort' and 'support'.

So it seems clear that prayer varies enormously according to social group and level of religious formation and commitment, and within different settings. Whilst it is not surprising that people's thoughts turn to illness and death in a hospital, it is less obvious that the same thing would be true for a cathedral – and yet it is. Does this indicate that people experience it as a liminal space in which the boundary between life and death is thin? Or that the space is associated with remembrance? Or that people still sense spiritual energies which can be drawn on for healing, often in relation to a shrine? Whatever the answer, it is clear that committed young Australian Catholics filling in a survey about prayer express a very different understanding and set of concerns than visitors to an English cathedral leaving prayer requests. Different again are the requests made online in a study discussed by Tania ap Siôn – here the most frequent requests relate not only to health and illness, but to growth, relationships and work.

Although considerable variation is evident with regard to both content and referent – the one who is prayed about – an overlapping finding is that people seem reluctant to pray directly for themselves. The online context mentioned by ap Siôn seems to make 'self-prayer' somewhat more acceptable, though presumably this has to do with the nature of the particular online site. When responding to a survey, Michael Mason's young Catholics say that if they pray for themselves, it is in relation to God – for example, in reflecting on sin or asking for guidance. And in the prayer requests offered by those segments of the general population studied by ap Siôn and Collins in the setting of a cathedral and hospital chapel, it is other people (and sometimes pets), which are the most common referent of prayer. In the English cathedral, for example, over 80 per cent of the prayers are for 'friends and family'. In the hospital, Collins finds that people are occasionally what he calls 'desperate enough' to resort to praying for themselves, but that when they do so, they often balance this by going on to include others, as in this – presumably Roman Catholic – example:

> Thank you to the Holy Family, all Angels, and Saints for prayers answered. Please let me be free of cancer to be well and healthy. God bless and protect us all always. Bless the surgeons, doctors nurses and everyone in this hospital for their kindness to all who enter here. God bless the families of all patients. Please give them strength and faith in you Dear God.

Thus 'prayer' seems to vary considerably depending on context and a person's religious background and socialisation, activism and orthodoxy – their degree of confirmation with the religion's authorities, including rites and formularies and group norms. The studies cited here suggest a number of hypotheses for more systematic investigation: for example, that activist Christians who are strongly committed to their religion pray for more 'pious' and less 'worldly' things than others, and that they are much more likely to pray to God.[2]

---

[2] And compare the survey of what British evangelicals pray for – in descending order, 'Ask God to bless your family', 'Confess and seek forgiveness for your sins', 'Try to listen to what God is saying', 'Ask God to help or heal people you know', 'Ask God to bless the work of your church', 'Ask for people to come to faith in Christ', 'Ask God to work in situations overseas', 'Ask God to bless your local community', 'Ask for help to overcome temptation', 'Ask for healing of your illness' (*21st Century Evangelicals* 2014), p. 18.

Varied Addressees

Even though the definition of prayer as 'attempts to communicate with God' makes monotheism the norm, the studies in this book uncover much greater variation in who or what is addressed in prayer. Certainly God or other 'super-social being(s)' – my term for beings other than and often 'greater' than living human ones (Woodhead 2011) – are addressed in many prayers, but in others the 'communication' is with a person (living or dead), a group, institution, or other 'agency'. And in many prayers there is no addressee at all – just a request or blessing or hope.

Again, setting and context clearly make a difference. In the hospital chapel, for example, the largest number of prayer requests are addressed to the chaplain, the next largest proportion to God, followed by those to a secular agency like 'the hospital staff'. Overall, about a third are overtly religious. Martin Stringer also reminds us of a form of prayer in which a woman 'chats' to her deceased grandmother, both in the Anglican graveyard in which she was buried, and at home whilst she is having a cigarette. As some of the authors mention, this practice of praying to deceased relatives and friends was also uncovered by Abby Day (2013) in her interview-based research amongst a sample of people living in Yorkshire.

Varied Emotions and Embodiments

Variation is also the norm in relation to the emotional and embodied dimensions of prayer studied in this book. What research like Julia Howell's on the recitation of traditional Sufi prayers in contemporary Indonesian rallies reminds us is not only that prayer can be a powerful sociopolitical force, but that the emotional tone of prayer is not simply dictated by the form or content of a prayer, but depends on a whole host of other factors, including the wider material, cultural and political contexts, the moods and intentions of those who pray and those who lead them, and the bodily expressions connected with prayer. Howell also shows that there can also be contradictions between these various elements, and that traditional forms of prayer can be 'repurposed' – reworked for new purposes. Thus a form of prayer designed to cultivate calm and meditative affect, for example, can be used to arouse 'hot' emotions, and vice versa.

Emir Mahieddin tells us about a similar phenomenon of emotional reordering and repurposing in the very different context of Swedish Pentecostalism. Here the intense affectivity associated with Pentecostal worship in most parts of the world has gradually given way in Sweden to a calm and cool form of congregational prayer and worship, as the religion has passed to new generations of Swedes. Insofar as more intense emotions like those associated with speaking in tongues are concerned, they tend to be reserved for more private settings – for prayer on one's own or in small groups. In other words, the emotional patterning of Pentecostal prayer and worship common elsewhere in the world is reversed: the emotionally expressive becomes a private rather than a public matter. The explanation, Mahieddin believes, has to do with Pentecostalism becoming conformable and acceptable to a Swedish society which is generally suspicious of intense displays of emotion, both in religious and other settings. At stake is not only social acceptability and congregational recruitment, but state recognition and funding.

Taken as a whole, the volume witnesses to a very wide range of 'prayer emotions'. It seems likely that *any* emotion can be associated with prayer, as Riis and Woodhead's (2012) approach to religious emotions would predict. Moreover, prayer emotions can be overtly and publically expressed or remain hidden and private, and can be of varying intensity. At one extreme are the intense and overtly expressed emotions of both joyfulness and sorrow associated with recent revivalist forms of religion, both Christian and Islamic. On the whole, these are concentrated in communal settings. At the other end of the spectrum are less visible emotions which may not be publically expressed at all – the altar-cleaning lady mentioned by Stringer who 'chats' with God, people who meditate in a quiet space, or the individuals who leave prayer requests in hospital chapels and cathedrals. In some cases, like that discussed by both Mahieddin and Althouse and Wilkinson, a group has transitioned from one emotional mode of prayer to another over time and under various wider pressures. What is most important to note is that there appears to be no necessary connection between the kind of prayer emotion (e.g. contrition or gratitude), the subjective intensity of emotion, and the expression of emotion – these are three separate dimensions.

Whilst the majority of authors find that emotion is an integral part of prayer, Carlo Genova is more cautious about this conclusion. For him what matters is social practice and embodiment. Prayer is a performative action. A person prays when she or he goes through the motions of praying – saying or listening to the words, making the bodily postures etc. – and it is not necessary for them to be able to formulate the 'meanings' involved. From this point of view, the possibly Protestant-derived view that prayer only really counts when the person who prays really 'means it' or feels something is a prejudice, and to say of some kinds of prayer that they are mere 'empty ritual' overlooks the fact that habitual, routine activities that do not prompt the individual to pose problems of explicit reflection still have an element of intentionality. Other chapters also stress the importance of bodily aspects of prayer and their repetition – such that prayer becomes something integral to the body, as well as laid down in memory.

Varied Uses

If Mauss is right that prayer 'is always, basically, an instrument of action' (2003: 22), the examples in this book suggest that there is no end to the uses to which it can be put. They make it clear that whilst prayer is deeply affected and shaped by wider social factors, it is also used as a tool to change both society and personal life. In this sense, prayer is powerful, and its power can be used for coercive as well as constructive purposes – as anyone who has been 'prayed for' or exorcised against their will, or found themselves trapped in a communal prayer to which they have moral objections, knows very well.

The sheer forcefulness of prayer, and its capacity for symbolic violence and for overwhelming the volition of people involved in public prayer, are discussed at various points in this book. Mahieddin, for example, reminds us of a Pentecostal view of prayer as a weapon in the ongoing spiritual warfare between good and evil, where the latter is identified with actual places and their inhabitants as well as 'powers and principalities' – with everything, in other words, which is believed to obstruct the progress of this particular kind of religion and its God (see also Butticci on the 'Mountain of Fire and Miracles Ministry' in Nigeria, in Giordan and Woodhead 2014). He also reminds us how an individual can force their way through social and other obstacles in doing 'God's work' (e.g. building an orphanage) by praying constantly and publically for this end, and interpreting positive events as answers to prayer which reveal God's support for the action in question, and negative events as obstacles to overcome, and deflections by evil forces.

Although he also considers Pentecostalism, Yannick Fer approaches the subject in a different way by arguing that the apparent freedom of the individual who prays, inspired by the Spirit alone, is in fact a learned skill in which what counts as authentic prayer is circumscribed by the community and its leaders. Even in prayer which is apparently free and spontaneous, the norms of the group and its leadership are being internalised. Few religious groups allow completely free spontaneous prayer; they offer guidance, discrimination and 'policing' of what counts as genuine prayer and answers to prayer.

Clearly there are strong articulations between a 'spiritual' subjective experience and 'religious' objective control. As Foucault's work would lead us to expect, prayer can be a powerful means of self-fashioning and disciplining. From the earliest age a child of either sex may, for example, internalise the authority of a father figure by praying to Him, and by hearing human and clerical 'fathers' lead prayer and establish its contents. By such means, different forms of paternalism and differentiated expectations of age and gender may be normalised. Some of the ways in which inequalities of age and gender are socially reflected and reinforced by prayer are made evident in Andrea Borella's chapter looking at prayer amongst the Amish – though Borella suggests that as well as reinforcing the status quo, silent prayer may provide individuals with a subjective space in which to escape from public norms and social pressures.

Whilst some aspects of the instrumentality of prayer may be invisible to the one who prays, others are not. In many examples in this book, prayer is knowingly employed as a form of coping and misfortune management. This is not necessarily an attempt to achieve a stated outcome, to coerce divine agency, or to conform the universe to one's desires. The studies in this volume show that people not only pray for an illness to end, they also pray that they may come to terms with it, or that good may come from it whatever the outcome. Some ask for change, but add the rider 'if God wills'. Others do indeed pray for real-world effects: from a parking space, to peace in the Middle East, to help with a church project. In these cases, the person who prays treats prayer as a tool in a wider process of world-transformation – in 'the daily labour of production and reproduction of the symbolic goods of God', as Mahieddin puts it. This goes beyond the view of prayer as merely a way of communicating or coping with circumstances, and elevates prayer to the status of a change agent. As a result, the boundary between 'prayer' and 'magic' becomes much more blurred than Durkheim and Mauss might like.

Common Findings

Alongside all this variety, it is also possible to discern some common themes in the various chapters' discussion of prayer. This is exactly what a sociological approach would expect. If prayer is always social in the way that Mauss argues, then the prayers of individuals in the same or similar social contexts are likely to exhibit commonalities. Rather than interpreting these as timeless aspects of prayer, or clues to a universal grammar of prayer, it demands less of the evidence to interpret them as features of prayer which are widespread in the late modern mainly Christian or post-Christian societies discussed here.

From Formalised to Less Scripted Prayer

One of the common findings is that formalised, laid-down, scripted forms of prayer are giving way to more informal modes. Whether or not the latter have their own less visible ways of 'scripting' prayer and the person who prays, it seems clear that liturgical prayer and set words and formulae for prayer have become less popular, especially with younger generations (unless repetitive forms are used in order to affect states of personal consciousness directly). In this respect, on the Amish forms of prayer discussed by Borella are an exception, since the community preserves more formal modes of prayer. But in the other studies, even when the formal protocols of prayer are clearly laid down – as, for example, on prayer request slips – people tend to interpret them in their own personal ways.

The prevalence of this departure from more formal modes of prayer is supported by findings from other studies, even amongst the more pious and orthodox. To give just one example, in a recent survey of British evangelical Christians only 17 per cent say that they find using written prayers or set liturgies helpful in praying, and only 10 per cent that they find postures like kneeling helpful. Just over one in five find using a church building or public prayer room beneficial, compared with 60 per cent (the largest proportion) who pray 'on the move', 48 per cent who make their own lists of people to pray for, 45 per cent who have a special place in their home to pray, 43 per cent who find it helpful to meditate on a verse of scripture, and 41 per cent who like music before or during prayer (*21st Century Evangelicals* 2014: 17).

This suggests not just a 'subjective turn' in praying, but an adaptation of prayer to the more fluid and mobile conditions characteristic of so much of modern life (Heelas and Woodhead 2005). Although the growing popularity of cathedral worship in Britain might seem like an exception to this preference for informality, it is notable that such growth is largely accounted for by the popularity of sung mid-week services of matins and evensong (Holmes and Kautzer 2014). Whilst formal in structure, these have much less by way of spoken liturgy and general 'words to follow' than many other church services of a liturgical nature. Moreover, the space and format allows many different forms of participation – including sitting silently, or even walking around the cathedral without participating fully in the service. In other words, people are not highly scripted, and there is a great deal of latitude to pray or contemplate or just be present in the way one wants to. In practice, 'peace and contemplation' are reported to be what is valued by the largest proportion of participants (Holmes and Kautzer 2014).

Personally-meaningful Experience

A related finding is that contemporary prayer is less likely to be valued as a bodily routine, discipline, form of ascetic self-denial, or matter of intellectual assent, than as a personally-meaningful experience with a close relation to an individual's own life concerns, hopes and fears. The view I once heard expressed in a seminary where the Principal responded to an ordinand who complained that he 'got nothing out of' morning prayers by saying 'that's the whole point', no longer seems to be widely shared.

This doesn't imply that people who pray are all seeking a particular kind of experience – not even a 'religious experience' – but simply that prayer is widely considered to be something meaningful to the one who prays, and that 'affect' (feeling, emotion) is an obvious way in which this is signalled. People want prayer to relate to their personal lives and deep concerns, rather than to other issues of a 'higher' and more impersonal or self-denying nature. This does not necessarily mean that prayer has to have deeply personal content, but that it should at least be conducive to personal growth and spiritual improvement (as with contemporary forms of meditation and mindfulness). There also seems to be an assumption that prayer is inherently personal, even if it takes place in a communal setting. In Christian terms, 'devotion' seems more popular than 'worship'.

In many ways then, prayer seems to have become its own reward, even if additional outcomes are sought. Ap Siôn mentions that a positive relationship between prayer and a sense of meaning in life has been noted in surveys of secondary school students in England and Wales. And a number of chapters in this book, including those by Cornelio and Mason, show that even amongst the more religiously committed, some of the most practised forms of prayer are those which place one's self and one's loved ones in relation with God – whether asking for guidance and help, in self-examination, or asking for blessing on self, friends and family. In contemporary societies, prayer seems to become something deeply personal and intimately related to one's own concerns – however 'selfless' and outward-looking those concerns may be.

Relational Prayer, Accessible Gods

There is little support in this book for Rudolph Otto's (1931) view of prayer as an encounter with the '*mysterium tremendum*' – an experience of 'communication' with a higher being who stands so far over and above the individual that the prayer takes the form of awe-filled reverence and submission. On the contrary, when God is the focus of the prayers discussed here, 'He' appears to be eminently accessible – so much so that for many of the more religious people discussed in this book, prayer seems to have a great deal to do with accessing God and communicating with Him in rather informal and direct ways.

For many contemporary religious believers, God is a very real presence who answers prayer and 'talks back' – not in mysterious ways, but in everyday terms which are immediately relevant to those to whom he relates (Luhrmann 2012). As Stringer reminds us in relation to contemporary Charismatic worship, even when God is approached as a mighty and transcendent being, it is possible to have a close and intense relationship with Him – He is not distant or overwhelming. This close relational aspect of prayer is underlined by the way in which answers to prayer are experienced as mediated by elements of people's everyday worlds – from phone texts to song lyrics to glimpsed billboard adverts. As Cornelio finds in his study of young Catholics in the Philippines: 'God does not speak in mysterious ways'.

Far from being veiled, hidden or mysterious, the studies that make up this book generally find that God comes close through prayer. Althouse and Wilkinson's description of 'prayer soaking' offers a vivid example, as does Stringer's account of the Catholic altar-cleaning lady who uses the opportunity to chat with God. Here there appears to be little difference in tone between chatting to God and chatting to one's gran. Both are easy to relate to, do not require deference, and are concerned for one's personal wellbeing. Even when the majesty and transcendence of God is the mode of prayer, God remains accessible – overwhelming by his presence and nearness rather than his distance, sternness and inaccessibility. As Stringer reminds us, there is no need to conflate God's transcendence with inaccessibility, or to assume that a being with whom one can 'chat' is necessarily an immanent one.

Prayer as Changing the Subject

To move to a more general level of reflection still – and to return to the observation with which I began this Conclusion – the chapters in this book may suggest a more general way of thinking about prayer as 'changing the subject'. This shift may involve one or more interrelated aspects.

For a start, prayer externalises or 'objectifies' the concerns of the person or people who pray. If I am anxious about the health of a loved one, for example, praying about it turns it into something external to me, from which I can gain some distance. To that extent, it alters my concern, makes it public, gives some control over it, and places it in a wider context. It 'gets it out'. Given that prayers often articulate fears and anxieties, prayer can therefore function as a coping mechanism which gives some means of cognitive and emotional control over a situation. At the very least, it can be a talking cure which is simpler to perform and considerably less expensive than psychotherapy. Moreover, by writing a prayer on a slip of paper and leaving it in a cathedral, or asking a chaplain to pray, or tying a ribbon on a sacred tree, one unobtrusively shares one's concerns with others and makes them pubic. All this is valid whether or not a person believes there is a God. The prayer can still be efficacious in purely human terms. If there is a God, so much the better: one shares one's concerns with the most powerful agent of all. If there is no God – well, nothing is lost. As Giuseppe Giordan says in the Introduction, 'you never know'.

Prayer also changes the subject by shifting the subjectivity of the one who prays, even to the extent that one is possessed by another subject. To use Cornelio's example of the Filipino girl excluded from further education by poverty who sits in a church and prays, this proves to be an effective way of seeing things in a broader perspective – in this case, from a God's eye view. In a sense the young woman entered into, or was possessed by, a higher perspective (whether of God, Mary, or another saint, depending on the referent(s) of her prayers). Here prayer enables someone to find a different meaning in the situation than when the latter was experienced in terms of one's own feelings of disappointment, anger or despair.

The picture which emerges from this book is not just of prayer as a way of acting on reality, but of prayer as a way of allowing reality – and different interpretations of reality – to act on, in, and through, the one who prays. The young Filipino girl might say that prayer enabled her to connect with a higher reality than her own, and to change the subject of her thoughts and feelings. When someone prays, he or she doesn't just relate to another being or beings, but may enter partially or wholly into another subjectivity. 'Having the mind of Christ', as St Paul put it, or 'seeing things from my late dad's perspective', as a bereaved person praying to her father might say. The idea that a person has only a single identity and a single subjectivity is challenged by the practice of prayer, which allows us to change our everyday subjectivity by allowing other people – or gods – to speak as one's own inner voice or conscience. To speak in tongues, for example, is to allow the Spirit to speak and pray through the believer, who is Spirit-possessed.

Prayer can also 'change the subject' by relating the person who prays to other humans (or animals, as in shamanism), and vice versa. The result may be an enlarged sympathy, imagination, field of emotions, consciousness and perception. Praying for a distant part of the world, or for a person whom one has never met are ways of broadening sympathies and 'expanding consciousness'.

Prayer to a 'third person' – like God – can also bind the 'first-' and 'second-' persons who pray to a 'third-person'. 'If your heart is as my heart, give me your hand', as John Wesley said to those who shared his love of Christ. In prayers to the same addressee, human others become non-other to one another by sharing in relationship with the one who is prayed to, and by experiencing themselves from that same third perspective. To some extent, their subjectivities converge. The effect can be particularly powerful in communal prayer, which can bind a group and alter feeling and attitudes. Even prayers said individually at the same time (e.g. a one minute silent prayer around the world), or shared on a prayer website, or viewed by others, can have some of this effect. Prayer can also foster the circulation of personal information in a group, thus enabling God to 'answer' individual needs through community activities experienced as an intimate conversation or answer from God (Luhrmann 2012).

This book also reminds us that it is not only by feelings but also by words and actions that prayer can change the subject. In terms of words, Margaret Archer's (2000) work on the social importance of the 'internal conversations' we constantly hold with ourselves and others 'in our head', gives a framework for thinking about how prayer can bring about a conversational and agential shift in the one who speaks from first-person to third-person – whether that third is God, a saint, ancestor, one's higher consciousness, the voice of 'the universe' etc. What is important is that the normal flow of internal conversation and inner narratives, and one's usual subjective vantage point is disrupted, either voluntarily or involuntarily. There is likely to be an associated emotional disruption in which one emotional state gives way or is supplemented, however briefly, to another.

Given that agential shift is involved, changing the subject involves relating to something or someone 'higher' or different from oneself and one's normal state of mind. There is some form of self-transcendence and suspension of one's normal emotionality, volition and desires, which become temporarily open to alteration. The use of the body to induce this agential shift, for example in the bodily postures of Muslim prayer, or the kneeling 'hands together, eyes closed' posture of some Christian prayer, or the use of psychotropic drugs like ayahuasca, can all play a part (Mellor and Schilling 1997).

In terms of the process involved, a three-stage scheme not unlike van Gennep's account of ritual (1908/1960) could be used to disaggregate and analyse this approach to prayer: stage of separation; liminal stage; stage of reintegration.

A Framework for the Sociology of Prayer

Taken together, the chapters in this and the previous volume also supply the ingredients for the construction of a general framework for the sociological study and interpretation of prayer. They do so by highlighting several dimensions of prayer.

First, prayer may be classified along a spectrum from the more private to the more social, always acknowledging that some element of each will be present in the other – for even in the most public prayer, the individual may pray privately; even in private prayer, social relations often structure prayer, and existing cultural forms shape its form.

Second, prayer varies by its relation to the body, bodily posture and ritual practice: the nature of Muslim prayer, for example, is distinct from Christian or Jewish prayer partly by virtue of the different bodily postures which are involved.

Third, prayer varies in relation to different material and spatial settings and symbolic objects. For example, prayers in front of a real or imagined image of a goddess in the setting of a Hindu temple are distinguished by those very factors from, say, Jewish prayer at the Wailing Wall in Jerusalem. Throughout this Conclusion we have noted how profoundly situation and context alters the form of prayer, what is prayed for, and who is prayed to (if anyone).

Fourth, prayer varies by the emotions which are associated with it, and can be classified in terms of their nature, intensity, privacy and expression.

Finally, prayer varies in terms of the social and super-social relations involved, and the nature of the subjectivities which are suspended, engendered and related. We have seen very clearly the great variation there can be in the nature of what or who is prayed about, with whom (real or virtual co-prayers), to whom (the addressee, whether human or divine agent), and for what end(s).

In the contemporary societies discussed here, the book reveals a preference for informal rather than formal and highly scripted or liturgical prayer, for mobile rather than static modes of prayer, and for prayer which is personally-meaningful and clearly related to personal life-concerns. I have also highlighted what appear to be considerable differences between the prayer of the committed and 'orthodox' members of a religion, and the more 'post-dogmatic' religious, spiritual, mixed and secular populations of post-Christian societies.

Back to Definitions

So what of the definition of prayer? The problem is that even the common features of prayer which I have pulled out from the chapters seem to be contingent and specific to certain societies, certain groups, and a certain point in history. 'Prayer as attempted communication with God' is also contingent – and perhaps not suitable for post-Christian societies. It works for the more committed Christian groups discussed here, but excludes others.

Nevertheless, we will always need some filter and some boundaries, or we would never know where to look and what to include and exclude. Definitions like 'attempted communication with God' are useful even when we have to criticise them, stretch them or apply them metaphorically. They can help us see similarities as well as differences between Christian prayer and Jewish *daven*, Hindu *puja*, Muslim *salat*, various forms of ancient and contemporary Buddhist meditation and mindfulness practice, and so on.

The interesting question is whether or not prayer in the sorts of societies discussed in this book has changed so much that we need a shift to a new definition or paradigm altogether. My view is that we do and, having the studies in this book and its companion in mind, I would favour a definition which captures more of the variety they reveal in prayer. A new definition might focus less on God and communication, and more on those activities (bodily and/or 'mental', public or private) in which individuals (alone or together) adjust or suspend their subjectivity. Part of what this involves is that they enter into a new frame of reference – one which is in some sense 'sacred': higher, more powerful, more meaningful, more truthful, than everyday existence. But in saying this, we also have to recognise that different social, cultural and theological frameworks determine whether certain activities and experiences can be considered genuinely 'prayerful' or not, and the concept of prayer – like that of religion, and in related ways – is always subject to negotiation and dispute (Beckford 2003).

In the previous volume, Michael Mason suggested that prayer confers an 'accent of reality' on the 'sacred' beings who are prayed to (Giordan and Woodhead 2013: 9–25). This accent can be intensified when prayer is collective, carried out by social authorities, constantly repeated, embodied, or made integral to everyday and domestic practices. The power of prayer, both constructive and coercive, can also be explained in these terms. Here I have developed a compatible approach by suggesting we also consider prayer as 'changing the subject' – whether in a meditation in which everyday thoughts and feelings are suspended or viewed with detachment, or in prayer in which the one who prays is possessed by another subjectivity, or simply by objectifying one's concerns on a prayer card in a cathedral and leaving them behind in a sacred shared space.

As traditional forms of religion lose their authority in many societies, and as new forms of religion, spirituality and 'non-religion' take their place, so prayer changes and diversifies accordingly. The old definitions which focus on petitions or communications with a personal God – often formalised and scripted – become limiting and restrictive unless understood as starting points and metaphors. What this volume suggests is that the concerns, referents, forms and locations of prayer may now have shifted and changed so significantly that we need to reinterpret and renew our concepts, definitions and theories to sensitise us to what has happened. There is enough continuity to mean that the old can still be helpful, but so much change that we also have to look afresh. This book helps us to do that, and represents a stepping stone in the ongoing task of constructing a sociology of prayer.

References

Archer, Margaret (2000). *Being Human. The Problem of Agency*. Cambridge: Cambridge University Press.

Beckford, James A. (2003). *Social Theory and Religion*. Cambridge: Cambridge University Press.

Collins-Mayo, S. (2008). '*Young People's Spirituality* and the *Meaning* of *Prayer*', in Abby *Day* (ed.), *Religion and the Individual, Aldershot: Ashgate*, pp. 33–46.

Day, Abby (2013). *Believing in Belonging: Belief and Social Identity in the Modern World*. Oxford: Oxford University Press.

Gennep, Arnold van (1908/1960). *The Rites of Passage*. London.

Giordan, Giuseppe and Linda Woodhead (eds) (2013). *Prayer in Religion and Spirituality*. Vol. 4, Annual Review of the Sociology of Religion. Leiden, Boston: Brill.

Heelas, Paul and Linda Woodhead (2005). *The Spiritual Revolution. Why Religion is Giving Way to Spirituality*. Oxford UK and Malden USA: Blackwell.

Holmes, John and Ben Kautzer (2014). *Cathedrals, Greater Churches and the Growth of the Church*. http://www.churchgrowthresearch.org.uk/UserFiles/File/Presentations/CGRP_Holmes.pdf (accessed 12 July 2014).

Luhrmann, Tanya (2012). *When God Talks Back. Understanding the American Evangelical Relationship with God*. New York: Vintage Books.

Mason, Michael (2013). 'Making the Sacred Real', in Giordan, Giuseppe and Linda Woodhead (eds) (2013), *Prayer in Religion and Spirituality*. Vol. 4, Annual Review of the Sociology of Religion. Leiden, Boston: Brill, pp. 9–25.

Mauss, Marcel (2003). *On Prayer*. Edited by William S.F. Pickering, Oxford: Berghahn.

Mellor, Philip and Chris Schilling (1997). *Re-forming the Body: Religion, Community and Modernity*. London: Sage.

Otto, Rudolf (1931). *The Idea of the Holy*. 6th edition, revised with additions. Translated by John W. Harvey. London: Humphrey Milford and Oxford University Press.

Riis and Woodhead (2012). *A Sociology of Religious Emotion*. Oxford: Oxford University Press.

21st Century Evangelicals: Time for discipleship? A Snapshot of the beliefs and values of evangelical Christians in the UK (2014). http://www.eauk. org/church/resources/snapshot/upload/Time-for-Discipleship-PDF.pdf (accessed 11 July 2014).

Woodhead, Linda (2011). 'Five Concepts of Religion'. *International Review of Sociology*, 21(1) 121–43.

Woodhead, Linda (2013). Survey of GB Beliefs and Values, YouGov for Westminster Faith Debates, data available at http://cdn.yougov.com/ cumulus_uploads/document/mm7go89rhi/YouGov-University%20 of%20Lancaster-Survey-Results-Faith-Matters-130130.pdf (accessed 11 July 2014).

Index